ORGANISATIONAL CAPABILITY AND COMPETITIVE ADVANTAGE

Organisational Capability and Competitive Advantage

Edited by

CHARLES HARVEY and
GEOFFREY JONES

Routledge
Taylor & Francis Group

LONDON AND NEW YORK

First published 1992 by
FRANK CASS AND COMPANY LIMITED

Published 2013 by Routledge
2 Park Square, Milton Park, Abingdon, Oxfordshire OX14 4RN
711 Third Avenue, New York, NY 10017

First issued in paperback 2014

Routledge is an imprint of the Taylor & Francis Group, an informa business

Copyright © 1992 Frank Cass & Co. Ltd.

British Library Cataloguing in Publication Data
Harvey, Charles, *1950–*
Organisational capability and competitive advantage.
I. Title II. Jones, Geoffrey, *1952–*
338.6048

Library of Congress Cataloging in Publication Data
Organisational capability and competitive advantage / edited by
Charles Harvey and Geoffrey Jones.
p. cm.
'This group of studies first appeared in a special issue of
Business history, vol. xxxiv, no. 1 (January 1992)' – Copr. p.
Includes bibliographical references and index.
1. Organizational effectiveness – Case studies. 2. Competition –
Case studies. 3. Industrial management – United States – Case
studies. 4. Industrial management – Great Britain – Case studies.
5. Industrial management – Japan – Case studies. I. Harvey, Charles.
1950–. II. Jones, Geoffrey.
HD58.9.072   1992
338—dc20   91–36279   CIP

ISBN 13: 978-0-714-63457-9 (hbk)
ISBN 13: 978-0-415-76121-5 (pbk)

This group of studies first appeared in a Special Issue of *Business History*,
Vol. XXXIV, No. 1 (January 1992), [Organisational Capability and
Competitive Advantage].

Contents

ABSTRACTS

Managerial Enterprises and Competitive Capabilities, *by Alfred D. Chandler, Jr.*

This article relates the managerial enterprise (a firm in which decisions as to current production and distribution and allocation of resources for future production and distribution are made by salaried managers with little or no equity in the firms they operate in) to competitive success in the new capital-intensive industries that began to appear in the United States and Western Europe after the completion of modern transportation and communication networks. It begins by examining the reasons for the rapid rise of managerial firms in these industries, the global oligopolistic competition that ensued, and the organisational capabilities such competition engendered. It then reviews the competitive performance of such firms in global markets in chemicals, metals, electrical equipment, and heavy and light machinery in the early years of the century, motor vehicles in the inter-war years, and computers and semiconductors after World War II. These managerial firms grew by moving into foreign or related product markets. World War I, the Great Depression and World War II held back the full competitive impact of such growth until the 1960s. The response of US industrial firms to this intensive international, inter-industry competition of the 1960s brought unprecedented changes on the competitive capabilities of US managerial enterprises in such capital-intensive industries.

Corporate Strategy and Accounting Systems: A Comparison of Developments at Two British Steel Firms, 1898–1914, *by Gordon Boyce*

Studies of dynamic American firms reveal that new accounting systems developed during the late nineteenth and early twentieth centuries represented important adjuncts to administrative innovations which supported strategies designed to secure sustainable competitive advantages. Investigations of British firms have not previously been undertaken to provide a basis for international comparison of costing methods and systems designs which arose during the 1890–1914 period when technological change, the rise of scientific management, and growing foreign competition called for new types of strategic decisions. The following article examines the interaction between strategic processes and systems development within two British steel firms which pursued divergent strategies during the same years that du Pont made its pioneering accounting innovations. The study draws attention to the impact of environmental conditions and firm-specific factors in influencing strategy, structure, and systems design.

The Neglected Intangible Asset: The Influence of the Trade Mark on the Rise of the Modern Corporation, *by Mira Wilkins*

Trade marks are, and have been since the late nineteenth century and throughout the twentieth century, vital business assets. The paper argues that they (along with brand names, trade names, and company names) have been of crucial importance to the rise of the modern corporation. US law and the courts have protected these property rights at the same time as the value of these assets to the modern firm has increased. The paper explains the significant role of trade marks in the evolution of the modern enterprise; provides historical data on US laws and court rulings; compares the trade mark and the patent; and indicates how, over time, the trade mark has contributed to efficiency gains in the modern firm.

Marketing in the Second Industrial Revolution: A Case Study of the Ferranti Group, 1949–63, *by Geoffrey Tweedale*

In the early 1950s the UK emerged as a world leader in the design and construction of electronic digital computers, a fact illustrated by Ferranti Ltd., the Manchester electronics firm. Ferranti achieved its dominant position with a blend of innovative technology and government support, but eventually found the computer business unprofitable. Marketing failures were partly responsible, particularly an obsession with technology and a failure to target the most profitable sectors of the industry. But paramount in the factors leading to Ferranti's sale of its computer interests were: firstly, the greater resources and market opportunities of the Americans; and secondly, the conservatism of the Ferranti family, who found the manufacture of defence computers a safer and more profitable alternative than the highly competitive data-processing market.

Industry Structure as a Competitive Advantage: The History of Japan's Post-war Steel Industry, *by Patricia A. O'Brien*

This article examines the role of the Japanese government in the development of Japan's post-war steel industry. It argues that the Japanese government's industrial policies facilitated the rapid growth and success of Japanese steel companies in the world market. During the early post-war years, the government instituted a set of comprehensive policies which constrained the supply of steel in Japan's market and contributed to the development of large-scale plants and the full exploitation of the economies of scale in steel manufacturing. The Japanese steel industry's sizable cost advantage, of course, derived from more than government policies alone. But, as this article will argue, through the Ministry of Trade and Industry, the Japanese government used its power to exploit the economics of capital-intensive industries and accelerate the formation of an efficient steel oligopoly in Japan.

Serving America's Business? Graduate Business Schools and American Business, *by Susan Ariel Aaronson*

The rise of graduate business schools occurred during a period of enormous growth, followed by dramatic decline in the fortunes of American business. Because so many M.B.A.-educated executives had difficulty managing their companies' response to dramatic changes in markets and technology, this study examines how business education has influenced managerial attitude and practices. Columbia and Harvard Business Schools were examined to see how, as well as how well, their educational approaches provided managers with the skills, information and confidence to make both entrepreneurial and operational decisions. Both schools effectively prepared their graduates for operational decisions, but did not successfully provide their managers with the skills and knowledge to facilitate entrepreneurial decisions. Moreover, the study also found that American business was not actively engaged in the direction of graduate business education. Thus, the reliance of American business upon graduate business schools may have had consequences for America's business.

Regulatory Responses to the Rise of the Market for Corporate Control in Britain in the 1950s, *by Richard Roberts*

This article examines the evolution of the regulation of takeovers in Britain in the 1950s. Takeovers began in the early 1950s arousing hostility from the authorities which regarded them as undermining economic policy. A series of bids culminating in the struggle for control of the Savoy Hotel in 1953 led to official directives which covertly curtailed the phenomenon by restricting funds for bidders. There was a second wave of bids in the late 1950s following the relaxation of restrictions on bank lending in 1958. The battles for British Aluminium and Watney Mann aroused public interest and put the restriction of takeovers on the political agenda in the run-up to the General Election of 1959. The response was the publication of a set of self-regulatory guidelines by City practitioners, which was ignored. It is argued that this was what the authorities intended since they had come to regard the threat of takeover as a useful discipline on management.

Introduction
Organisational Capability
and Competitive Advantage

CHARLES HARVEY and GEOFFREY JONES

Royal Holloway and Bedford New College, London
University of Reading

The reputations of academic institutions are made or broken by the scholarly achievements of key individuals. Creativity and intellectual ambition may be fostered by good management and the provision of resources, but the quality and originality of scholarship still depends in large measure on individual ability and application. Thus, the Harvard Business School may count itself fortunate to have had the services of prolific authors like Alfred Chandler and Michael Porter, whose intellectual influence has been rising throughout the world. Both Chandler and Porter have produced a series of three conceptually united books, culminating in 1990 with the publication of two epic works: Chandler's *Scale and Scope* (860 pages) and Porter's *The Competitive Advantage of Nations* (855 pages).[1] These ambitious and wide ranging studies are certain to have a major impact on the intellectual climate of the 1990s. No business economist, strategist or historian can afford to fail to take note of the arguments and evidence brought forward in them, and likewise business leaders and policy makers would be wise to give serious consideration to their conclusions.

What is so important about the scholarship of Chandler and Porter, is their success in explaining why particular firms and industries grow strong in some nations and not others, and why some national economies advance while others remain static or experience relative decline. Both authors take the large-scale firm as the natural starting point for detailed analysis; reasoning that it is the individual firm that is in the front line in the competitive process, and that the success or failure of large enterprises ultimately dictates the fate of modern corporate economies. In both cases, the consideration of firms leads naturally to the consideration of industries – seen by Porter as the arenas in which firms compete – and thence to the clusters of industries at the heart of various national economies. Chandler's historical analysis is based on the experiences of firms in the United States, Britain and Germany that were big enough to rank amongst the 200 largest industrial enterprises in those countries at one of three benchmark years between 1913 and 1953. Porter's contemporary analysis is based upon the experiences of clusters of firms in globally competitive industries in ten countries. A comparative approach is used by both authors to illuminate concepts, prove models and draw generalisations.

Chandler is one of the pioneers of comparative business history. His first great achievement was to recognise the importance of organisation building and professional management to the growth and performance of modern enterprises. In *Strategy and Structure*[2] (1962) he compared and contrasted the experiences of four leading US corporations in devising multi-level hierarchical administrative structures in the first half of the twentieth century. A number of general propositions emerged; most notably that new organisational structures result from changes in the strategic direction of firms.

> The thesis is that . . . structure follows strategy and that the most complex type of structure is the result of the concatenation of several basic strategies. *Expansion of volume* led to the creation of an administrative office to handle one function in one local area. Growth through *geographical dispersion* brought the need for a departmental structure and headquarters to handle several local field units. The decision to expand into new types of functions called for the building of a central office and a multidepartmental structure, while the developing of new lines of products or continued growth on a national or international scale brought forth the formation of the multidivisional structure with a general office to administer the different divisions.[3]

The idea that there is a natural logic to organisation building is one that Chandler returns to time and time again in each of his later books.

The full significance of the idea was demonstrated by Chandler in his second great work, *The Visible Hand*,[4] published in 1977. In this, Chandler documents and explains the rise of large scale industrial enterprises in the US before 1940. The central idea is that firms grew large when a new breed of professional managers, working within hierarchical business structures, took over from markets responsibility for coordinating flows of goods and services throughout the economy. Following orthodox transactions costs logic, it is argued that firms internalised activities when it became cost effective to do so. Thus the growth of large enterprises, and the emergence of oligopolistic market structures, should be seen as economically rational and very much in the national interest. The arguments of economists and historians who attach more weight to the pursuit and exploitation of monopoly power when explaining the rise of big business are dismissed as lacking in both evidence and intellectual substance.

These arguments are refined and subtly extended in *Scale and Scope*. Firms that rise to the fore in an industry are those that make a substantial three-pronged investment in production, distribution and management at a critical early stage, when markets are growing rapidly and developing technologies present opportunities to reap significant economies of scale and scope. The *first movers* in an industry are able to push down unit costs through investment in new capital-intensive plant and matching distribution systems. But, in practice, the goal of stealing a march over the competition can only be realised if firms also invest in building an efficient organisation staffed by competent managers. The development of organisational capabilities is seen by Chandler as crucial to the health of the enterprise in the short, medium and long terms. It is through effective business systems and managers that firms achieve high rates of throughput and realise the potential for cost cutting and product development held out by new technologies. In this way, profit margins are improved and firms acquire the financial resources for reinvestment in new plant and diversification. Weaker competitors are eliminated, entry to the industry is made more difficult and oligopolistic competition becomes the norm. Thus, *first movers*, providing they continue to improve their organisational capabilities through investment in management and business systems, will tend to retain their position as industry leaders.

In his contribution to this volume, Chandler expounds his ideas on organisational capability and substantiates his arguments through reference to a number of important cases. These range from Standard Oil and the German chemical manufacturers of the late nineteenth century through to the global expansion of IBM since the late 1950s. It is shown that the first firms to make a 'three-pronged set of investments in manufacturing, marketing, and management essential to exploit fully the economies of scale and scope quickly dominated their industries and continued to do so for decades'. Chandler goes on to show how the first movers in various industries transformed them such that they became dominated by a few large firms which competed not through price but through quality and continued product improvement and development. Success came to be judged by market share. Oligopolistic competition sharpened the product-specific capabilities of workers and managers. These capabilities plus retained earnings became the basis for future growth. Most grew through expansion into new markets. Geographically distant expansion was based upon 'competitive advantage of organisational capabilities developed from exploiting economies of scale', and expansion into related industries through exploiting the economies of scope.

Important lessons are drawn from this analysis. If the required three-pronged investments were not made by entrepreneurs at the crucial time, then 'neither the enterprises nor the industries in which they operated became globally competitive in national or international markets'. And it becomes more difficult with time to enter dynamic industries as lagging firms lack the organisational capabilities needed to catch up. Hence the failure of British firms in a whole string of modern industries, from synthetic dyestuffs to computers: industries in which an early lead and other natural advantages were lost through a lack of investment in physical and human resources. British failure is contrasted with German success since the late nineteenth century in building well organised and professionally managed business organisations.

Chandler has not had the last word on the subject of organisational capability. His dominant concern remains the creation of managerial hierarchies, and he has relatively little to say on the subject of the business systems. Yet systems are developed and refined by firms on the basis of experience, and effective systems are an important source of organisational capability. Accounting and information systems, production and operating systems, marketing systems and human resource systems may all differ between the firms in an industry. They are potential sources of organisational strength or weakness. Leading firms, with low unit costs and high levels of productivity, generally have efficient business systems which capture accumulated knowledge and experience. It is at the systems level that much of the variation in performance between firms can be explained.

The importance of business systems as a key to corporate performance and behaviour is the theme of Gordon Boyce's article in this collection. He shows, with reference to du Ponts, how an 'integrated accounting infrastructure . . . enabled management to win sustainable economies of scale and scope within a multi-function, multi-purpose enterprise and thereby transform the structure of the American explosives industry'. Having established that accounting systems matter, Boyce goes on to consider in some detail the methods of two British iron and steel firms – South Durham Steel (SDS) and Cargo Fleet Iron (CFI) – in the early twentieth century. He argues that differences in practice between the horizontal combine SDS and the vertically integrated CFI were largely a function of corporate strategy, and that performance in both cases may have been improved through the more systematic analysis of internally and externally generated cost data. This essay, it might be added, demonstrates some of the complexities of comparative analysis at a higher level of specificity than that undertaken by grand generalisers such as Chandler and Porter.

Mira Wilkins' article, like that of Boyce, seeks to extend the intellectual universe created by Chandler. Her argument is that more than technology and organisation are required for first moving firms to prosper. Modern corporations, she reasons, must positively attract customers to them, otherwise they 'would be unable to take advantage of increasing returns to scale and scope'. The trade mark (trade name, brand name and company name) is held up as critical to the process of attracting customers, as it conveys vital information about what is being purchased and it safeguards the producer's 'skill and industry'. As modern enterprises emerged towards the end of the nineteenth century, they sought and received protection for trade marks under the law. The trade mark thus became a crucial asset which raised barriers to entry in many industries. To numerous enterprises, like Sears, Holiday Inn and McDonald's, the 'trade name seems even more fundamental than new technology'. This should be seen in a positive light, argues Wilkins, since trade marks help lower costs and increase output by encouraging higher rates of throughput, reducing promotional costs and lowering costs of borrowing. The consumer also benefits from better information and higher standards. 'In short, in many ways, involving the lowering of costs of production, costs of distribution, and costs to the consumer, the use of the trade mark provides for the efficiency gains of the modern corporation'.

In his study of the Ferranti computer group in the 1950s and early 1960s, Geoffrey Tweedale provides evidence which supports and extends the case for British entrepreneurial failure made by Chandler. Ferranti was a pioneer in the digital computer industry with significant technological advantages, but it conspicuously failed to make the first mover investments in production, distribution and management necessary for continued commercial success. The firm was eventually eclipsed by IBM and the other emerging giants of the US industry and it sold its computer division in 1963. In a splendidly balanced conclusion, Tweedale brings out the important point that while the Ferranti computer business may have suffered from weak leadership and consequent underinvestment, it did not have the key advantage which IBM and other US firms had: government agency support on a massive scale for the emergence of a self sustaining national industry. In this case at least, economies of scale and scope resulted from implicit subsidy and intervention in the first instance, as much as from the actions of far thinking business leaders.

The analytical framework offered by Chandler, as the Ferranti case illustrates, is not all embracing; attaching relatively little weight to wider environmental influences on the competitive strength of firms, industries and nations. This is recognised by Porter who notes in *The Competitive Advantage of Nations* that Chandler's research 'stresses the development of internal skills and managerial capabilities in the growth of successful international competitors'. His own work, on the other hand, 'is more on the environment surrounding firms, and how this influences the creation of strategy, skills, organisational arrangements, and success in particular fields'.[5]

Like Chandler, Porter has developed a set of techniques and models for the analysis of competitive processes, corporate growth and industrial development. In *Competitive Strategy*[6] (1980), his concern was with the analysis of industrial structure and competitor behaviour, and with the formulation of corporate strategy. Firms might gain competitive advantage – the ability to earn above industry average profits – through one of three strategies: cost leadership, product differentiation, or focusing on a particular segment of the market. In *Competitive Advantage*[7] (1985), his concern was to demonstrate how firms might implement one of these three strategies and sustain a competitive advantage over the medium and long term. His main conceptual advance was the introduction of the concept of the value chain. All firms are seen to engage in two sets of activities, one primary, the other supporting. Primary activities are inbound logistics, operations, outbound logistics, marketing and sales, and after-sales care. Support activities involve planning, finance, human resource management, technological development and procurement. A firm might be perceived as the sum of its activities, and it can secure competitive advantage by performing any or all of these activities better than its competitors. Firms create value by performing activities and the value created by the firm is reflected in the price buyers are willing to pay for its product or services. A profitable firm is one in which the cost of performing its activities is lower that the value of its output. Competitive advantage is gained when a firm either performs activities more efficiently than its competitors (cost leadership strategy) or it creates a higher value for buyers and commands a premium price (product differentiation strategy).

The general applicability of these ideas can be seen with reference to the articles already introduced by Boyce, Wilkins and Tweedale. Boyce is considering the strategy and cost accounting systems of two firms with cost leadership strategies, one more explicitly so than the other. Wilkins is concerned primarily with firms with product differentiation strategies and the means of implementing these to secure competitive advantage. Tweedale concludes his article on an up beat note. Ferranti, in selling its commercial computer business, did not retreat from the computer business entirely. It decided on a focus strategy, concentrating its efforts on the market for defence computers and control systems. It emerged as an industry leader in this field; in the process partly justifying the investment decisions of its senior managers.

The behaviour and performance of individual firms is much easier to explain than that of national economies. Porter, like Chandler, takes the *micro* to *macro* leap through a crude form of aggregation. In extending his analytical scope in *The Competitive Advantage of Nations*, he equates national economic success with the success of home based firms in globally competitive industries. He is impressed by the fact that the internationally competitive firms in an industry tend to cluster together in a few nations and often in a few regions within nations. This clustering is explained with reference to four determinants of national competitive advantage: factor conditions, demand conditions, the existence or otherwise of supporting and related industries, and micro-level factors such as corporate strategy, structure and rivalry. Not all determinants have to be present to make for an internationally competitive cluster, but evidently the likelihood of clustering is greatest when factors of production (such as skilled labour) are in abundant supply, when home demand is strong, when there are many firms in related and supplying industries, and when there is vigorous competition between efficient firms in the home market. It follows that successful national economies are those with numerous and related clusters of firms in globally competitive industries. Japan, Germany and the United States are leaders of the world economy because of the existence of numerous clusters in those countries, whereas a nation like Britain is suffering from a decline in the number of important clusters in the home economy.

Porter builds upon his earlier work in stressing the importance of corporate strategy, structure and rivalry as a determinant of national competitive advantage. He extends the range of his analysis through the introduction of the three other environmental determinants. Government is not considered as a determinant in its own right; 'its role is ultimately a partial one'.[8] Its proper role is seen as supporting industry through the promotion of education, scientific research and infrastructure investment, through the promotion of competition, and through the provision of information and promotional services. The approach of the Japanese Ministry of International Trade and Industry (MITI) is applauded in correctly highlighting for business leaders the 'important priorities and challenges they face'.[9] Direct intervention is seen as a mistake the Japanese have successfully avoided.

The valuable research published in this volume by Patricia O'Brien, a colleague of Chandler and Porter, suggests that at a critical stage in Japanese economic development – during the reconstruction of the early post-war years – MITI took a far more determinedly interventionist stance that Porter suggests. O'Brien's thesis is that Japanese government policies in steel 'helped the industry develop a competitive advantage by shaping the industry's structure'. MITI understood the importance of exploiting economies of scale through ensuring high throughput, and accordingly sought to regulate capacity. It did this through various levers and was particular successful in the 1950s in structuring the industry on oligopolistic lines. Its direct control declined from the 1960s onwards but by then the structure of the industry was fixed; with a balance struck between corporate rivalry and the recognition of mutual interest in achieving the right balance between capacity and demand. The result was the emergence of Japan as the world's leading steel producer. The view that MITI played an important role in the Japanese economic miracle, associated with the work of Chalmers Johnson, is often contested in Japan, and even by some recent American writers.[10] O'Brien's careful and well-researched essay is a powerful restatement of the traditional western assessment.

O'Brien's work points out the practical and intellectual dangers of universal policy prescriptions. So too does the article in this volume by Susan Aaronson on the management training provided by leading US business schools between 1945 and 1960. America's competitive decline in recent decades has led to a re-assessment of the value of its system of management education. Unkind observers have noted a striking correlation between economic success – as seen in Japan and Germany – and the absence of MBA-type training for future managers. Robert Locke has recently explored these matters in depth on a comparative basis.[11] Aaronson extends the criticism of the conventional wisdom that more investment in management education will yield a national competitive advantage. She puts forward the critical thesis that at the time 'American business grew reliant on graduate business schools for their managerial pool, MBA students gained managerial training twice remove from real-world experience'. Columbia and Harvard may have trained students to make operational decisions, but they were much less successful in helping their graduates develop an entrepreneurial outlook. It is somewhat paradoxical that management education in Britain proliferated – the number of British students graduating with MBAs from British business schools rose from 1,100 in 1980 to 4,500 in 1991 – just as American researchers like Aaronson were developing a powerful critique of the MBA concept.

Likewise, the research of Richard Roberts, published in the final essay in this volume, opens up a new area of academic enquiry with considerable policy implications. In this original essay, based upon official sources, Roberts examines official British and City of London reactions to the emergence for a market for corporate control (take-overs) in the 1950s and early 1960s. The article indicates the importance of national politico-institutional traditions – in this case self-regulation – in shaping attitudes and government policy. Roberts notes but does not enter into the controversial debate concerning take-over movements and the organisational capability of British firms. Chandler is not so reserved. In his essay he concludes with a sharp attack on the short-termism and financial manipulation which in his view has been a source of economic debilitation in Britain and the US in recent times. According to this view, many take-overs have been made without reference to the underlying economic logic of corporate growth; consequently they have failed to yield economies of scale and scope – hence the rising number of disinvestments in both countries. This argument is part of a wider critique of British and US firms offered by Chandler which highlights their inability to sustain organisational capability and competitive advantage. On this matter, Chandler finds a strong ally in Porter, who is equally critical of economic trends in the US and (more so) in Britain.

Alfred Chandler and Michael Porter are two of the greatest living thinkers on capitalism and the processes of global competition. Their works are coherent and thought provoking, and they have popularised concepts which might have remained buried in more formal, less well written, works of scholarship. Their work is supported by an outstanding generation of American academic writers on business who have set the international agenda for research. In business history alone, the publications of Mira Wilkins on multinationals, Thomas K. McCraw on regulation, Lou Galambos on public policy, Richard Tedlow on marketing, Robert Locke on management education, Bill Lazonick on competitive advantage, and many others, are unmatched in Europe and Japan, whose business historians are often reduced to carping criticisms of the bold generalisations of the Americans. There is an urgent need for non-American perceptions of business, past and present, to be assessed with the weight and authority of a Chandler or Porter.

In the meantime, such concepts as organisational capability and competitive advantage, popularised by Chandler and Porter, and explored in this volume, remain amongst our most potent and valued tools in the analysis of modern business. It is hoped that the essays in this collection will help clarify and develop our understanding of how firms and nations compete successfully or fail in an increasingly competitive world.

NOTES

1. A.D. Chandler, *Scale and Scope: The Dynamics of Industrial Capitalism* (Cambridge, MA, 1990); M.E. Porter, *The Competitive Advantage of Nations* (London, 1990).
2. A.D. Chandler, *Strategy and Structure: Chapters in the History of the American Industrial Enterprise* (Cambridge, MA, 1962).
3. Chandler, *Strategy and Structure*, p.14.
4. A.D. Chandler, *The Visible Hand: The Managerial Revolution in American Business* (Cambridge, MA, 1977).
5. Porter, *Competitive Advantage of Nations*, p.786.
6. M.E. Porter, *Competitive Strategy: Techniques for Analyzing Industries and Competitors* (New York, 1980).
7. M.E. Porter, *Competitive Advantage: Creating and Sustaining Superior Performance* (New York, 1985).
8. Porter, *Competitive Advantage of Nations*, p.680.
9. Porter, *Competitive Advantage of Nations*, p.681.
10. Chalmers Johnson, *MITI and the Japanese Miracle: The Growth of Industrial Policy, 1925–1975* (Stanford, 1982). For a contrary viewpoint, see David Friedman, *The Misunderstood Miracle: Industrial Development and Political Change in Japan* (Ithaca, 1989).
11. Robert Locke, *Management and Higher Education Since 1940: The Influence of America and Japan on West Germany, Great Britain, and France* (Cambridge, 1989).

Managerial Enterprise and Competitive Capabilities

ALFRED D. CHANDLER, JR.

Harvard Business School

For the past century large managerial enterprises have been engines of economic growth and transformation in modern economies. These enterprises were created and continued to grow in much the same ways; and that pattern of creation and growth was based on a powerful economic logic. By following the logic of that dynamic, the decisions of entrepreneurs and managers helped to make Germany Europe's most powerful industrial nation before World War I, the United States the most productive in the world from the 1920s to the 1960s, and since the 1960s Japan their most successful competitor.

Departure from the dynamic – the ignoring of its logic – has been equally significant: since the 1960s, it has been largely responsible for the loss of competitive capabilities in such vital American industries as semiconductors, machine tools and consumer electronics and for the weakening of competitive abilities in metals and in machinery, including electrical equipment. On the other hand, in other industries, particularly computers and chemicals, managers sticking to that logic have maintained their competitive power at home and abroad. Finally, individual companies in machinery and metals, by staying with the logic or returning to it, have been able to maintain or retain their competitive strength.

This article begins by reviewing the pattern of the creation and evolution of managerial industrial enterprises and the logic behind that pattern. It then examines specific historical developments in the industries most critical to the growth of modern industrial economies – chemicals, electrical equipment, machinery (light and heavy), metals, motor vehicles and computers. In all of these managers followed the logic of the pattern outlined. It next looks at the competitive performance – success and failure – in those same industries in the past quarter of a century. Its conclusion suggests the long-term implications of the dynamic and the deviations from its logic for maintaining the competitive capabilities of vital American industries.

The New Institution

By managerial enterprise I mean simply those industrial concerns where decisions as to current production and distribution and those involving investments in facilities and personnel for future production and distribution are made by a hierarchy of lower, middle and top salaried managers. Although such hierarchical organisations were common in military, government, and religious institutions in earlier centuries, they did not appear in commerce and industry until the coming of the railroads in the United States and Europe in the mid-nineteenth century. Before that time owners of business enterprise managed and managers owned.

Such managerial enterprises appeared in production and distribution shortly after they did in transportation and communication. In production they came suddenly in the 1880s and 1890s. From then on they continued to cluster in new capital-intensive industries with similar characteristics. And they were born and grew in much the same manner. From the start such hierarchies of salaried managers were governed by a board of directors consisting of inside directors – full-time senior managers – and outside directors – usually part-time representatives of owners.

Tables 1 and 2 indicate the industries in which large managerial firms have always clustered. Table 1 gives the location country by country and industry by industry in 1973 for all enterprises employing more than 20,000 persons. Seventy per cent of these enterprises clustered in seven of 20 manufacturing groups of the US Standard Industrial Classification – in food, chemicals, oil, primary metals and the three machinery groups. Just over 24 per cent of these were in subcategories of six other two-digit industries which had the same capital-intensive characteristics – cigarettes in tobacco, tires in rubber, newsprint in paper, plate and flat glass in stone, clay and glass, cans and razor blades in fabricated metals, mass-produced cameras in instruments. Only just over five per cent were in the more labour intensive industries – apparel, textiles, lumber, furniture, publishing and printing, leather, and miscellaneous. Table 2 shows that the pattern of concentration was much the same in the United States throughout the twentieth century. This, too, was the case for the 200 largest enterprises in the same years in Great Britain, Germany, France and Japan.

As the Nobel Prize winner, Simon Kuznets, emphasized in his *Economic Growth of Nations*, these capital-intensive industries in which the large firms clustered were the fastest growing of their day; while the labour intensive ones in which few such firms appeared were, in Kuznets'

TABLE 1

DISTRIBUTION OF WORLD'S LARGEST INDUSTRIAL ENTERPRISES WITH MORE
THAN 20,000 EMPLOYEES, BY INDUSTRY AND COUNTRY, 1973[a]

Group	Industry	United States	Outside United States	Great Britain	West Germany	Japan	France	Others	Total
20	Food	22	17	13	0	1	1	2	39
21	Tobacco	3	4	3	1	0	0	0	7
22	Textiles	7	6	3	0	2	1	0	13
23	Apparel	6	0	0	0	0	0	0	6
24	Lumber	4	2	0	0	0	0	2	6
25	Furniture	0	0	0	0	0	0	0	0
26	Paper	7	3	3	0	0	0	0	10
27	Printing and publishing	0	0	0	0	0	0	0	0
28	Chemicals	24	28	4	5	3	6	10	52
29	Petroleum	14	12	2	0	0	2	8	26
30	Rubber	5	5	1	1	1	1	1	10
31	Leather	2	0	0	0	0	0	0	2
32	Stone, clay and glass	7	8	3	0	0	3	2	15
33	Primary metals	13	35	2	9	5	4	15	48
34	Fabricated metals	8	6	5	1	0	0	0	14
35	Machinery	22	12	2	3	2	0	5	34
36	Electrical machinery	20	25	4	5	7	2	7	45
37	Transportation equipment	22	23	3	3	7	4	6	45
38	Instruments[b]	4	1	0	0	0	0	0	5
39	Miscellaneous	2	0	0	0	0	0	0	2
—	Conglomerate	19	3	2	1	0	0	0	22
	Total	211	190	50	29	28	24	59	401

Notes: a. The *Fortune* lists include enterprises of non-communist countries only.
b. Medical equipment and supplies, photographic equipment and supplies, and watches and clocks.

Sources: Compiled from 'The Fortune Directory of the 500 Largest Industrial Corporations', *Fortune* (May 1974), pp.230–57: 'The Fortune Directory of the 300 Largest Industrial Corporations outside the US', *Fortune* (August 1974), pp.174–81.

words, 'lagging industries'. In the economies of the United States, Great Britain, and Germany these capital-intensive industries, in turn, made manufacturing the fastest growing subdivision of the industrial sector which also included mining, construction, utilities, and transportation and communication. In the three economies the industrial sector, in its turn, grew faster than either the agricultural or service sectors. And these three economies until the 1930s accounted for close to two-thirds of the world's industrial output. In this sense large managerial enterprises have been primary engines of economic growth for the past century.[1]

Why, then, did these enterprises appear suddenly in the 1880s and 1890s in capital-intensive high-growth industries? They did so because in those industries such enterprises enjoyed the cost advantages of the economies of scale and scope. In those industries larger plants had significant cost advantages over smaller ones in producing a single line of products. The cost per unit dropped much more quickly as volume of output increased than was the case in the labour-intensive industries. Besides such economies of scale large works also often utilised the economies of scope – those that resulted from making different products in one factory using much the same raw and semifinished materials and the same intermediate processes of production.[2]

Such potential cost advantages of scale and scope, however, could only be fully realized if a constant flow of materials was maintained to assure capacity utilisation. If the volume of flow fell below rated capacity, then the actual cost per unit quickly rose. It did so because fixed costs remained high and sunk costs – the original capital investment – were larger than they were in the more labour-intensive industries.

TABLE 2

DISTRIBUTION OF THE 200 LARGEST INDUSTRIAL ENTERPRISES IN THE UNITED STATES, BY INDUSTRY, 1917–73[a]

Group	Industry	1917	1930	1948	1973
20	Food	29	31	27	22
21	Tobacco	6	5	5	3
22	Textiles	6	4	8	3
23	Apparel	3	0	0	0
24	Lumber	3	4	2	4
25	Furniture	0	1	1	0
26	Paper	5	8	6	9
27	Printing and publishing	2	2	2	1
28	Chemicals	20	20	23	28
29	Petroleum	22	26	22	22
30	Rubber	5	5	5	5
31	Leather	4	2	2	0
32	Stone, clay and glass	5	8	6	7
33	Primary metals	31	23	23	19
34	Fabricated metals	11	10	6	5
35	Machinery	17	19	23	16
36	Electrical machinery	5	5	7	13
37	Transportation equipment	24	23	29	19
38	Instruments	1	2	1	4
39	Miscellaneous	1	2	2	1
—	Conglomerate	0	0	0	19
	Total	200	200	200	200

Note: a. See Table 1 notes.
Sources: Appendixes A.1-A.3 for 1917, 1930, and 1948 from Chandler, *Scale and Scope*; figures for 1973 compiled from *Fortune* (May 1974), pp.230–57.

The advantages of the economies of scale and scope can be illustrated by cost figures of more than a century ago – those from two of the very first modern managerial industrial enterprises – the Standard Oil Co. (its successor, Exxon, is still the world's largest oil company) and the oldest and still the world's largest chemical companies – the German firms, Bayer, BASF and Hoechst. John D. Rockefeller built the world's largest refinery in Cleveland only a few years after oil was discovered in north-eastern Pennsylvania. By increasing capacity from 500 barrels a day to over 1,500 barrels his enterprise reduced the cost of making a gallon of kerosene from 5¢ in 1870 to 2.5¢ in 1879. In 1881 Rockefeller's Standard Oil and allied companies formed the Standard Oil Trust. Their aim was not to obtain a monopoly. Linked by financial ties, they already controlled close to 90 per cent of the kerosene produced in the United States. Instead, the Trust was formed to provide the legal instrument that permitted the refining facilities of the many companies to be placed under a single management. The new enterprise quickly concentrated close to a quarter of the world's production into three 6,000 barrel refineries, resulting in economies of scale which helped the enterprise to reduce its unit cost per gallon to 0.534¢ in 1884 and to 0.425¢ in 1885. At the same time profit per gallon rose from 0.0534¢ in 1884 to 1.004¢ in 1885. At that cost Standard Oil's American-made kerosene was able to undersell that made from Russian oil in Europe and that made from South-east Asian oil in China, and also to produce profits that created at least three of the world's largest industrial fortunes.

When the three German companies began production of a new-man-made dye, red alizarin, its price was close to 200 marks per kilo. By 1878 the price had fallen to 23 marks per kilo, and by 1886 it had dropped to nine marks. Comparable price reductions were made in other dyes. The addition of new dyes and then pharmaceuticals added little cost to the production of each item and the additions permitted a reduction in the total unit cost of the others. By the 1880s a large German plant was producing more than 500 different dyes and pharmaceuticals at unit costs far below that of smaller competitors.

The story of oil and chemicals was repeated in the same years in other industries using new capital-intensive technologies of production including steel, copper, aluminium, glass, rubber, branded packaged food and drug products, and a wide variety of machinery. And they suddenly appeared in the 1880s and the 1890s because the completion and integration of modern transportation and communication networks – the railroad, the telegraph, the steamship, and the cable – made possible for the first time in history the high-volume, high-speed, flow of goods and messages without which substantial economies of scale and scope could not be realized. Transportation that depended on the power of animals, wind, and current was too slow and too uncertain to maintain the level of flow necessary to achieve the potential cost advantages of the new technologies.

In all these industries, however, the new large plants were able to maintain the cost advantages of scale and scope only if the entrepreneurs who built them made two other sets of investments. They had to create a national and then international marketing and distributing organisation, and they had to recruit teams of lower and middle managers to co-ordinate the flow of products through the processes of production and distribution and top managers to coordinate and monitor current operations and to plan and allocate resources for future activities. The first to make such a three-pronged set of investments in manufacturing, marketing, and management essential to exploit fully the economies of scale and scope quickly dominated their industries and continued to do so for decades.

It is important here to distinguish between the *inventors* of a product or process, the *pioneers* who first commercialise such an innovation, and the *first movers* who made the three-pronged investment essential to exploit fully the economies of scale or scope. For example, in mainframe computers several pioneers made investments large enough to market the innovation on a national scale. But it was IBM's massive investments in the production, distribution and management of its System 360 that made it the first mover in the industry. And what IBM did in computers, Rockefeller did in oil and the three German companies in chemicals.

The tripartite investment gave the first movers powerful advantages; to benefit from comparable costs, challengers had to construct plants of comparable size, and to do so after the first movers had already begun to work out the bugs in the new production processes. The challengers had to create distribution and selling organisations to capture markets where first movers were already established. They had to recruit management teams to compete with those already well down the learning curve in their specialised activities of production, distribution, and (in technologically advanced industries) research and development. Challengers did appear, but they were only a few.

The three-pronged investment by the first movers (as in the case of German chemicals there were often more than one) transformed the structure of industries. The new capital-intensive industries were quickly dominated by a small number of large managerial enterprises which competed for market share and profit in a new oligopolistic manner. Price remained a significant competitive weapon, but these firms competed more forcefully through functional and strategic efficiency; that is, b carrying out processes of production and distribution more capably by improving both product and process through systematical research and development, by locating more suitable sources of supply, by providing more effective marketing services, by product differentiation (in branded packaged products primarily through advertising), and finally by moving more quickly into expanding markets and out of declining ones. The test of such competition was changing market share, and in the new oligopolistic industries market share and profits changed constantly.

Such oligopolistic competition sharpened the product-specific capabilities of workers and managers. Such capabilities, plus the retained earnings from profits of the new capital-intensive technologies, became the basis for the continuing growth of these managerial enterprises. Firms did grow by combining with competitors (horizontal combination) or by moving backward to control materials and forward to control outlets (vertical integration), but they took these routes usually in response to specific situations. For most, the continuing long-term strategy of growth was expansion into new markets – either into new geographical areas or into related product markets. The move into geographically distant markets was normally based on competitive advantage of organisational capabilities developed from exploiting economies of scale. Moves into related industries rested more on those advantages developed from the exploitation of the economies of scope. Such organizational capabilities honed by oligopolistic competition provided the dynamic for the continuing growth of such firms, of the industries which they dominated, and of the national economies in which they operated.

The Historical Experience to World War II

Of all the new capital-intensive industries in what historians have properly called the Second Industrial Revolution – those that permitted the exploitation of the cost advantages of scale and scope – the chemical industry was the most technologically advanced and provided the widest range of new industrial and consumer products including man-made dyes, medicines, fertilizers, textiles, film, and other materials. The first major products of the new industry were synthetic dyes.

Here the British entrepreneurs were the pioneers. An Englishman, William Perkin, invented the first such dyes. The world's largest market for man-made dyes remained until after World War II the huge British textile industry. Dyes were made from coal, and Britain had the largest supplies of high quality coal in Europe. In the 1870s, Britain had almost every comparative advantage in the new dye industry. It lacked only experienced chemists, and British entrepreneurs had little difficulty in hiring trained German chemists to their factories. By any economic criteria the British entrepreneurs should have quickly dominated the world in this new industry. But they failed to make the essential investments in production, distribution and management. Instead the Germans – Bayer, BASF, and Hoesch and three smaller enterprises – made the first mover investments.[3]

The Bayer experience makes the point. In the 1880s Frederick Bayer & Co. was a relatively small pioneer. In that decade under the guidance of a young chemist, Carl Duisburg, still in his twenties, the company, exploiting economies of scope, developed new dyes and then pharmaceuticals. In 1891 it decided to expand by purchasing a dye maker on the Rhine near Cologne – a better location for receiving high movements of supplies into and finished goods out of the works than the original works at Eberfeld. At first the plan was to enlarge the Leverkusen plant, but then Duisburg convinced his colleagues to scrap its existing facilities and build a giant new works that would meet the company's needs for the next half-century.

Duisburg designed the new works to assure a steady flow of materials from their arrival at the works through the processes of production to storage and shipment of the final products. There were to be five processing departments, a sixth department consisting of the many workshops and offices required to service the processing plants, and Department VII, Central Administration. Department I, which included raw-material storage and the pump house and concentrated on the production of inorganic chemicals, was situated along the Rhine wharf. Separated from it by a street 120 feet wide (such streets separated all the departments) was Department II, which produced the organic intermediates. Then came Department III, making alizarin and azo dye stuffs. Department IV produced aniline dyes. Department V made pharmaceuticals. The last row back from the river consisted of the grinding and mixing plants, the refrigeration facilities, the power station, and the packaging and other works that made up Department VI. Along the wide streets ran the canals to supply the water needed in processing, the gas and electric lines, and 40 miles of railway tracks.

By this plan each of the five production departments was to have its own laboratories and engineering staff, for Duisberg thought it essential 'to place all chemists working in the same area in a common laboratory, so as to make possible a common working of various people, and encourage each individual by mutual stimulation'. The offices of the production engineers were to be close to the chemical laboratories so 'that works chemists can at any time get into direct communicatio with the works engineers'.[4] When completed the works covered 760 acres, and employed close to 8,000 workers. There was no comparable chemical establishment anywhere in the world except those of BASF and Hoechst. Today Leverkusen is still one of the most efficient chemical works in the world. Its laboratories became and remained amongst the most innovative in the world, producing a stream of new dyes, pharmaceuticals, films, fertilizers, varnishes, resins, and other chemical products.

By the time the Leverkusen works was in operation, Bayer's global sales force of experienced chemists were contacting and working with more than 20,000 customers; for every user of dyes in cloth, leather, paper, and other materials had to be taught how to apply the new products that had very different properties from natural dyes. And by the turn of the century Bayer and the other German chemical leaders had created the largest and most carefully defined managerial hierarchies the world had yet seen.

As might be expected, the resulting German competitive advantages quickly demolished Britain's economic comparative advantages. In 1913 160,000 tons of dyes were produced. Of these the German firms made 140,000 tons (72 per cent being produced by the Big Three); 10,000 more were produced by Swiss neighbours up the Rhine.[5] Total British production was 4,400 tons. The story was much the same for pharmaceuticals, films, agricultural chemicals, and electro-chemicals.

The electrical equipment industry, while employing a smaller number of professionally trained technicians and scientists, was even more of a transformer of economic life than chemicals. Not only did the new industry provide new sources of light and power that so altered urban living and transportation, but it changed the ways of the working place. Moreover, a new electrolytic process transformed and greatly reduced costs of producing copper, aluminum, and several chemicals. In this industry British pioneers were as active as those in Germany and the United States. But within a decade after the establishment by Thomas Edison of the first central power station (it was in New York City) two first movers in the United States – General Electric and Westinghouse – and two in Germany – Siemens and AEG – had made the investments in production and distribution necessary to exploit the economies of scale and scope.

Again, the German story is illustrative. In 1903, after merging with a major competitor, Siemens embarked on a ten year plan of systematising and rationalising production by concentrating production in what became the world's largest industrial complex under a single management. Where Bayer had built a single giant works, Siemens constructed several – one employing more than 8,000 workers for telecommunication equipment and instruments, and somewhat smaller ones for large machinery, small motors, dynamos, electrochemicals, and cables. Employing more than 20,000 workers and covering several square miles, the district of Berlin which this complex dominated soon became officially designated as Siemensstadt. As in the case of Bayer this massive investment in production was financed primarily from retained earnings. In these same years, its rival AEG built a comparable though somewhat less massive set of works only a few miles away. Nothing comparable occurred in Britain, even though Sir William Mather, senior partner of Mather & Platt, one of the largest British textile machinery manufacturers, had obtained the Edison patents at the same time as had Rathenau at AEG.

As a result, by 1913 two-thirds of the electrical equipment machinery made in British factories by British labour was produced by subsidiaries of General Electric, Westinghouse and Siemens. AEG sold more products in Britain than did the largest British firm. Mather & Platt had become a minor producer of electrical equipment for factories. From the 1890s on continuing research and development to improve existing products and develop new ones was carried out in Schenectady, Pittsburgh and Berlin, but not in Britain.

What was true of chemicals was also true of steel, copper and other metals, and in heavy and light machinery. In metals, the British pioneered, but the Germans and Americans made the necessary investments that quickly drove the British from international markets. In machinery, the British did not even try. The Germans quickly dominated the production of heavy processing machinery and equipment for the new industries of the Second Industrial Revolution, and for many of the old; while the Americans acquired a near global monopoly in machinery which was produced in volume by fabricating and assembling standardised parts, a process that by the 1880s was already known as 'the American system of manufacturing'.[6]

In office machinery, such first movers as Burroughs Adding Machine, National Cash Register, the Remington Typewriter Co., and the Computing-Tabulating-Recording Co. (later renamed International Business Machines) all dominated their industries world wide until well after World War II. In sewing machines the Singer Sewing Machine and in agricultural equipment McCormick Harvesting Machine were world leaders. Indeed in 1913 the two largest commercial enterprises in imperial Russia were Singer and International Harvester. (The latter was a 1902 merger in which the McCormick company was the major player.) By then Singer produced 79,000 machines annually in its Moscow factory with a work force of 2,500 wage earners and 300 salaried employees; while its sales force of more than 25,000 workers covered the vast territory from the Sea of Japan to the Baltic. For both companies their Russian operations were smaller than those of their other European business based on Singer's large factories in Scotland and Germany and Harvester's major plant in Germany. By World War I, American firms had achieved comparable global competitive power in the production of elevators (Otis Elevator), pumps (Worthington Pump), boilers (Babcock & Wilcox), printing presses (Merganthaler Linotype) and heating equipment (American Radiator). On the other hand, American machine tool makers which provided much of the equipment used by these companies in their processes of production, did not make large investments in production, distribution, and management. That industry continued to consist of a sizable number of small, mostly family-owned firms.[7]

In the inter-war years chemical, electrical equipment and machinery industries continued to be major drivers of economic growth. As late as 1946, 45 per cent of scientific personnel in American industry were employed in the first two of these industries – 30 per cent in chemicals, and 15 per cent in electrical equipment.[8] The chemical industry in the United States prospered as such pre-World War I firms as Du Pont, Dow, Monsanto, and two major mergers (Union Carbide in 1917 and Allied Chemical in 1920) expanded into new markets based on the organisational capabilities they had developed in the exploitation of scale and scope. So, too, in Britain formation of Imperial Chemical Industries in 1925 permitted the British industry to begin to challenge the Germans. But in other key industries – electrical equipment, heavy industrial and light mass produced machinery – British enterprises never became major contenders.

After World War I, the automobile industry surpassed all others as the prime source of economic growth and transformation. By 1908, less than a decade after the automobile was first sold commercially, the world's two largest automobile companies were the Ford Motor Co. and General Motors. It was Ford which made the first mover investments. With the building of the Highland Park factory where the moving assembly line was adopted in 1913, the creation of a national and international marketing organisation, and the recruitment of a team of excellent managers, Ford had even a stronger world-wide monopoly of low priced cars than did the American light machinery makers in their industries. Comparable investments in middle priced and high priced automobiles were made in the 1920s by General Motors and then by Chrysler. Both soon successfully challenged Ford in the low price range

– GM with Chevrolet and Chrysler with Plymouth. By developing a full line of cars (and so to benefit more extensively from the economies of scale) both were able to remain profitable when the drastic drop in demand in the 1930s meant that the smaller middle priced manufacturers could no longer remain viable as automobile makers, with only Willys (it became American Motors) surviving beyond the early 1950s (thanks to its production of the military Jeep). By 1929 the United States produced 85 per cent of the world's automobiles and much of the remaining 15 per cent were produced by subsidiaries of American companies abroad. Ford and General Motors were among the leading car producers in Britain and Germany. In 1928 all but 347 of the 25,000 automobiles produced in Japan were assembled by General Motors and Ford.[9]

In automobiles, functional and strategic competition led to rapid shifts in market share and profits. Henry Ford destroyed his first mover advantages by firing his most effective executives (several went to General Motors), and his company's share of the market dropped from 55 per cent in 1921 to 19 per cent in 1940; while General Motors' share rose from 11 per cent to 45 per cent and Chrysler, after acquiring Dodge in 1925, from four per cent to 24 per cent in 1940. From 1927 until 1937 Ford's loses were about $100 million. In the same depression years General Motors profits after taxes were just under $2 billion! (In the early 1930s annual GNP dropped to below $100 billion.) Only after Henry Ford died and after his son hired a group of General Motors managers to restructure his company did Ford begin to regain competitive strength and profits.

Historical Experience Following World War II

In the years after World War II, as the information revolution transformed industries and economies, the computer industry took on the role that the automobile had had in the 1920s and the chemical, electrical and machinery industries in the years before World War I. The beginnings and the processes of growth of the leaders in this industry were similar to those of earlier industries with one striking different – most pioneers were not, as they had been in the past, entrepreneurs. Instead they were long-established managerial enterprises in closely related industries.

The first to appreciate the opportunities for the commercial application of the giant costly computers initially developed for scientific and military purposes were American business machine companies. In 1950 Remington Rand, the nation's leading typewriter company, began to develop UNIVAC, the first computer designed for business uses. (In 1955 Remington Rand merged with Sperry, a large defence contractor, to form Sperry Rand in order to obtain greater capabilities in research and production of electronic products.) Other leading business machinery firms – IBM, Burroughs Adding Machine, National Cash Register, and Honeywell – quickly followed. (Honeywell, a maker of heat control systems, had in 1934 challenged IBM by acquiring a small tabulating computing company.) Other pioneers were large established enterprises with electronic capabilities – Raytheon, General Electric, RCA, and Philco. The only new firm to compete with the pioneering mainframe producers was Control Data. All these pioneers made substantial investments in producing and distributing the new machine.[10]

But IBM was the first pioneer to make the investments that transformed it into the industry's first mover, much as Ford, Rockefeller and the leading American and German chemical, machinery and metal companies had done in earlier years. The strategy of IBM's top managers, particularly Thomas Watson, Jr., was to reach as wide a commercial market as possible by utilising the cost advantages of the economies of scale. This called for all-purpose machines, whose development demanded not only the standardisation of machines and components but also compatibility between different closely related products. Several years of intensive investment in research and then in production led in 1964 to the marketing of the System 360, a broad line of compatible mainframe computers with peripherals for a wide range of uses. The massive investment in research and production, the swift expansion of the company's international marketing organisation, and the impressive increase in the size of its management gave IBM the dominance in the industry that it retains today.[11]

With the one exception of Control Data, IBM's successful competitors continued to be business machine companies. Like Remington Rand, these three each acquired electronic companies in order to improve their production and research competences. On the other hand, the electronic companies dropped out. Raytheon and General Electric sold their operations to Honeywell, RCA's computer activities were acquired by Sperry Rand, and Philco dropped its computer operations soon after it was taken over by the Ford Motor Co.

In mini- and micro-computers, entrepreneurial firms played a greater role, for while the established business machinery firms were concentrating on developing the capabilities of the mainframe, other opportunities emerged for machines using different technologies for different markets. In minicomputers – low cost machines for specific purposes, particularly scientific and academic – the first mover was Ken Olsen's Digital Equipment (DEC), which after several years of development, began volume production of the PDP-8 line in 1965.

Again, heavy investment in production was accompanied by the creation of a world-wide marketing network and a comparable increase in the size of management. In 1968 Edson de Castro, the engineer who headed the design team for the PDP-8, left DEC to form Data General and made a comparable set of investments. However, a third pioneer, Scientific Data Systems (SDS), failed to do so. After it was taken over by Xerox in 1969, it soon disappeared from the scene.

The most successful challengers to DEC and Data General were not entrepreneurial enterprises but established managerial ones. By 1980 DEC ranked second and Data General fourth in revenues generated. IBM was first, Burroughs third, and Hewlett Packard, an established producer of electronic measuring and testing instruments, fifth. The sixth was Wang Laboratories, a first mover with a new product for a different market – word processing and office systems. And these six accounted for 75 per cent of revenues generated in the minicomputer branch of the industry.[12]

The pattern is much the same in personal (micro) computers. These machines employed a still different architecture for a still different market – the individual user. The first entrepreneurial firms to make extensive three-pronged inter-related investments – Apple Computer, Tandy (Radio Shack), and Commodore – accounted by 1980 for 72 per cent of dollar sales in the United States. By then, three pioneers which together in 1976 accounted for 50 per cent of sales, but which failed to make such investments, had already dropped by the wayside. Two years later, however, three established firms – IBM, the Nippon Electric Co. (NEC) of Tokyo and Hewlett Packard – moved in. By 1982 they accounted for 35 per cent of sales; driving the market share of the three entrepreneurial first movers down to 48 per cent.[13]

Like the American machinery firms of earlier years, these computer companies quickly moved abroad. IBM almost immediately became the leading producer of mainframe computers in Europe. DEC led in microcomputers. By the mid-1980s Apple, IBM and NEC produced half the world's output of personal computers. All but one of the successful European or Japanese competitors were created by long-established enterprises. True to form, British pioneers failed to make the necessary investments. So by 1974 only a little over a quarter of all installations in Britain were from British producers.[14]

This brief review of the patterns of growth of the managerial enterprises that dominated the past century's most vital industries demonstrates the logic behind these patterns by emphasising three points.

First, unless the necessary investments in production, marketing, and management were made to exploit fully the cost advantages of scale and scope, neither the enterprises nor the industries in which they operated became competitive in national and international markets. To remain competitive, entrepreneurs in a new capital-intensive industry had to create enterprises administered by teams of lower, middle, and top managers.

The second point is that the opportunity to make such investments and to create such organisations was short-lived. Once the opportunity was lost, it was difficult for an enterprise and its national industry to regain competitive capabilities, even in its own domestic market. The British created such capabilities in chemicals with the formation of ICI, but they never developed a strong competitive edge in electrical equipment, heavy and light machinery, automobiles, and computers. Nor did they in steel, copper, or other metals.

The third point is that the first movers and the few successful challengers continued to grow by moving abroad and into related industries. The Americans became multinational in light machinery, automobiles, and computers using capabilities based on the economies of scale. The German and American electrical companies and the German and then American chemical companies also became multi-industrial by moving into related product markets based on the capabilities developed in using the economies of scope. These patterns of growth, based on organisational capabilities developed by exploiting the cost advantages of scale and scope, intensified inter-firm competition. The full impact of international and inter-industry competition created by such growth, however, was held back by world events. World War I and the massive inflation and military occupation of the Ruhr and the Rhineland that followed kept German companies out of international markets for almost a decade. They returned with impressive strength between 1925 and 1929, only to be reined in again by the coming of the Great Depression, then Hitler's command economy and the disastrous Second World War. Depression, global war and post-war recovery also dampened or redirected the growth of American enterprises and those of the smaller number of managerial enterprises in European nations other than Germany. It was not, therefore, until the 1960s, after the economic health of the European nations had been fully restored, and after Japan, following a massive transfer of technology, began to industrialise rapidly, that the international competition which had been developing before 1914 became a full-fledged reality. In the same post-World War II years, unprecedented investments in research and development intensified inter-industry competition in the United States and Europe.

The American Response to Intensified Competition

Because American enterprises had become so numerous in the capital-intensive industries at home, as well as abroad (Table 1) and because the American market was the world's largest and richest, the new competition provided many American enterprises in these industries with the greatest challenge that they had to face since their establishment decades earlier. The challenge was unexpected, as the American economy of the 1960s was prosperous. Even so, markets became saturated. With capacity underutilised, costs rose.

Many American managers responded as they had in the past, and as the office machinery firms did in the 1960s, by re-investing to improve their capabilities in their own and closely related industries. Many others, however, began to grow by moving for the first time into industries where their enterprise had no particular competitive advantage. These companies were cash-laden precisely because the post-war years of American hegemony had been so prosperous. Moreover, because they had had little competition abroad since well before World War II, and because they were being told by academic practitioners of management science that management was a general skill, many – but certainly not all – had come to believe that if they were successful managers in their own industries, they could be just as successful in others. So they sought to invest retained earnings in industries that appeared to show a greater or even potential than their own, even though those industries were only distantly related or even unrelated to their companies' core capabilities. Because of their lack of knowledge of the operations of their target industries, they obtained facilities and personnel through acquisitions or occasionally merger rather than, as had been the case in earlier moves into related industries, through direct investment, that is by building of their own factories and hiring or transferring their own workers and managers.

By the late 1960s, the drive for growth through acquisition and merger had become almost a mania. The number of acquisitions and mergers rose from just over 2,000 in 1965 to over 6,000 in 1969, dropping back to 2,861 by 1974. During the period 1963–72 close to three-quarters of the assets acquired were for product diversification. Half of these were in unrelated product lines. In the years 1973–77 half of all assets acquired through merger and acquisition came from those in unrelated industries.[15]

Such unprecedented diversification led to another new phenomenon. That was the separation between top management at the corporate office – the executives responsible for co-ordinating, managing, and planning and allocating resources for the enterprise as a whole – and the middle managers responsible for maintaining the competitive capabilities of the operating divisions in the battle for market share and profits.

Massive diversification led to such separation for two reasons. First, the top managers often had little specific knowledge of, and experience with, the technological processes and markets of many of the divisions or subsidiaries they had acquired. The second was simply that the large number of different businesses acquired created an extraordinary overload in decision-making at the corporate office. Whereas before World War II the corporate office of large diversified international enterprises rarely managed more than ten divisions and only the largest as many as 25, by 1969 numerous companies were operating from 40 to 70 divisions and a few had even more.[16]

Because few senior executives had the training or experience necessary to evaluate the proposals and monitor the performance of so many divisions in so many different activities, they had to rely more and more on impersonal statistics. As Thomas Johnson and Robert Kaplan point out in *Relevance Lost: The Rise and Fall of Managerial Accounting*, such data were becoming increasingly less pertinent to controlling costs realistically and understanding the complexities of competitive battles.[17]

Managerial weaknesses resulting from the separation of top and operating management quickly led to another new phenomenon – the selling off of operating units in unheard-of numbers. Before the mid-1960s, divestitures were rare. By the early 1970s they had become commonplace. In 1965 there was only one divestiture for every 11 mergers; in 1969, at the height of the merger boom, the ratio was 1 to 8; by 1970, 1 to 2.4; and then, for the four years 1974 to 1977, the ratio was close to or even under 1 to 2.[18]

The unprecedented number of mergers and acquisitions followed so shortly by an unprecedented number of divestitures helped to bring into being another new phenomenon – the buying and selling of corporations as an established business, and a most lucrative one at that. Although the industrialists pioneered this business, the financial community prospered from it. This brand-new business was further stimulated by an unprecedented change in the nature of 'ownership' of American industrial companies, that is in the holders, buyers, and sellers of their shares. Before World War II the majority of securities were held by relatively wealthy individuals and families. Even as late as 1952 only 4.2 per cent of the United States population held corporate securities – a figure which included owners of mutual funds.[19] The major institutional investors were insurance companies and trust departments of banks. Such institutional investors, like wealthy individuals, normally invested for the long-term – for growth and assets rather than current dividends.

After World War II, increasingly large amounts of the voting shares of American industrial enterprises were held in the portfolios of pension and mutual funds. These funds had their beginnings in the 1920s, but grew little in the depressed years of the 1930s. By the 1960s, however, they had come into their own. The success of the managers of these funds was measured by their ability to have the value (dividends and appreciation) of their portfolios outperform the Standard & Poor index of the value of 500 companies. To perform satisfactorily they had constantly to buy and sell securities – transactions made more on the basis of short-term performance than on long-term potential. As time passed these portfolio managers – the new owners of American industry – increasingly traded securities in large blocks of 10,000 shares or more.

As the number of such funds and the volume of the securities they individually traded increased, both block sales and the turnover of securities traded rose rapidly. The proportion of the volume of shares traded annually on the New York Stock Exchange to total shares listed grew from 12 per cent and 16 per cent in the early 1960s to over 50 per cent by the 1980s. Block trading accounted for only 3.1 per cent of total sales on the New York Stock Exchange in 1965. By 1985 it accounted for 51 per cent of sales. In those years, too, the volume of total transactions rose on the Exchange rose from close to half a billion shares annually in the early 1950s to three billion at the end of the decade and to 27.5 billion by 1985.[20]

The great increase in the total volume of transactions, the rise in the turnover rate, and the growth of block sales made possible still another new phenomenon – the coming of an institutionalised market for corporate control. For the first time individuals, groups, and companies could obtain control of well-established enterprises in industries in which the buyers had no previous connection simply by purchasing their shares on the stock exchange. Large blocks of stock were being traded regularly; and buyers had little difficulty in raising funds for these purchases from financial institutions and financiers.

Thus the diversification of the 1960s, the divestitures of the 1970s, the business of buying and selling corporations stimulated by the shift in ownership, and finally the coming of the market for corporate control greatly facilitated the ease in which the modern managerial enterprise could be restructured. Such firms could now be bought, sold, split up, and recombined in ways that would have been impossible before the acquisition wave of the 1960s.

By the mid-1970s the intensified competition which had led to a rejection of the logic behind the dynamic of growth demanded extensive re-investment in reshaping and rationalising product-specific facilities and skills if industries were to maintain and regain competitiveness. At the same time this deviation made necessary the restructuring of enterprises which had grown so large and unwieldy through unbridled diversification. But the return to the logic through restructuring of enterprises and of industries was now clearly affected by the desires of investment banks and other financial institutions to maintain the new and profitable business of buying and selling companies and the needs for pension and mutual fund managers to maintain the current value of their portfolios.

Competitive Performance since the 1960s

What impact did the new developments have on the competitive performance of industries which were central to economic growth and competition in modern industrial urban economies? What relationships did they have to the ability of the chemical and computer industries to retain their competitive capabilities; to the abilities of the automobile and lesser extent metal industries to restore theirs, and to the failure of such industries as semiconductors (so closely allied to computers) and machine tools (so closely allied to the machinery industry) to maintain theirs? Answers to these questions are particularly important, as all these industries faced the same external environment – inflation and oil shocks in the 1970s, rising costs of capital, the fluctuating dollar, and anti-trust and other government regulatory legislation.

The American computer industry remains strong and competitive. The major players have changed little in the past decade. Of the 20 largest producers of hardware in 1987, only two had been founded in the 1980s. One, Compaq (ranked 14) was the single successful challenger in existing sectors (in this case microcomputers). It announced in its first annual report a strategy of 'thinking of itself as a major company in its formative stage rather than a small company with big plans'. It has invested accordingly. The other, Sun Microsystems, number 20 in size (and like one smaller competitor, Apollo) followed the pattern of entrepreneurial start-ups in the past, developing a new architecture for a new market – in this case workstations.[21]

Business machinery firms still dominate mainframe production and have major positions in the other two major sectors of the industry:

Sperry Rand and Burroughs in 1986 merged to form UNISYS making it the second largest computer producer in the United States. The disappearance of the electronic companies suggests weaknesses of the highly diversified enterprise and of diversification into unrelated industries. GE, RCA, Ford with Philco, Xerox with SDS, by relying on profit centres and statistical cost controls, exited because they failed to put the resources into computer lines necessary to compete with the business machine companies and the few entrepreneurial firms which made first mover investments. On the other hand, Hewlett Packard, for 30 years a highly successful producer of electronic instruments, and even less diversified than the machinery firms, did make the investments necessary to become a major player in mini and microcomputers. In minicomputers, Digital has made a comeback through its VAX networking systems. The most important challenger, besides established foreign firms, is a venerable managerial enterprise from a related industry – AT&T with its UNIX operating system that permits portability of software across hardware of many different manufacturers.[22]

In 1987, American companies still enjoyed just under 60 per cent of the European market for mainframe and minicomputers, and just over 20 per cent of the Japanese. In Europe IBM's market share was 35 per cent, DEC's seven per cent, UNISYS' five per cent and Hewlett Packard's three per cent. In Japan IBM had 15 per cent, UNISYS three per cent, and NCR two per cent. In microcomputers Apple and IBM, together with NEC, accounted for 50 per cent of the world market. Except in some peripherals foreign competition in the United States remained limited.[23]

In semiconductors the story has been very different. This industry, which supplies critical components for telecommunications, factory automation, robotics, airspace, and production controls as well as for computers, was created in the United States. In the mid-1970s, the pioneering American firms held 60 per cent of the world market, 95 per cent of the domestic market, half the European market and a quarter of the Japanese. By 1987 their share of the world market share was reduced to 40 per cent, while the Japanese share had risen to 50 per cent. By then the United States had become a net importer, with the Japanese supplying 25 per cent of its market. The Japanese controlled over 80 per cent of the world's sales of dynamic random access memory (DRAMs) which had been invented by an American company, Intel. Intel, Motorola and Texas Instruments have moved into the most technically advanced sectors, producing particularly advanced microprocessors. Even here they are being challenged by the Japanese. IBM, now the only world class producer of semiconductors in the United

States, is working with the Defense Department through SEMATECH, a consortium of American companies, to try to save the industry.[24]

What happened? Again the diversified electronics firms – RCA and GE – with the greatest capabilities for production and continuing research pulled out, while Ford's takeover of Philco destroyed the potential there. More serious, however, was the failure of the pioneering firms to make the investments in production, distribution and management essential to become first movers. If IBM is the prototype of the giant managerial enterprise as first mover, surely the semiconductor companies in California's Silicon Valley epitomise entrepreneurial enterprise. Instead of making the long-term investments, creating the necessary organisational capabilities and continuing to reinvest, these entrepreneurial enterprises remained small or sold out, often to the Japanese. Repeatedly groups of engineers left their companies to start new ones. Both old and new failed to make the necessary long-term commitments.

In Japan, on the other hand, large established firms did make the investments needed to become first movers in the new industry and did develop the organisational capabilities that permitted them so quickly to destroy American competitive advantages. As an MIT study on American productivity notes: 'The rapidity of the Japanese advance and the American retreat and the emphasis of the Japanese on those sectors with the greatest potential for the future suggests that without dramatic structural changes, the decline of the US industry will not only continue but will accelerate'.[25] But if the experience of the entrepreneurial chemical, electrical, and machinery firms in Britain in the 1880s and 1890s provides any indication, such restructuring is difficult and the opportunity to regain competitiveness is fleeting.

In light machinery, the response to intensified competition varied. The experience of sewing machines and agricultural machinery contrasted sharply from that of business machines. In both the leading firms have been destroyed. In sewing machines the American industry's capabilities deteriorated when Singer, the dominant firm, diversified into machine tools and several defence-related industries in which it had few strong organisational capabilities. Soon it dropped out of the sewing machine business altogether. As defence demands fell off so did Singer's profits. In 1987 a takeover specialist, Paul A. Bilzern, financed by Shearson and T. Boone Pickens, obtained the company. He had sold off eight of the remaining 12 divisions before he was convicted of fraud and sued by the Federal Government for over $30 million.[26]

In agricultural and construction equipment (International Harvester had moved into the latter in the 1920s) American firms did better. John

Deere, Caterpillar, and other leading firms reinvested in improving product and process. International Harvester, however, was not dismembered by a corporate raider but by a highly touted business manager who came from Xerox with the largest salary yet offered a CEO in the United States. To increase shareholder value he concentrated on cutting costs, including a reduction of wages that led to a bitter strike. In the resulting sell-off in 1984 and 1985, American companies purchased the operating divisions of Harvester – Caterpillar acquired the Turbine Division, and Tenneco, a conglomerate, its agricultural equipment operations. As Tenneco already owned a long-established agricultural equipment enterprise, J.I. Case, it began to rationalise facilities and personnel in ways to regain competitive strength.[27]

In machine tools, on which American machinery, automobile, and other industries depend as much as does the computer industries on semiconductors, the story has relevant similarities to that of semiconductors. In both the pioneers failed to become first movers. The older industry had long been operated through small enterprises, many of which were in the 1960s still owned and managed by the founders' families. These firms had not made the investments necessary to exploit fully either the economies of scope, as had German machinery firms earlier in the century, nor to exploit the economies of scale, as the Japanese did after World War II. Conglomerates such as Textron and Houdaille moved in, consolidating many small firms. By 1982 85 per cent of American machine tool production was concentrated in 12 firms. But the conglomerates did not rationalise the consolidated facilities, as Tenneco has begun to do in farm machinery, or invest in new ones. Instead they used the firms as cash cows to generate income to be re-invested in other industries. When demand fell off in this cyclical business, they spun them off. As a result of this failure to restructure and re-invest, the United States share of world production dropped from 25 per cent in the mid-1960s to less than 10 per cent in 1986. More significant for an industry which, like semiconductors, remains critical to the productivity of the wide variety of other industries, was the fact that the United States imported 50 per cent of its machine tools in 1986, compared with four per cent in the mid-1960s.[28]

The post-1960s history of the motor vehicle industry remains one functional and strategic competition for market share. Diversification and mergers and acquisition have played only a small role. True, Ford's acquisition of Philco eliminated a potentially strong international electronics competitor. But the decline of the market share held by the American Big Three resulted largely from the ability of European and then Japanese firms to produce better products in terms of performance, price, and customer satisfaction, much as General Motors and Chrysler had done in competing with Ford and the smaller producers of middle-priced cars during the 1920s and the 1930s.

The new challengers in the United States and world markets were, of course, not small American entrepreneurial firms but established foreign managerial enterprises. Once their domestic markets had become large enough to assure a volume sufficient to reduce costs to a competitive level, these managerial firms began to move into the rich American market. American car makers, committed to high dividends and high wages, were slow to respond. By the 1980s, however, they were beginning to restructure their enterprises and their industries, improving product and process and their relationships with suppliers and dealers; and adjusting strategies and structures. So at present they are beginning to regain market share at home and abroad. According to the MIT's commission on productivity: 'The American-owned *firms* are now headed in the right direction, and the American based *industry* (including Japanese firms operating in the United States) is improving its international competitive position very rapidly'. Moreover the subsidiaries of General Motors and Ford were still strong competitors in Europe and Australia and all of the 'Big Three' had close links (strategic alliances) with Japanese firms.[29]

Until very recently, the venerable first movers in the electrical equipment industry, General Electric and Westinghouse, remained strong in their core products – systems generating and transforming electric power; electric motors, engines, components and other industrial products; and some long-established consumer appliances. While GE remains a world leader in the industry, in 1990 Westinghouse, which had disposed of its lighting division in 1986 to an American firm, sold off its electrical equipment and elevator divisions to Swiss companies. The proceeds of these sales were used to purchase businesses, largely in the service sector, where Westinghouse had not yet developed competitive capabilities. As its CEO, John C. Marous, explained to a reporter from the *Wall Street Journal*, his company was:

> boxed in by the rules of US capitalism. While European companies don't expect more than 12 per cent, he says, and the Japanese are even satisfied with 10 per cent or even as little as five per cent, if a product has a long lifecycle, American companies faced with a threat of takeover must do far better. 'Competition is tilted in favor of foreigners', declares Mr Marous, who has pushed Westinghouse to achieve a 22 per cent on equity last year.[30]

In this way pressure from the institutionalised market for corporate control pushed Westinghouse to abandon the long-term logic of industrial success – the logic which GE continued to follow by reinvesting heavily in those operating divisions in which it had the strongest competitive capabilities.

In consumer electronics – radio, television, and video equipment – the performance of the leaders and the smaller competitors has been uncommonly poor. Here over-diversification in the 1960s and 1970s appears to have been the culprit. GE and RCA became widely diversified and failed to concentrate resources on product development in consumer electronics; Philco and Admiral were acquired by firms (Ford and Rockwell, respectively) that had no experience in the industry. And Magnavox and Sylvania were purchased by the Dutch firm Philips. So by 1985 only 23 per cent of consumer electronic sales in the United States were for products made in American factories.[31]

Let me close this historical overview with a success story – that of the chemical industry, the industry that was hardest hit by the intensified competition of recent years. It remains one of the most significant generators of economic growth and transformation. In 1987 its US sales totalled $210 billion, as compared to auto sales of $125.6 billion. Its output of textiles far surpassed those produced by cotton, wool, and silk combined – products that had been the basis of powerful economies in the past. Its drug and pharmaceutical plants provided much of the world's medicine; its fertilizers had made possible the green revolution in many parts of the world; and its wide variety of other products had become essential in the production processes of its many and varied industries as those of the electrical and electronics industries. For a century the most research-intensive of all industries, its companies continued to expand by exploiting the economies of scope and entering markets related to their distinctive core production and research technologies. After World War II, American companies moved into Europe and European companies into the United States more than they had before 1939. Moreover, as the industry was dependent on oil for its basic raw materials, it suffered more than others from the sharp increase in oil prices in the 1970s.

As the leading managerial enterprises reshaped their own product lines and their organisational strategies, they restructured their industry. They narrowed their product lines, spinning off many of the commodity products, particularly petrochemicals, concentrated on expanding their output in existing higher value-added specialties and moving into new ones best fitted to their capabilities, including pharmaceuticals, biotechnical products and advanced materials. Thus, Dow's portion of commodities produced dropped from 63 per cent to 35 per cent in five years and Monsanto from 61 per cent to 35 per cent in four. As chemical companies reduced capacity much of petrochemical output was taken over by long-established oil companies. That is, the chemical companies moved into markets where they could utilise organisational capabilities developed to exploit economies of scope; and the oil companies into the petrochemicals where they could exploit capabilities based on understanding the economies of scale. Such restructuring based on long-term strategic plans involved heavy direct investment in new products and processes and the acquisition of pioneering firms in the growth areas as well as the divestiture of declining product lines. This restructuring was carried out almost wholly by the managerial enterprises that had long dominated their national industries – Bayer, BASF, and Hoechst in Germany; Ciba–Geigy in Switzerland; ICI in Britain; and in the United States Du Pont, Union Carbide, Dow, Monsanto (Allied Chemical, the most enthusiastic diversifier in the industry, is no longer a major player), and smaller, but still large, managerial enterprises such as Hercules, Rohm & Haas, and American Cyanamide. New start-up firms played almost no role; though a very few smaller firms were created to operate and occasionally consolidate the spun-off petrochemical activities. The United States remains an exporter of chemicals. Japanese firms have yet to become serious competitors in American or international markets.[32]

The Logic of Competitive Success and Failure

In the capital intensive industries, particularly those whose product and processes are technologically complex, the managerial enterprise has continued to dominate. (In this article I am speaking only of the capital-intensive industries that have been at the centre of growth and industrial competitiveness for the past century.) Such firms continued to grow by moving into new geographical and related product markets. Such growth continued to be based on the maintenance and improvement of product-specific facilities and skills whose activities were co-ordinated, monitored and planned by experienced full-time managers. And the test of such capabilities is their ability to compete functionally and strategically for market share.

The success and failure of American managers in competing for market share at home and abroad since the 1960s emphasises that those who ignore the logic of this dynamic do so, not necessarily at their own peril, but at the peril of the continuing long-term productivity and profitability of their enterprises, and of the industries and the national economies in which they operate. The failure of entrepreneurs to make the large long-term investments in manufacturing, marketing and management which are essential to create the capabilities needed to compete globally has meant that they and their enterprises lost out to those that did, both abroad and at home. This was as true of the entrepreneurs of Silicon Valley in semiconductors in the 1970s as it was of the entrepreneurs in Britain in chemicals, electrical equipment, machinery and metals in the 1880s and 1890s.

Similarly, the failure of managerial enterprises to improve their capabilities once created meant that they lost out in functional and strategic competition for market share to those that did. Just as General Motors and Chrysler took market share and profits from Ford by enhancing their organisational capabilities while Ford let its deteriorate, so too European and then Japanese automobile makers captured share and profit from the American 'Big Three' in the 1970s by improving their functional facilities and skills and by devising more effective long-term strategies for maintaining and gaining market share. And just as Ford regained its capabilities in the 1940s and 1950s, so too the Americans began to come back in the late 1980s.

The automobile story emphasizes that, while co-ordinated capabilities developed within the managerial enterprise are essential to competitive success, these managerial enterprises, like any human institution, can stagnate. Ford in the 1920s and the American 'Big Three' in the 1970s made wrong-headed decisions as to their markets, suppliers, dealers, and the activities of their competitors. In both cases, by improving process and product and restructuring their organizations, they were able to regain their capabilities and their competitive strength. The patterns of competition in automobiles have been much the same in nearly all capital-intensive and oligopolistic industries for the past century. Once established, a small number continued to dominate, with the market share and profitability changing constantly. Here the discipline of the market helped to enforce the logic of the dynamic of industrial growth.

More serious to the long-term health of enterprises and industries was the deliberate ignoring of that logic by managers who decided on a strategy of growth of acquiring companies in business in which they had little or no product-specific organizational capabilities that gave them a competitive edge. Such moves weakened the competitive strength of many American companies and industries. The American electrical and electronics companies had as great a potential for success in computers as did American machinery companies, and as great a potential for success in semiconductors and consumer electronics as did the large electrical and electronic companies in Europe and Japan. They failed in good part because these were only one of many product lines. So their top managers were unable to devote the time and resources necessary to compete effectively in computers, semiconductors, and consumer electronics. Nor did the top executives at Ford and Xerox have the capabilities to maintain the competitiveness of Philco and SDS. So, too, Singer's move away from its basic business was the beginning of its end. In comparable fashion, ITT, which had been since the 1920s a world-wide producer of telephone equipment was, after its diversification spree, out of that business. The conglomerates helped to bring down the machine tool industry. Finally, the diversification of automobile and machinery companies into unrelated industries made them much more vulnerable to the European and Japanese invasion of their market. By pulling back and concentrating on improving their functional capabilities, they are now beginning to regain competitive strength.

Ignoring the logic of industrial growth had even more far-reaching consequences than the destruction of the capabilities of a number of major American enterprises and industries. It led to changes in the capital markets that further encouraged inattention to the basic functions of managerial enterprises and to the maintenance of national competitive capabilities in global markets. The extraordinary number of acquisitions made in the late 1960s into unrelated and more distantly related industries, followed by a totally unprecedented number of divestitures in the early 1970s, suggest that many managers quickly realised the hazards of ignoring the logic. But it also made it clear that often more money was to be made in buying and selling companies than in operating them. Indeed, the new business turned many financial institutions, particularly investment banks, from carrying out what had been for almost a century their basic function, that of providing funds to supplement retained earnings in the reinvestment of facilities and skills essential to maintain competitive capabilities – a function that financial institutions in Japan and continental Europe continue to perform effectively. The new business, often personally as profitable to managers involved as to the financial institutions, was further encouraged by the new owners of American industry: the managers of portfolio and pension funds whose abilities were constantly tested by comparisons with their performance to the Standard & Poor indices. As time passed even the language of the financial community – such terms as 'bust-up takeovers', 'putting companies into play', and 'break-up value' – indicated that long-term investment was no longer the major concern of financial intermediaries. This trend away from the realities of global competition has been further stimulated by business schools and the business press. Just as in the 1960s the schools encouraged the hubris of American managers by teaching that those who learned the general principles of management need not be intimately concerned with its product-specific content; so the current discussion of shareholder value focuses on the obtaining of profit rather than on the product-specific capabilities necessary to achieve that profit – capabilities that differ considerably from industry to industry.

All this is not to say that the increased flexibility of the processes and products of the financial markets is not of significant value in restructuring American enterprises and industries so that they can regain or maintain their long-term competitive capabilities. The success of the chemical industry is a case in point. It is only to say that, as the experience of chemicals indicates, such flexibility is valuable only when capital is raised and businesses are bought and sold to enhance facilities and skills according to a carefully considered long-term strategy. Nor is this to say that conglomerates cannot play a significant role in maintaining and developing capabilities, as the case of Tenneco in agricultural implements suggests. Indeed, as long as the conglomerate operates a relatively small number of divisions and its full-time executives concentrate on maintaining those divisions' competitive capabilities, such executives can provide a more effective and more immediate discipline over managerial inertia than can the product markets. Nor is this to say that outside directors representing financial institutions or large stockholders do not have an important role in reviving stagnating companies whose capabilities have deteriorated, by bringing in outsiders, perhaps even from another industry, to turn the company around. The basic task of conglomerate managers, outside directors and a new CEO must, however, be to recruit managers who have the experience and skills essential to understand the enterprise's technologically complex products and processes, the intricacies of its many markets, and the activities of its competitors in these markets.

Individual financiers, managers and shareholders have often profited from ignoring the dynamics of managerial enterprises in capital-intensive industries, but the consequences of such actions have been serious to the long-term health of enterprises and industries involved. That logic has been ignored when managers and financiers view the assets of an enterprise as merely the value of existing facilities, and when they consider the employees and managers in terms of costs of wages and salaries instead of product-specific skills to be enhanced. The consequences can be particularly serious when deals involving the buying and selling of companies are based on such assumptions. It is ignored, too, when the goal of those involved in that buying and selling is the profit to be made from the transactions themselves rather than that made from the resulting improvements in the competitive capabilities of the enterprises involved in the transaction. The long-term consequences can be dangerous too when the transactions burden the enterprise involved with heavy debts whose interest reduces the funds essential for reinvestment in facilities and skills. They are serious too when the managers sacrifice funds needed to maintain and improve capabilities, to meet shareholder demands for higher dividends.

Why then should the weakening of organisational capabilities of managerial enterprises weaken the competitive strength of national industries and economies? The reason is that the development, production and distribution of goods for national and global markets must be a co-operative effort. It requires the carrying out of a wide variety of activities that in turn call for different facilities and skills. And only when these facilities and skills and the flow of goods through their processes of production and distribution are carefully co-ordinated can the activities be integrated in ways to reduce price, assure quality, and provide services essential to reach those markets. Such co-operative efforts are so profitable that if entrepreneurial enterprises fail to become managerial and managerial enterprises fail to maintain and nourish their competitive capabilities, they lose market share and profits to managerial enterprises from other nations and from related industries that do. At least that has been the experience in the industries that have done the most to transform the world since the coming of modern transportation and communication more than a century ago.

NOTES

This article was presented at the Business History Seminar at the Harvard Business School in September 1989. Very much reworked, it appeared as 'The Enduring Logic of Industrial Success', *Harvard Business Review*, Vol.90 (1990), pp.130–40. Because it was greatly shortened, because much of the basic data was deleted and because the data was not documented, it seemed worthwhile to have the original text published. Parts of this piece have been used in 'Learning and Technological Change: The Perspective from Business History', in R. Thomson (ed.) *Learning and Technological Change*, to be published by Macmillan, and in 'Competitive Performance of U.S. Industrial Enterprises: A Historical Perspective, 1880s–1990s' in M. Porter (ed.), *Time Horizons in American Industry*, to be published by the Harvard Business School Press. Both the title of the article and of the book are tentative.

1. S. Kuznets, *Economic Growth of Nations: Total Output and Productivity* (Cambridge, MA, 1971), pp.144–51, 160–1, 316–9; W.W. Rostow, *The World Economy: History and Prospects* (Austin, TX, 1978), pp.52–3.
2. The following paragraphs are based on A.D. Chandler, Jr., *Scale and Scope: The Dynamics of Industrial Capitalism* (Cambridge, MA, 1990), Ch.2.
3. For the British failure and German success in chemicals, pharmaceuticals, electrical equipment and other machinery and metals, see ibid., Ch.7 (particularly pp.274–86) and Ch.12 (particularly pp.463–86).
4. These two quotations are cited in ibid., p.476 from Carl Duisberg, 'Memorandum on the Construction and Organization of the Dye Works [Farben Fabriken], at Leverkusen', p.3 (Bayer Archives).

5. L.F. Haber, *The Chemical Industry, 1900–1930: International Growth and Techno-logical Change* (Oxford, 1971), pp.121, 145, 179.
6. Chandler, *Scale and Scope*, Ch.6 for the dominance of US firms in light volume produced machinery.
7. M. Dertouzos *et al.*, *Made in America: Regaining the Competitive Edge* (Cambridge, MA, 1989), p.234.
8. Chandler, *Scale and Scope*, p.171. The collective history of the leaders of the US chemical industry in the inter-war years is told in ibid., pp.170–90.
9. Ibid., pp.205–8 for this paragraph and the next.
10. For information on computers, see K. Flamm, *Creating the Computer: Government, Industry and High Technology* (Washington, DC, 1987), Chs. 4–6 and for the history of individual companies, J. Cortada, *Historical Dictionary of Data Processing Organizations* (New York, 1987).
11. R. Sobel, *I.B.M.: Colossus in Transition* (New York, 1981), Ch.10.
12. *Datamation*, Vol.29 (1983), p.92.
13. Chandler, *Scale and Scope*, pp.611–12.
14. Flamm, *Creating the Computer*, pp.168, 201.
15. D.S. Ravenscraft and F.M. Scherer, *Mergers, Sell-offs, and Economic Efficiency* (Washington, D.C., 1987), Ch.6.
16. For extent of diversification see A.D. Chandler and R.S. Tedlow, *The Coming of Managerial Capitalism: A Casebook on the History of American Economic Institutions* (Homewood, IL, 1985), pp.765–75.
17. T. Johnson and R. Kaplan, *Relevance Lost: The Rise and Fall of Managerial Accounting* (Boston, MA, 1987). As the book points out 'contemporary cost accounting and management control systems . . . are no longer providing accurate signals about the efficiency and profitability of internally managed transactions . . . Without receipt of appropriate cost and profitability information, the availability of the "visible hand" to effectively manage the myriad of transactions that occur in a complex hierarchy has been severely compromised'. Particularly useful are Ch.6, 'From Cost Management to Cost Accounting: Relevance Lost', and Ch.7, 'Cost Accounting and Decision Making: Academics Strive for Relevance'.
18. W.T. Grimm & Co., *Mergerstat Review, 1987* (Chicago, IL, 1988), pp.103–4.
19. New York Stock Exchange, *Share Ownership, 1980* (New York, 1981), p.1.
20. New York Stock Exchange, *New York Stock Exchange Fact Book, 1987* (New York, 1987) pp.70–1.
21. This information is taken from *Datamation*, Vol.34 (1988), p.30.
22. Flamm, *Creating the Computer*, pp.17, 102–127.
23. Ibid., pp.168, 201.
24. Dertouzos *et al.*, *Made in America*, pp.248–61. The US has remained strong in microprocessing chips but recently a Japanese firm, Kubota, purchased 20 per cent of MIPS Computer Systems, the first merchant vendor to commercialize an advanced microprocessor chip for reduced-instruction-set computing (RISC). In return, MIPS shares its technology with Kubota; while Matsushita manufactures the devices (pp.259–60).
25. Ibid., p.251.
26. *New York Times*, 3 May 1989, p.D19; 28 Sept. 1989, p.D1.
27. Marsh, *A Corporate Tragedy: The Agony of International Harvester Company* (Garden City, NY, 1987). Describes in detail the disintegration of this great American firm. Particularly useful are Chs.11–17. Valuable too is an article comparing Deere to Harvester in *Sales and Management*, Vol.32 (1985), pp.30–3. For Tenneco see, besides annual reports, *New York Times* (30 Dec. 1990), pp.D3–4.
28. Dertouzos *et al.*, *Made in America*, pp.232–3; M. Holland, *When the Machine Stoppes: A Cautionary Tale From Industrial America* (Boston, MA, 1989) provides a graphic account of the destruction of an innovating and well managed machine tool maker – Burgmaster Corporation.
29. Dertouzos *et al.*, *Made in America*, pp.171–87. The quotation is from p.187.

30. *Wall Street Journal*, 24 Jan. 1990, p.A4. For GE's continuing strength in the core lines see the company's annual report for 1989. This paragraph was revised after the completion of the original draft.

31. More detailed than Detouzos *et al.*, *Made in America*, pp.217–31 is 'The Decline of US Consumer Electronics Manufacturing: History, Hypothesis, and Realities', *The Working Papers of the MIT Commission on Industrial Productivity*, Vol.1, (Cambridge, MA, 1989), especially pp.15–21, 45.

32. As in the case of consumer electronics, the *Working Papers of the MIT, Commission*, Vol.1, 'The Transformation of the US Chemicals Industry' provides much more information on individual companies than does the summary volume *Made in America*. J.L. Bower, *When Markets Quake: The Management Challenge of Restructuring Industry* (Boston, MA, 1986), especially Chs.4–6 adds valuable information.

Corporate Strategy and Accounting Systems: A Comparison of Developments at Two British Steel Firms, 1898–1914

GORDON BOYCE

Victoria University of Wellington

Alfred D. Chandler Jr.'s comparative analysis of how organisational innovations within large-scale firms contributed to variations in international competitiveness has naturally encouraged accounting historians to investigate how new accounting systems played a supporting role in shaping corporate performance. Chandler's numerous references to new accounting methods that accompanied organisational change in the United States and H.T. Johnson's case studies of firms that pioneered systems designs have led many to suspect that British accounting practice, like organisational forms, probably lagged behind developments in the US.[1] However, we cannot confirm or refute the validity of this suspicion insofar as it relates to the pre-war era, when the relative decline of Britain's competitiveness coincided with salient administrative changes and the rise of oligopoly in US industry, because our knowledge of British and American accounting practice is drawn from different sources.

Scholars of British accounting between 1880 and 1914 have investigated the causality underlying the emergence and diffusion of new techniques using textbooks and the records of professional groups. The initial appearance of costing manuals in the 1880s led David Solomons to suggest that British management made little use of cost accounts for decision making until compelled do so by increasing competition.[2] S.P. Garner attributed the rise of specialist accounting literature to the growing capital intensity of industry which stimulated greater concern for costs.[3] More recently, Robert Locke has drawn attention to the absence in Britain of those professional and institutional links that played important roles in disseminating new cost concepts among managers, engineers and accountants in Germany and the US.[4]

Johnson and Kaplan's studies of innovative, and hence possibly unrepresentative, American firms between 1860 and 1920 revealed both a trend of cumulative sophistication in costing methods and systems design as well as lines of diffusion running from the railroads to steelmaking, explosives, and automobile manufacturing. Following Chandler they argue that differences in environmental conditions induced distinct patterns of corporate growth which in turn shaped national trends in systems development. Market and technological factors in the US exposed important economies that could be secured by internalising within the firm functions previously co-ordinated by markets. The resultant administrative complexity generated demand for improved accounting controls. With little firm evidence to support them, Johnson and Kaplan drew the inference that efficient market mechanisms in Britain encouraged persistent structural fragmentation and the proliferation of single-function firms that needed comparatively simple costing methods.[5]

Detailed case studies of British firms exist, but overwhelmingly they examine accounting practices during the Industrial Revolution era.[6] In a survey of these investigations, Edwards and Newell drew attention to an array of surprisingly advanced techniques, including some used by innovative American firms after 1900.[7] These sophisticated calculations were usually found in *ad hoc* reports used for decision making rather than in production ledgers. Edwards and Newell suggested that assessments of accounting expertise rely too much on evidence drawn from control records which are more likely to survive than special planning reports. The discovery of *ad hoc* calculations reveals that British businessmen used cost data to develop strategy long before 1880 and by implication undermines arguments that attribute innovations to a single factor, such as competition, capital intensity or internal organisation. Edwards and Newell suggested that accounting techniques arose in a contingent demand-induced manner in response to the diverse requirements of planning and control.

To develop an accurate basis for drawing international comparisons of accounting practice we need case studies of British firms from the pre-war era when technological change, the rise of scientific management and growing competition called for new types of strategic decisions. The present investigation examines the relationship between the strategies and accounting procedures as reflected in the planning reports and control systems of two British steel firms that operated within the same environment, shared a common pool of accounting expertise, and yet developed different policies. South Durham Steel and Iron (SDS) followed a passive strategy based on horizontal merger, while Cargo Fleet Iron (CFI) initiated a bold course of process integration designed to change industrial structure. These Northern steel firms pursued their divergent strategies at the same time that du Pont made its pioneering accounting innovations.

The first section below traces the relationship between strategy and systems development in single- and multi-function American firms before 1914 in order to establish the comparative context needed to assess the procedures employed by SDS and CFI. The second part of the study describes the features of the subject companies' environment: market conditions, technological changes and shifts in the organisation of the Northern steel industry. The last two sections analyse the systems and strategies employed by SDS and CFI.

I

In the 1850s and 1860s, single-function American textile firms, like Lyman Mills, employed 'conversion cost' accounting to calculate input costs (labour and materials) in terms of a unit of output (yards or pounds).[8] By measuring the expense of transforming material into finished products, 'conversion cost' methods enabled management to monitor production efficiency, but Johnson reports that the firm did not use this data to make pricing decisions, to evaluate alternative production policies, to assess new technology or to inform other strategic decisions. As a price taking firm, Lymans sought to improve the efficiency of its internal operations, rather than challenge external conditions.[9]

In contrast, Andrew Carnegie used his elaborate cost system which, following railroad technique focused mainly on prime costs and excluded overheads, to formulate an innovative strategy through which he exerted a dynamic influence on his business environment.[10] After 1870, Carnegie based prices on costs, a practice which was central to his policy of capturing market share by paring expenses and running his mills at capacity. By employing his system to assess the cost impact of different input mixes and process and product improvements, the steelmaker was able to perfect the mass production techniques which later served as a foundation for extending his control over purchasing and sales functions and inducing broader structural change in the industry.[11]

Carnegie's capital accounting methods were also based on railway practice. Like the Pennsylvania Railroad, he used 'renewal' methods, that is he charged repairs and maintenance to the operating account and did not treat depreciation in a systematic fashion.[12] As a result, profits, capital consumption and asset values were understated. These practices did not impair Carnegie's strategy which focused on reducing prime costs.

The scientific management movement developed new concepts that helped to extend and refine internal accounting controls. Frederick

Taylor sought to improve process efficiency by developing standard rates based on 'best practice' labour and material usage and by implementing more accurate statistical process controls.[13] Alexander Hamilton Church extended these innovations to costing to devise ways of assessing not just process efficiency, but overall *commercial* efficiency. By breaking down costs more rigorously and by determining indirect shop charges, overheads and selling expenses for individual products, rather than averaging these costs over all types of output, Church helped to link product cost information more precisely to profit and loss.[14] These practices also enabled management to set prices more accurately and thereby improve the precision of product strategies. Church and Henry Gantt also devised ways to calculate standard costs from a given percentage of capacity utilisation in order to relate fluctuations in unit costs to variations in throughput.[15] With this *corpus* of techniques firms could develop comprehensive product strategies to win higher levels of capacity utilisation and economies of scope.

The du Pont cousins learned of these new costing techniques from their contacts with steel firms that had been advised by Taylor.[16] They applied these methods and devised other systems innovations to pursue a strategy similar to that of Carnegie: run the mills full to achieve low costs needed to win a large and stable market share. However, the cousins sought to attain these objectives by rationalising plants following horizontal merger while simultaneously extending functional controls. To develop multi-function capabilities within a multi-product operation the du Ponts made strategic and tactical decisions that required new types of accounting information.

At the strategic level, the cousins had to decide how much capital to allocate to individual functional departments and to ascertain whether retained profits or outside funds would be used to support growth. Their methods were also conditioned by the need to service debt incurred in financing the purchase of the family firm. Therefore, in capital accounting they abandoned the 'renewal' method and devised methods of providing for the addition and removal of plant and then used a consistent method for treating depreciation in order to establish a more accurate value for the firm's assets.[17] This made it possible to express earnings as a percentage of investment (ROI), to assess alternative allocative proposals in uniform terms, to monitor coverage of interest costs, and to evaluate the efficiency of *capital* utilisation. The cousins drew up estimates of monthly spending and compared these with net earnings forecasts developed from sales projections in order to control capital spending and to evaluate the merit of using additional external finance.

At the tactical level, the du Ponts devised separate bases for evaluating and controlling functional activities: ROI for manufacturing, pre-set targets for sales, and purchasing limits established by sales forecasts. In production they rationalised plants and set product policies by compiling costs for each mill and product in a more rigorous way than Carnegie by assigning overheads, depreciation, and selling and purchasing expenses for each unit of output and across the product range.[18] In time, these unit cost figures were compared to a pre-set basis that was calculated from a standard operating volume (percentage of capacity utilisation). In sales, management used a 15 per cent ROI target to set price and volume guidelines for branch offices and products. Sales and manufacturing were integrated through the use of monthly sales forecasts and daily reports from the branches. After 1907, du Pont dovetailed purchasing with manufacturing and sales by establishing stock limits set by monthly sales forecasts. The system that arose from these strategic and tactical decisions represented an integrated accounting infrastructure that enabled management to win sustainable economies of scale and scope within a multi-function, multi-product enterprise and thereby transform the structure of the American explosives industry.

II

By the 1860s the North East Coast district had established world leadership in iron production by developing new blast furnace technology and exploiting the abundant but low quality ores of Cleveland.[19] The rapid growth of the 1860s produced some large firms, notably Bell Brothers and Bolckow Vaughan, but these concerns co-existed with numerous small-scale operators. The subsequent rise of bessemer steelmaking supported new entry thereby fragmenting the industry further. After 1880 shifts in technology and demand conditions did not induce structural change.

Demand for the region's traditional product – rails – grew more slowly after 1880. However, the expansion of shipbuilding and engineering called for increased output of plates and angles and thereby helped to sustain a moderate rate of growth throughout the Northern steel industry. (In 1990 the North still accounted for 29 per cent of the UK's total steel output.) The new basis of demand also protected the region's steelmakers from direct competition with American and German imports which won a permanent position in Britain during the late 1890s. Thus, neither imports nor abrupt shifts in the regional market disturbed the industry's structure.

The gradual alteration in local demand also required a change in steelmaking process, but the timing of developments in related equipment prevented this technological shift from inducing greater concentration. Large-scale rail manufacturing had been based on the Bessemer system, but for quality and metallurgical reasons plate making involved the adoption of the acid open-hearth process. However, the change in technique took place *before* the invention of ancilliary equipment which supported the integration of hematite iron production and acid open-hearth steelmaking. In the absence of economies of process integration, the expansion of the open-hearth sector caused a proliferation of blast furnace operators who smelted imported hematite ores, unintegrated acid open-hearth steel makers and rerollers.

While these trends in technological development limited the extent to which firms could emulate the first phase of Carnegie's strategy by perfecting mass-production through process integration, existing commercial practices prevented them from following the second stage of the American steelmaker's strategy – developing functional co-ordination. These market-related impediments included price-fixing organisations, close delivery or quality-based ties between existing producers and their large customers, the entrenched intermediary position that merchants occupied between manufacturers and small clients, and the established custom whereby consumers of steel placed orders to secure price but submitted size specifications only when they required delivery. These practices and the state of steelmaking technology supported the continued existence of an industrial structure that consisted of large and small single-function firms.

At the turn of the century, the technological basis of the open-hearth sector was radically transformed by Benjamin Talbot's invention of a continuous basic process. The Talbot system made it commercially possible to refine iron made from the cheap, low quality ore of the North and to employ the ancilliary equipment that American's had developed during the 1890s to secure economies of process integration. Thus, a window of opportunity appeared for firms to adopt innovative mass-production strategies that might induce structural change. However, the number of companies that could respond to the technological shift was limited by the ownership of local ore deposits, existing plant configurations, and the financial strength of individual enterprises.

In 1900, two of the region's three large firms possessed the best ores. One of these, Dorman Long & Co., purchased Bells in 1899 to secure ore needed for basic open-hearth steelmaking. However, the firm failed to rationalise its collection of plant and duplicated modernisation schemes produced inconclusive results. Dorman's manufactured both acid and basic steel for the rail and angle sectors of the market. Bolckow Vaughan also owned local ore but had a heavy investment in Bessemer technology. During the 1890s, piecemeal modernisation created an unbalanced plant that made angles, rails and a small quantity of plate. The third major regional producer, Consett Iron, did not own local ore mines and did not venture into basic open-hearth production. Instead, this firm imported hematite ore to manufacture acid steel plates. Behind these three major firms trailed a large number of small unintegrated operators, and from their ranks emerged the two companies that form of the subject of this study.

Two Northern shipbuilders, Sir William Gray and Sir Christopher Furness (later Lord) independently acquired CFI and the constituent parts of SDS in order to implement divergent strategies in response to opportunities exposed by Talbot's system and the fragmented structure of the local industry. Gray formed SDS in 1898 to execute a policy of horizontal combination which was designed to fulfill two objectives. First, Sir William combined his son's plate mill with two others in order to protect his family's investment by reducing local competition which undermined the stability of the regional price-fixing association. Second, as a customer who paid regulated prices, Gray sought to participate on a larger basis in suppliers' profits which he hoped to enhance by closing one plant to concentrate production during periods of slack demand and by gradually modernising SDS' facilities to cut costs. Each of SDS's plants operated acid open-hearth steel furnaces and plate mills: none possessed blast furnaces or mines. At 300,000 tons p.a., SDS's finishing capacity was about the same as Consett's, the North's other specialised platemaker, but larger than Bolkow's. In 1900, Gray strengthened his firm's commercial position by joining forces with Furness, and together they floated SDS as a public company.

Before this, Furness had been supporting the growth of his shipping and shipbuilding operations by acquiring coalmines, engineering works, and another steel firm.[20] This latter company, the Weardale Steel Coal and Coke Co., was a collection of unbalanced assets: large coal mines, small iron and steel making facilities, and a mill that rolled a small tonnage of boiler plates of acid steel. Weardale's future viability as a steel producer was undermined by its inland location. To remedy this disadvantage the firm bought CFI in 1900. CFI's obsolete blast furnaces occupied an ideal coastal site where Furness planned to build a fully integrated plant that incorporated Talbot's system. The new plant, which could make 125,000 tons p.a., would be supplied by CFI's iron mine and Weardale's collieries, while the latter firm's mill would be moved to the new site to undertake large-scale ship plate production.

Thus, SDS and CFI developed divergent strategies in light of their environment and resource sets. CFI sought to confront those conditions that hindered mass-production: SDS pursued horizontal growth and a cost cutting policy. (These strategies also set the two firms on a collision course in the plate market, but conflict was averted in 1904 by an exchange of shares and CFI's abandonment of plate making in favour of angle production.) The challenge facing the management of these firms was to devise systems tailored to the requirements of their distinct policies.

III

To carry out its horizontal strategy SDS needed a system that supported rapid adjustment to abrupt shifts in short-term conditions. 'Responsive' capability was important for two reasons. First, being derived from a capital goods industry, demand for ship plates was volatile, and the price of inputs, especially hematite iron, fluctuated widely. Second, Gray and Furness expected SDS to contend with these conditions without further financial assistance because they needed their private resources to support other rapidly growing businesses. In light of these considerations, this section examines the accounting expertise reflected in (1) the system that SDS used to monitor transaction flows, production, and liquidity and (2) special planning reports.

SDS's strategy did not require a system that supported rigorous functional co-ordination. The shipbuilders guaranteed the firm a sizeable share of the local market, and they did not plan to attack the prices set by the Plate Makers' Association (PMA) or to undertake direct selling.[21] Therefore, unlike du Pont, which did confront a price-fixing association, SDS did not need to establish either a sales organisation or a system that integrated sales and manufacturing. The technological divisibilities of acid open-hearth steelmaking did not generate significant economies that could be won by exerting systematic co-ordination over the flow of inputs to the steel furnaces. Nor did SDS have to integrate backwards in response to supply threats. Thus, the shipbuilders did not plan to modify existing competitive relations and lines of input distribution, and SDS remained a single-function horizontal combine that monitored, but could not internalise, transactional flows between manufacturing, sales, and supply.

To provide this monitoring function for SDS's three plants, Furness and Gray formed a centralised organisation managed by C.J. Bagley.[22] The new manager watched two sets of statistics to evaluate the likely impact of changing demand on production. First, he gained an overall view of market trends from Lloyd's weekly list of ships building in the UK.[23] This data was not used to set sales targets of the type that du Pont developed from ROI objectives because, as long as it was a member of the PMA, SDS could not influence its share of the market. Second, Bagley monitored the size of SDS's Order Book, that is the tonnage of sales recorded, and he divided this aggregate figure by the mills' annual capacity to compute how many months work the firm had available. However, this gave him only a rough indication of when he might have to close a plant to run the others at peak levels. Order Book size reflected the duration of *potential* full capacity operations, the *actual* number of months that SDS could run full depended on specification flows which the firm could not control.[24]

SDS did not tie purchasing to sales using formal administrative means of the type employed by du Pont. While the cousins set a fixed ratio of stock levels to forecasted sales, Bagley bought inputs under the supervision of the Board which shifted price and quantity guidelines at irregular intervals as demand and material prices changed.[25] SDS's procedures reflected both its inability to influence and thereby forecast sales and its owners' desire to monitor liquidity directly. Developing the capacity to respond to shifts in the firm's cash position made sense given lags between orders and specifications. The Board usually bought inputs when sales were booked, rather than when specifications came in, so that material costs were related directly to selling prices and the firm was insulated from the effects of fluctuating iron prices. However, this meant that the firm carried material which could not be processed immediately.[26] These circumstances made it impossible for the Board to build safeguards and delegate purchasing in the same way that the du Ponts did in order to manage financial resources systematically. Instead, SDS tailored its system to give the owners flexibility and hands-on control.

With data on purchases and sales, Bagley made rough estimates of future profits by subtracting material and production costs from average unit plate prices and multiplying by each operating mill's capacity.[27] SDS's records contain no profit or cost projections based on different levels of throughput. Even though estimates using standard rates have been found before 1800, Bagley employed full running as the basis for both routine and special reports because the owners shut mills to concentrate output during slumps. There was no compelling reason to monitor the relationship between volume and profits more precisely. Bagley's method of calculation reflects the responsive rather than anticipatory character of the firm's policy.

SDS used a production cost control system devised by W.B. Peat, a well-known professional accountant. The works submitted uniform weekly cost reports which recorded the cost of each manufacturing stage and each product for all three plants.[28] These data were compiled within the 'Analysis of Accounts' which management used for production and product decisions as well as for identifying areas of excessive cost.

The format of the Analysis was designed to facilitate the comparison of works' performance according to each process and product, rather than assessment of cost variations and operating ratios along a vertical production flow. Separate folios were devoted to costs incurred according to each product and manufacturing stage with expense items listed side by side for each plant. Thus, the cost of labour in steelmaking at each works could be compared at a glance whereas determining the relationship between steelmaking expenses and final product cost involved consulting six different folios. The Analysis did not record the volume of plant output because SDS did not operate fully integrated works which required close monitoring of the links between costs and volume. (For special reports Bagley consulted the Auditors' records which listed volume according to product and plant.)[29] In keeping with overall firm strategy, the Analysis was oriented toward comparing plant performance rather than evaluating the continuity of operations.

Within each folio, unit costs were broken down according to materials, labour, salaries, 'general charges' and repairs. The overhead items were computed by dividing a lump sum by aggregate output. Depreciation was not accounted for in the ledger. The inclusion of overheads was a departure from Carnegie's single-minded focus on prime costs, but the form of calculation and the omission of depreciation left SDS behind du Pont's standards.

The design of the Analysis and the information it included show that this ledger was intended to supply management with cost data for short-term decisions. It was not set up to support a long-term strategy like du Pont's, which pursued economies of scale through post-merger rationalisation. By excluding asset values and depreciation, the ledger did not treat individual plants as profit centres for which ROI could be used to inform decisions concerning which works to close permanently and where to concentrate investment. Since Furness used ROI to allocate investment among his shipping lines, SDS's officials were probably aware of the calculation, but did not employ it because their policy was to close a plant *temporarily* during recessions in order to concentrate production, lower costs, and win high profit margins by running the remaining facilities at capacity.[30] When specification submissions increased and intensified competition over delivery time during booms, the manager reactivated idle plant.[31] The Analysis' comparative data concerning prime costs and overheads helped Bagley to cope with fluctuating demand.[32]

The Analysis also provided a rough guide for product decisions, but SDS's strategy was not intended to achieve economies of scope; instead over time management reduced the range of the firm's product line. While depreciation and overheads were not allocated systematically to specific products, Bagley was able in a rough way to determine profits on intermediary processes, to decide when to concentrate production of subsidiary products, when to discontinue making specific items, and to formulate make or buy decisions.[33] Since these concerns were secondary to SDS's main priority and since prices were not based on costs, but rather set by Makers' Associations, improving the accuracy of the statistics to inform long-term decisions was not vital. Thus, as an instrument of production control, the Analysis was not intended to help SDS capture economies of scale or scope over the long-term.

SDS's capital accounting procedures and investment strategies reflected the same short-term orientation. Like many American and British firms in the late 1800s, SDS employed the 'renewal' method of capital accounting. Thus, Gray and Furness established an initial value for the firm's assets when they promoted SDS, and each year they added amounts spent on new equipment. The 'Summary of Capital Expenditure' recorded separately the value of new assets included at each of the three plants during the course of the financial year.[34] These data were summed and added to the total asset figure recorded in the balance sheet. The Directors then deducted depreciation, but only from the aggregated balance sheet figure not from the plant-level sums. Moreover, the amount of depreciation was not established by any systematic method. Rather, the Board allocated a round figure the size of which fluctuated according to annual profit levels.[35] These procedures made it clearly impossible to treat the works as independent profit centres, to determine precise asset values, and to use accurate ROI figures for each facility or the firm as a whole as a basis for rationalisation decisions. However, these were not vital considerations given the owners' strategy and their desire to preserve liquidity.

In keeping with its short-term orientation, the Board's main priority in allocating new investment was to commit funds to projects that would reduce operating expenses enough to recover their cost in one year.[36] Gray and Furness did not set a target profit margin towards which to direct these cost reducing investment decisions because they did not intend to concentrate fund allocation. Instead, using comparative data from the Analysis to identify areas of excessive cost the Board committed investment primarily to the two most modern facilities, but continued to siphon off funds to the Moor works to keep them operational so that SDS could compete on delivery during booms. Over time, SDS developed a 'flat-bottomed' cost curve to contend with fluctuating demand.

The short-term focus of investment policy is also reflected in the way in which the Directors determined the amount of spending. The Board sanctioned expenditure on an annual basis as profits allowed: in good years large sums were allocated, in poor years spending fell. With investment linked closely to fluctuating trade conditions, SDS's current prosperity determined its long-term profitability.[37] Only once during the 1898–1914 period – when the Directors authorised the construction of new steel furnaces – did the firm issue fresh capital (£100,000), and even then the additional funds were intended to supplement retained earnings.[38] Even though the absence of appropriate data for assessing investment proposals in precise ROI terms meant that decision makers lacked the means to evaluate the costs and benefits of using retained earnings or external finance to support SDS's long-term development, it was clearly their intention to keep SDS on a self-financing basis and as a result their attention was focused on short-term operating and profitability considerations.

SDS's investment horizon did not create demand for an accounting system that supported long-term planning capability. Annual improvement projects were small in scale, short in duration, and were carried out while the works were operating. As a result, there was little need for a formal capital budgeting and expenditure control system. Cost over runs sometimes occurred, but they were small and could be covered by overdraft borrowing or, after 1910, by reducing SDS's substantial cash surplus. The possibility of a serious working capital crisis arising from projects that involved relatively small sums (£20–30,000) was quite slim.[39] Bagley made rough comparisons of anticipated and actual cost savings arising from specific plant alterations, but with such a wide variety of projects there was no obvious way in which this exercise could be used to improve the accuracy of future planning. In short, the incremental, rather than fundamental nature of plant additions and the small amounts of capital involved created little need for an accounting infrastructure that could increase the efficiency of capital resource utilisation.

Between 1898 and 1914, the Board considered only two major proposals. Details concerning the construction of two Talbot furnaces have not survived, but estimates for a larger and more important project – the building of coke and iron making plant needed to adopt full-scale basic open-hearth steelmaking – reveals the accounting context within which SDS evaluated strategic options. Ben Talbot, CFI's Manager and the inventor of the continuous process, furnished SDS with these figures:[40]

Total cost of coke ovens, blast furnaces and conversion to basic practice	£700,000
Savings (£0.75 per ton at 175,000 tons p.a.)	131,250
Less depreciation at 7.5 per cent	37,000
[rounded to]	94,000
Add saving of £0.25 per ton on the use of cheaper ores	43,750
Total annual reduction in cost	127,750

(Investment recovered in 6 years after allowing for depreciation.)

The Directors evaluated the project in the same terms – pay back period – that they used to assess short-term investment plans. Their attention continued to be focused on liquidity and short-term cost reduction. With this data the Board could have calculated ROI (18 per cent), but given its emphasis on self-financing there was little need to do so in order to assess the viability of external financing.[41] Moreover, at this time the firm did not possess the resource set to implement the proposal. Lacking a mine and intimidated by the project's large cost, which would have increased well beyond the initial estimates if SDS purchased the ore supplies needed to implement the scheme, the Board retained its original strategy of incremental improvements until World War I brought tax incentives that facilitated internal financing.[42]

In conclusion, SDS's owners remained committed to a conservative policy, and their system was overwhelmingly orientated toward short-term concerns. SDS's routine cost accounts went beyond Carnegie's preoccupation with prime costs, but they fell short of the sophistication of du Pont's integrated system. Special reports seldom arose in response to questions of a fundamental strategic nature, and the answers provided, though imprecise in comparison with those obtained by du Pont, were adequate in terms of the owners' objectives. With no change in strategy there was no need to alter the format of SDS's control systems or to improve the accuracy of the data used in special reports.

As it stood, the firm's strategy was the exact opposite of that pursued by Carnegie and du Pont. Instead of trying to win scale advantages that would generate the large and stable market share needed for full running, while leaving competitors to cope with swings in demand, SDS absorbed the impact of market fluctuations itself. Firm-specific factors (an inappropriate resource set and a conservative financial strategy) and objective circumstances (technological divisibilities and market conditions that impeded the extension of functional controls) shaped this strategy. Yet, SDS's heavily depreciated plant and flat-bottomed cost curve, enabled it to cope with its cyclical market. Financing major additions with outside funds, especially debt, would have reduced its responsive capability. While Gray and Furness pursued a policy that was not adventurous, it was lucrative: SDS was Britain's second most profitable steel firm in the pre-war era.[43]

IV

In contrast to SDS's responsive horizontal policy, CFI devised an aggressive first-mover assault aimed at breaking those constraints that hindered the mass-production of open-hearth steel. Its owners believed that CFI possessed the resource set required to become an ultra-efficient single-product (plate) firm that could cut prices, run at full capacity, and let rivals cope with fluctuating demand. Thus, they sought to replicate the first stage of Carnegie's strategy by securing scale economies through process integration.

Carrying out this innovative policy required special planning reports and, given the radical extension of CFI's production facilities, a new comprehensive control system. To *formulate* strategy, CFI's Board needed reports that furnished accurate estimates of their firm's production costs and information about competitors' expenses.[44] These figures would provide a basis for anticipating the effect that CFI's competition would have on regional prices and, in turn, its own profit margins. The planners also needed precise estimates concerning the cost of building a balanced facility capable of achieving optimal scale economies.

To *execute* their scheme CFI's owners had to establish a system that differed markedly from SDS's. CFI required an infrastructure that would enable the management to exercise close control over works branches that carried out a series of vertically related processes, rather than to compare costs incurred at similar plants. Initially, CFI needed an organisational structure which delineated areas of authority from which accounting data for planning and control purposes would flow upwards to the chief decision-makers.[45] The links between organisation and systems were particularly important because, unlike SDS which took over commercially viable facilities, CFI had to build a brand new plant and, therefore, required budgeting and expenditure controls and strong works-level planning capabilities.

In terms of functional controls, it was initially necessary for CFI's executives – unlike their counterparts at SDS – to develop accounting procedures that could link part of the supply area with manufacturing. Management needed to set up a system that would co-ordinate the Liverton iron mine's activities with the operations of the new plant.

However, since CFI did not own a coal mine, it did not need to extend its backward functional controls further. To achieve the firm's initial goal – perfecting mass-production – its planners did not require accounting systems that would co-ordinate production and sales. The firm could rely on custom from Furness's yards to absorb its annual make (125,000 tons). However, if CFI's owners intended to expand the firm's market share further and confront remaining constraints facing British steelmakers – manufacturers' associations, close producer–customer ties, and fragmented order and specification flows – CFI would have to modify both its organisational structure and systems to support direct selling and to co-ordinate sales, purchasing, and production.

E.L. Pease (CFI's first Chairman) drew up the initial planning reports.[46] He projected an annual capacity of 125,000 tons of plate at a cost of 77 s. per ton. At the current market price, which he erroneously expected to remain the same, Pease anticipated a profit margin of £1 per ton. The works would cost £400,000. While the projections included rough depreciation estimates (see below), the managers did not use ROI (31 per cent) to assess the viability of the project, because they were not considering alternative schemes and did not plan to use outside capital. CFI's parent, Weardale Steel, would finance the new plant.

In keeping with the integrated nature of CFI's operations, Pease developed his production cost estimates in a cumulative fashion by first computing the cost of winning ore from Liverton and then projecting this fundamental expense through the entire sequence of manufacturing. This serial calculation also included estimates (based on definite offers) for coal and other materials. The costs at each stage from coking to rolling were compiled from material conversion ratios provided by equipment makers and other steel firms. Unlike the standard rates used in US industry, CFI's ratios were based on full capacity operations. Given the firm's strategy, using this rate of utilisation for estimating made sense, but it was projected through the production sequence only as far as steel making: plate rolling was not included. The omission is telling: it reveals that management did not confront the imbalance that it was planning into the works. The capacity of Weardale's mill was twice that of the rest of the plant.

Pease's estimates provided for overheads and depreciation but did not do so in a systematic manner. The report used a variety of bases for calculating overheads, perhaps following the sources of information available.[47] Depreciation was allocated directly to coking alone because the ovens were subject to heavy wear. For the other departments Pease arbitrarily set rounded sums for depreciation and after dividing these figures by full capacity output, he added the result to the total unit costs.

Thus, rather than factoring depreciation directly into unit costs like du Pont, CFI's planner adhered to the 'renewal' method and 'tacked on' this expense to final unit costs to determine a net profit margin. Though imprecise by standards set by Du Pont, this practice was more advanced than that of Carnegie and it suited the basis of CFI's strategy given the expectation that the firm's costs would establish regional prices. Whereas SDS adhered to PMA prices and exhibited a short-term perspective, CFI had a longer-run policy.

Pease's capital cost estimates and spending controls showed serious weaknesses. Capital costs were broken down according to equipment type and works department.[48] These estimates also included amounts paid up to November 1902, and a schedule of anticipated monthly payments running from November 1902 to January 1904. However, the schedule did not cross-reference payments on specific plant components with amounts falling due each month, so that management could not monitor construction in direct relation to expenditure. Ominously, there was no comparison of estimated and actual payments for the 1 November 1902 to February 1903 period revealing a four month gap in reporting.

Overall, Pease's plan supported the formulation of an innovative strategy because it traced production costs cumulatively through the entire manufacturing sequence and because it provided comparative data drawn from other firms for every department except mining and ironmaking. While the estimates were based on full capacity operations (with the exception of rolling) this assumption was logical given the intention to run full and cut prices. Thus, the sponsors of the project could obtain an immediate grasp of the scale economies which formed the central objective of their strategy. For nearly every stage of production, they could also ascertain the resultant competitive advantage that the plant would win over rivals.

Nevertheless, the projections exhibited serious limitations. First, the estimates were based on an unbalanced plant, and the addition of the upstream equipment needed to round out the works would have radically changed the scope of the project.[49] Second, Pease's estimates were based on the assumption that each week the Liverton Mine could produce 7,000 tons of ore containing 37 per cent iron at a cost of 6s. per ton, but he did not consider the effects of deviations from these parameters. Third, with his attention captivated by a unique opportunity to win extraordinarily low costs, Pease developed a rigid production plan by building his projections from the 'bottom up' to arrive at a maximum profit margin. In contrast, du Pont began with a financial target, based on ROI criteria because they had to service their capital, and then worked backwards. Since CFI's owners used internal funds, they did not have to be concerned with ROI. But given its basic strategy the firm needed some sort of profit objective that took into account competitors' pricing reactions. In short, Pease did not transform his production plan into a commercial scheme. Finally, Pease's capital spending and control arrangements exhibited serious defects, and he did not include contingencies for cost overruns or equipment changes.

As they stood, CFI's cost estimates rested on two critical assumptions. Over the long-term Liverton could meet cost, quality and output targets. Further, the estimates assumed full capacity operations. The effects of deviations from these two conditions on down stream activities were not considered.

Soon after development began on the basis of Pease's estimates, it became apparent that CFI's existing organisational structure and accounting procedures could not control capital spending. By October 1903, CFI had almost exhausted Weardale's reserves. In response to this problem, doubts about the viability of producing plates and lingering concern about Liverton's potential, Furness appointed a 'Committee of Experts', drawn from CFI, Weardale, and SDS, to re-examine the entire project.

The Experts drew up another comprehensive planning report which concurred largely with Pease's estimate of production expenses but revised construction costs upward by 16 per cent.[50] Including earlier escalations, capital costs amounted to twice the initial £400,000, but the causes of the over run cannot be traced because Pease and the Experts used different categories for compiling equipment costs. The Committee also recommended that CFI abandon plate making in favour of sections, so that the firm would manufacture products that complemented rather than competed with those of SDS. This shift in policy required a different rolling plant and raised costs by a further £184,000. Perhaps following the parameters laid down in the original scheme, the Experts planned for a section mill that had the same capacity (5,000 tons per week) as Weardale's plate mill. As a result the imbalance in CFI's plant was not corrected.

The Committee's report recomputed past spending and total estimated expenditure needed to complete the works. However, since it did not include a schedule of anticipated monthly payments cross-referenced with specific plant components, the report did not correct those defects in CFI's capital spending controls that prevented executives from monitoring construction in direct relation to expenditure. This problem was remedied – ten months later – when an 'Approximate Statement of Payments' was drawn up, but the equipment categories used were not the same as those in the earlier reports.[51] Thus, CFI's capital cost projections resemble a series of independent estimates which displayed no continuity. The inconsistent methods of calculation prevented management from identifying reasons for inaccuracies and ensuring that errors were not repeated.

In 1904–5, the Board discovered further mistakes, the correction of which increased building costs further. In response CFI departed from its earlier policy and borrowed heavily from outside sources.[52] Debt servicing raised the firm's fixed costs and eroded its competitive advantages relative to competitors who operated heavily depreciated plant. (In contrast Carnegie was able to control spending and could therefore continue to use internal funds; this policy strengthened his position in the 1890s when he faced over capitalised rivals.)[53] While CFI's owners recognised the danger of growing debt, the costing system that they initially designed did not quantify the consequences in terms of unit costs and prices.[54] The du Ponts exchanged bonds for the family firm and therefore devised a system that accounted for the cost of capital, while Carnegie did not need such a framework as long as he eschewed borrowing and retained his prime cost advantage. CFI did not adjust its system to accommodate its new financial policy.

CFI's anticipated production cost advantage did not materilise after manufacturing began in 1906. Recognition of the reasons was not hindered by defects in the firm's production cost controls but rather by the way in which they were used before Benjamin Talbot became Manager in 1907. Earlier management did not use the original estimates as standards against which actual cost figures could be compared in order to identify the causes of deviations even though the production records were compiled in the same way as the original projections. (In designing their cost system, CFI's managers consulted the format that W.B. Peat devised for SDS.)[55] Instead, historic or past cost trends were employed as a comparative yardstick. Thus, CFI's executives came to use a 'floating' standard rather than a fixed point of reference to assess operating performance.[56]

When Talbot took over in 1907, he began centralising CFI's organisation and opened up blocked communication flows that prevented problem recognition.[57] One of the first things he did was to compare the actual costs and the composition of furnace burdens with the estimates, and he immediately realised that too much foreign ore was being charged to compensate for the poorer-than-expected quality of Liverton ore.[58] He changed mining procedures at Liverton, but he could not reduce costs to the levels in the original estimates because of the declining quality of the deposit. It became apparent that the CFI project had been founded on a false assumption:

Liverton could not provide a sound basis for the firm's long-term development.

This realisation induced the new manager to devise operating ratios to assess the impact of Liverton's performance on CFI's overall cost structure. He determined that 1d. of extra cost per ton of ore raised iron expenses by 1s., and one per cent variations in iron content caused changes of 1s. per ton of steel.[59] Realising that the volume of mine output had an important impact on total costs, he quantified the cost reducing effects of increased output and priced outside ore sales below cost to reduce CFI's total expenses.[60] Talbot used these ratios and *ad hoc* calculations, instead of standard rates or full capacity operations, because CFI had departed from its original production strategy.

When Furness recognised that CFI could not achieve the competitive advantage needed to cut prices and win economies of scale in a single product field, he adopted a more passive policy of joining rather than fighting manufacturers' associations. The broadening of CFI's product line following the decision to make sections instead of plate also influenced this strategy.[61] As a result, there were fewer incentives for Talbot to develop a system that rigorously correlated volume and costs, although he did determine that CFI's break even point was 3,000 tons per week and used this as a general performance objective.[62]

Having failed to replicate the first stage of Carnegie's strategy and lost its ability to influence prices and sales, CFI did not need to extend its accounting controls to win economies of functional co-ordination. Talbot hired a new purchasing officer and a sales representative (CFI continued to sell extensively through agents) and centralised their reporting flows, but the functional organisation remained rudimentary. CFI did not sell direct and, therefore, did not need to dovetail purchasing and sales using systematic methods like those developed by du Pont.

In turn, without integrated functional controls, CFI could not develop accurate financial projections of the type that du Pont employed to support long-term planning. A Finance Committee received data concerning receivables, payables, sales booked and overdraft levels. With this information it could monitor changes in cash flow, but could not project future trends because the firm could not forecast sales. After CFI overcame its debt crisis in 1910, overdraft facilities provided a working capital cushion.

Operating rather than financial considerations dictated the direction of new investment. After CFI's productive core was operating, the need to increase primary iron and steel capacity to make fuller use of the rolling mill became the main consideration. Talbot assessed proposals according to payback or savings per ton rather than ROI criteria because he did not have to select from a range of investment alternatives and because liquidity and cost reduction remained important.[63] Moreover, CFI used retained profits instead of outside capital to pay for improvements. There was no reason to devise new capital accounting procedures in order to calculate ROI. The firm employed 'renewal' methods and, like SDS, used 'depreciation' write offs to finance extensions.

Talbot also reformed procedures for the reporting of capital spending. In 1912, he introduced monthly statements showing amounts approved for construction to date, plus new authorisations for the current month, less total payments made to date, leaving the figure still owed.[64] With this data the Directors could monitor overall expenditure, but lacking estimates of future monthly profits they could not correlate capital spending systematically with financial projections.[65] Since the firm did not win the anticipated cost advantage and remained exposed to the lag between order and specification submissions, management could not base profit estimates on full capacity operations. Thus, as CFI retreated from its aggressive strategy, Talbot modified aspects of its systems in accordance with environmental conditions and the firm's reduced capabilities.

V

The findings of this case study suggest that firm-specific resource sets as well as environmental conditions influence strategy formulation. Policy unfolds as management recognises complementarities between external circumstances and corporate attributes. Externally oriented communication channels reveal the existence of productive opportunities while a firm's internal information flows, including those that convey accounting data, indicate whether or not the company's resources qualify it to exploit specific opportunities. Thus, systems provide inputs into strategy formulation and their form evolves in line with the requirements of policy implementation.

In this regard, systems represent an important adjunct to administrative structure. CFI encountered difficulties because it did not adjust its organisation and accounting controls to fit its policy. Pease did not use targets articulated in the original estimates to evaluate production cost data in order to assess the effectiveness of policy execution, and he failed to develop controls for monitoring capital expenditure in direct relation to construction. As a result, he obtained a false impression of the firm's capability. Talbot, who had observed Carnegie's methods while managing American steel firms, undertook rudimentary organisational reforms and identified the sources of CFI's problems, but without an absolute cost advantage the firm could not overcome those environmental conditions that constrained structural change. SDS pursued a less adventurous policy which did not require innovations in organisation or systems.

Concerning the relationship between planning reports and accounting controls, these cases indicate that similar types of calculations were needed to determine whether parameters laid down in planning estimates were achieved. The differences that Edwards and Newell observed in the techniques employed in *ad hoc* reports and systems used by early firms may not have had debilitating consequences when technology, market conditions, and relatively low levels of managerial complexity generated little need for close interaction between planning and control. By the late nineteenth century, environmental conditions and the availability of high volume technology generated demand for accounting techniques that facilitated more comprehensive control. However, only firms like CFI, which pursued dynamic strategies and undertook complicated development schemes, needed such sophisticated controls. SDS required only simple procedures to link plans for incremental improvements to less complicated production records.

Overall, the accounting techniques employed by these two firms were not as advanced as those devised by du Pont, but they exceeded the sophistication of Carnegie's practices. While both British steel firms made provision for overheads, they accounted for depreciation in 'renewal' fashion. Unlike du Pont, SDS and CFI did not face environmental conditions that exposed economies which could be secured by linking functional areas with accounting controls. The owners of the two firms knew about, but did not employ, ROI techniques because they relied primarily on retained earnings for investment and did not consider a range of investment proposals. Even though SDS and CFI shared the same information sources, which on the surface resembled the accounting–engineering–management links found in the US, these specialised single-function firms had no reason to use more advanced techniques. While this study has provided some firm-level insights concerning the relationship between accounting systems and strategy formulation during an important period in Britain's economic history, further evidence from company records is needed to assess the representativeness of the practices described here.

NOTES

The author thanks the editors and an anonymous referee for their valuable criticisms and acknowledges the helpful comments made by Professor A.J. van Zijl and members of the Accounting Group when an earlier draft was presented at Victoria University of Wellington.

1. Alfred D. Chandler, Jr., *The Visible Hand: The Managerial Revolution in American Business* (Cambridge, MA, 1977) and *Scale and Scope: The Dynamics of Industrial Capitalism* (Cambridge, MA., 1990). For Johnson's case studies see, H. Thomas Johnson and Robert S. Kaplan, *Relevance Lost: The Rise and Fall of Management Accounting* (Boston, 1987).
2. D. Solomons, 'The Historical Development of Costing', in Solomons (ed.), *Studies in Cost Analysis* (Homewood, IL, 1968), pp.17–19.
3. S.P. Garner, *Evolution of Cost Accounting* (Alabama, 1954), Ch.2.
4. Robert R. Locke, 'Cost Accounting: An Institutional Yardstick for Measuring British Entrepreneurial Performance circa 1914', *Accounting Historians Journal*, Vol.6 (1979), pp.1–22 and *The End of the Practical Man. Entrepreneurship and Higher Education in Germany, France, and Great Britain 1880–1940* (Greenwich, CT, 1984).
5. See also, Edgar Jones, *Accountancy and the British Economy* (London, 1981). and H.T. Johnson 'Toward a New Understanding of Nineteenth Century Cost Accounting', *The Accounting Review*, Vol.LVI (1981), pp.510–18.
6. Examples include, R.K. Fleischman and Lee D. Parker, 'Managerial Accounting Early in the British Industrial Revolution: The Carron Company, A Case Study', *Accounting and Business Research*, Vol.20 (1990), pp.211–21; N. McKendrick, 'Josiah Wedgwood and Cost Accounting in the Industrial Revolution', *Economic History Review*, 2nd series, Vol.XXIII (1970), pp.45–67; and Willard E. Stone, 'An Early English Cotton Mill Cost Accounting System: Charlton Mills, 1810–1889', *Accounting and Business Research*, Vol.13 (1973), pp.71–78.
7. J.R. Edwards and E. Newell, 'The Development of Industrial Cost and Management Accounting before 1850: A Survey of the Evidence', *Business History*, Vol.33 No.1 (1991), pp.36–47.
8. H.T. Johnson, 'Early Cost Accounting for Internal Management Control: Lyman Mills in the 1850s', *Business History Review*, Vol.52 (1972), pp.466–74 and *Relevance Lost*, pp.21–31.
9. Lymans like Charlton Mills also developed integrated financial and cost accounts. Concerning the potential problems arising from inventory evaluation, see *Relevance Lost*, pp.131–35. In Britain, demand for audited financial reports grew comparatively early with the rise of the securities market. Because British firms were single-function entities, auditors could obtain all the information they needed from the general ledger which recorded profit and loss arising from market transactions. Consequently, there was no need to use the two sets of books as an internal check. (*Relevance Lost*, pp.41–4).
10. For analyses of Carnegie's accounting methods see, Joseph F. Wall, *Andrew Carnegie* (New York), pp.314–16, 329, 336, and 342; Harold Livesay, *Andrew Carnegie and the Rise of Big Business* (Boston, 1975), pp.84–9; and Chandler, *Visible Hand*, pp.259–69. Edgar Jones reports that it was not until 1900 that major British railroads, like the North Eastern, developed accurate cost data for systematic rate setting (*Accountancy*, pp.115–6).
11. Chandler, *Visible Hand*, pp.268 and 360–61 and Livesay, pp.149–66. We do not know what accounting means Carnegie used to support functional co-ordination.
12. Chandler, *Visible Hand*, pp.111–2 and 115. British railways began to account for depreciation in the 1830–50 period (Edwards and Newell, 'Development of Industrial . . .', pp.52–3).
13. Chandler, *Visible Hand*, pp.272–78.
14. Marion Jelinck, 'Toward Systematic Management: Alexander Hamilton Church', *Business History Review*, Vol.54 (Spring, 1980), pp.63–79 and Johnston and Kaplan, pp.47–58. In contrast, American Tobacco reported sales and advertising costs and

Armour devised rough estimates for overheads and assessed selling costs at a flat 5% rate (Chandler, *Visible Hand*, pp.386 and 431).

15. Chandler, *Visible Hand*, pp.277–8.
16. Chandler, *Visible Hand*, p.415; H.T. Johnson, 'Management Accounting in an Early Integrated Industrial: E.I. du Pont de Namours Powder Company, 1903–12', *Business History Review*, Vol.49 (1975), pp.184–204; *Relevance Lost*, pp.61–92; and M. Massouh, 'Technological and Managerial Innovation: The Johnson Company, 1883–1898', *Business History Review*, Vol.50 (1976), p.46.
17. Thus, the du Ponts calculated depreciation from historic cost: some accountants advocate the use of replacement value as the basis for depreciation.
18. Chandler, *Visible Hand*, p.415 and Johnson 'Du Pont', p.193 n. 29.
19. This discussion of the Northern steel industry is based on B. Elbaum, 'The Steel Industry Before World War I', in Bernard Elbaum and William Lazonick (eds), *The Decline of the British Economy* (Oxford, 1986), pp.51–81; Steven Tolliday, *Business, Banking, and Politics: The Case of British Steel, 1918–1939* (Cambridge, MA, 1987); pp.46–81; and G. Boyce, 'The Development of the Cargo Fleet Iron Company, 1900–1914', *Business History Review*, Vol.63 (1989), pp.839–75.
20. For a description of Furness' business career, see G. Boyce, 'The Growth and Dissolution of a Large-scale Business Enterprise: The Furness Interest 1892–1919' (unpublished Ph.D. thesis, London School of Economics, 1984).
21. The shipyards controlled by Furness and Gray gave SDS preference at equal price. Thus, as long as the PMA remained intact, SDS received all of their orders.
22. SDS Directors Minutes [hereafter DM] 20 and 31 Dec. 1898 and 7 Feb. 1899. British Steel Corporation, Northern Regional Records Centre, Middlesbrough. Accession Number 04893 [all SDS and CFI records are housed at the BSC NRRC]
23. SDS Correspondence (Letter Book 2132) Sladden to Gray 28 Sept. 1899.
24. Bagley could only 'press' yards for submissions. He used the methods described above to calculate how many tons of specifications SDS needed to receive in order to run full. See, SDS DM 28 March 1908, 24 July 1912, and 27 Aug. 1913.
25. These changing parameters are reported throughout SDS DM.
26. Due to lags in payments from clients and to suppliers, slow specification flows squeezed SDS's cash position from two sides. Purchasing warrants could alleviate this pressure, and overdraft facilities provided a cushion at the cost of interest. SDS never stood out of the market on the expectation of falls in iron prices.
27. He assumed that SDS would receive enough specifications to run full in the forecast period. SDS DM 29 Sept. 1903, 19 Oct. 1903, 28 Nov. 1904, 19 June 1905, 27 March 1906, and 24 April 1911.
28. Analysis of Accounts, BSC 04908. About 75% of SDS's output consisted of steel plate.
29. SDS Auditors' Reports BSC 04879.
30. See Furness, Withy & Co. Directors Minutes 20 Aug. 1907 and Prince Line accounts National Maritime Museum, Greenwich [FWS B/6/1 & B/7/1].
31. Bagley did not account for the cost of idle capacity even though he recognised that SDS incurred closure and start-up expenses. He did, however, devise rough figures for profits and output lost due to strikes and breakdowns using full capacity operations as a standard. SDS DM 29 Sept. 1903, 9 Feb. 1904, and 23 Feb. 1911.
32. SDS DM 22 July 1904, 28 Nov. 1907, 28 March 1908, and 29 May 1912.
33. SDS DM 12 October 1900, 17 Feb. 1903, and 23 July 1913. The du Ponts could not accurately perform make or buy calculations either since they did not assign depreciation to intermediate products, but this did not hinder the formulation of final product strategy. (Johnson, 'Du Pont', p.202).
34. The Summary was included as a separate part of the Analysis.
35. SDS DM passim and Shareholders Minutes BSC 04908.
36. SDS DM 24 Jan. 1900, 21 Feb. 1901, 7 Dec. 1903, 4 Feb. 1905, 16 Nov. 1905, 27 Jan. 1910, 28 Nov. 1910, 27 July 1911, 28 Sept. 1911, 28 Sept. 1912, and 26 Nov. 1913.

37. To reduce expenditure on vital projects during poor years, the Board allowed Bagley to cannibalise the Moor works, thereby raising future restart costs. SDS DM 27 Jan. 1910 and 22 Jan. 1913.
38. SDS DM 22 June 1906 and Circular to Shareholders (BSC 03362).
39. Cost overruns recorded in SDS DM 17 Feb. 1903 29 March 1906, and 28 Nov. 1907 amounted to £3–4,500 at a time when the firm had reserves of £100,000.
40. SDS DM 26 June 1912.
41. The firm's method of capital accounting also prevented the Directors from comparing the ROI of this project with SDS's investment in existing plant.
42. SDS leased Weardale's blast furnace (DM 17 Jan. 1917) and bought iron makers Cochranes and Seaton Carew, undoubtedly with the aid of Excess Profit Duty rebates, to overcome supply threats brought about by a regional imbalance in iron and steel capacity arising from wartime construction. [W.G. Willis, *History of South Durham Steel & Iron Co., Ltd.* (Portsmouth, 1969), pp.15–6.]
43. Consett was the most profitable firm. H.W. Richardson and J.M. Bass, 'The Profitability of Consett Iron Company before 1914', *Business History*, Vol.7 No.2 (1965), p.72.
44. Carnegie joined the Bessemer Pool to obtain cost data about his competitors. (Chandler, *Visible Hand*, p.268).
45. Boyce, 'The Development of the Cargo Fleet Iron Co.', pp.848–60.
46. Pease's plan of Feb. 1903 [BSC 07710] refers to an earlier set of estimates which has not survived.
47. Different methods were used to compute these expenses for the various departments: for mining and coking costs carefully estimated figures were divided by output; in iron making a round sum was used; in steel making Pease relied on Frodingham's costs, and used SDS's figures for rolling.
48. Capital costs were included in the Feb. 1903 plan (BSC 07710).
49. There is no evidence that the owners planned to build the additional plant which would have doubled capital costs.
50. Report of the Expert Committee BSC 07710.
51. The Approximate Statement is included in BSC 07710.
52. Boyce, 'Cargo Fleet', pp.860–73.
53. Livesay, *Andrew Carnegie*, pp.182–6.
54. For Talbot's view, see CFI DM [BSC 04906] 16 April 1908.
55. CFI DM 4 Nov. 1904.
56. This is reflected in the 'Summaries of Costs, Prices, and Profits' (BSC 04877) and the Manager's reports appended to CFI DM passim
57. Boyce 'Cargo Fleet', pp.855–60.
58. Talbot to Furness 3 Dec. 1908 BSC 04119 (file 203).
59. CFI Committee Minutes [hereafter CFI CM] BSC 04906 12 July 1911.
60. Since depreciation was not included, CFI may have lost money on these outside sales. (CM 1 Nov. and 28 Dec. 1910.)
61. CFI joined all associations that regulated its products and therefore could not follow competitors who joined some but not all groups so that they could win high margins on some products and 'dump' output in other markets to achieve higher throughput. Talbot and Furness disagreed on this policy. but lack of a cost advantage made it necessary. (DM 10 Apr. 1908; CM 10 June 1911)
62. DM 22 June 1908 ff.
63. DM 14 Aug. 1907, 1 Nov. 1910, 23 July 1913, CM 12 July 1911, 13 Dec. 1911, 17 July 1912, and 23 April 1913.
64. DM 29 May 1912 ff.
65. The Board received profit and sales data for the current month.

The Neglected Intangible Asset: The Influence of the Trade Mark on the Rise of the Modern Corporation

MIRA WILKINS

Florida International University

Trade marks are – and have been since the late nineteenth and throughout the twentieth century – significant business assets; this paper argues that they have played a critical role in the rise of the modern multifunctional, multiplant, multiproduct, multiregional, multinational enterprise. Yet, they have not – nor have brand names, trade names, and company names (and following the lead of the legal scholars I use these terms interchangeably herein) – been systematically studied by economic or business historians, even though much has been written by other scholars on these intangible assets.[1] Most economic and business historians recognize the importance of intangible property rights, in general. Thus, Douglass C. North and Barry R. Weingast have written, 'For economic growth to occur the sovereign or government must not merely establish the relevant set of rights, but make a commitment to them'.[2] As I will show, the United States did this in the late nineteenth and early twentieth century in relation to trade mark protection.

In this paper I will: (1) explain the importance of trade marks to the coming of age of the modern managerial corporation; (2) present a brief chronology of the principal US laws and some major court rulings in US trade mark history with the aim of demonstrating the correspondence between the increase in the value of this asset to the modern firm and the development of legal support for it; (3) analyse the unique and crucial characteristics of the trade mark, comparing it with the patent; and (4) indicate how the trade mark promotes economic efficiency gains through time. While this article focuses on the growth of American business and modern US legal history, the argument pertains to the rise of the modern corporation in general; and indeed I do consider the experiences in the United States of non-US based multinationals. This paper, moreover, should make it evident why developed countries have nationally and internationally known trademarked products (the names of which can be legally defended in the courts) and less developed ones lack such trademarked goods and services and protection of the property rights.[3]

II

When economic and business historians discuss the rise of the modern corporation, our debt goes to the pioneering work of Alfred D. Chandler, Jr. Chandler has emphasized what he calls the 'technological and organizational underpinnings' of the modern corporation. He has insisted that by taking advantage of new technology and through organisational innovations, the modern corporation has created efficiencies.[4] The modern corporation – in Chandler's view – benefits from economies of scale and scope.[5] Yet, the large modern corporation (often a multinational one) has required more than advanced technology and more than organisation to persist and to succeed. Unless it had volume sales, there could be neither economies of scale or scope (production and distribution economies would go unrealized); organisation was not required if the enterprise could not obtain a market for its output. By definition, sales were necessary for survival. The argument of this paper is that if a firm is to attract customers *to it*, it must draw those buyers to some 'name' that is unique and known. Without the distinctive trade mark, brand name, trade name, or company name (as noted, I use these words as equivalents), it would be impossible to pull consumers to the particular goods or services of an enterprise and the firm would be unable to take advantage of the increasing returns to scale and scope. A company's advertising is pointless with no name to promote.

Indeed, the very endurance of the firm seems linked with a name or names that over long periods continue to bring in customers. If one views an enterprise as having the advantage of knowledge accumulated and transmitted cheaply through time within the firm, it has to be a given that the output of that firm must be desired by buyers. The name embodies the company's reputation and offers information to the customer that sustains the enterprise. To quote Harold Demsetz, a property rights system that provides trade mark protection encourages 'investment in "permanence", and discourages investment in fly-by night operations'.[6]

The giant American-headquartered corporations that emerged in the late nineteenth century offered a range of new products that benefited from economies of large-scale output. To sell sewing machines, harvesters, cash registers and so forth, there had to be trade names. These were advertised products. Standard Oil, which took advantage of major economies of scale, adopted the name 'Standard' to connote a standard quality product.[7] All the US companies in the late nineteenth and early twentieth century that became multinational enterprises – based on their sales abroad – offered trademarked goods. So, too, all the successful European multinationals that invested in the United States in this same period sold trademarked products.[8] For reasons that will become apparent, the trade mark became especially valuable to multinational corporations.

Trade marks are *not* new to modern managerial enterprises, nor are they necessarily confined to major enterprises. Archaeologists have found potters' marks on pots at least 4,000 years old from a region that became part of ancient Greece.[9] The mark seems to have identified the producer. Yet, there is no evidence then or subsequently, as Greek civilisation developed, of Greek laws granting exclusivity to trade marks.[10] Likewise, a small business – a dressmaker, today or in years past, for example – has her name that recommends customers to her; her reputation (the product she provides; her skill and industry) attracts purchasers to her dressmaking services. The property right, her name – the intangible asset – does not, however, require legal defence, for the close nexus between seller and buyer growing out of the one-to-one exchange is sufficient to assure that property right. In a parallel manner, she does not need to protect her skills with patents (nor can she do so, since her method is not 'new and nonobvious' and does not meet other specifications for a patent)[11] nor must she establish a corporate entity that is a 'legal person'.

By contrast, the big modern corporation (by virtue of its large output) is characterised by a separation of producer and consumer through a distribution chain. This is even more true of the multinational enterprise than of the purely domestic one. The goods maker's name and reputation are not known to the purchaser through the intimacy of personal familiarity between seller and buyer. Yet, the need to differentiate the product – to draw customers to the firm's products rather than to competitors' output – remains (and indeed with a firm's economies of scale or scope becomes imperative) even though the name and reputation are no longer sustained by personal connections. Repeat-purchases (those made *again* by a single buyer and those made by *different* buyers on the basis of earlier buyers' information) of a particular firm's offerings are impossible if there is no brand name identification.

When the separation between producer and buyer occurs, the name and reputation become intangible property rights that *require legal support*. The modern firm uses the corporate form to attract and to manage capital. Patents assure the corporation (or individual) legal rights to inventions. The trade mark, the trade name, similarly calls for legal backing. The need to define and to defend in the courts the trade mark – as a corporate property right – becomes a *new* and significant feature of modern giant enterprise. The latter must stop others from free-riding on, or debasing, this asset. Since the consumer relies on the name in the transaction, free-riding and debasing become threats to the modern firm. Indeed, as we will show, the rise and development of the large enterprise in the late nineteenth and early twentieth centuries coincided with the major change from a common law acceptance of trade names to statutes, rules, and court decisions and from an arena with few to many cases.

Trade marks were sometimes adopted and promoted very early in the history of the modern firm, sometimes later. More systematic investigation is required on the use and timing of trade marks *by industry*; there were variations. With one set of products, the eye sees them as alike; the trade mark tells of differences. With a second set of products, the eye sees differences; the trademark confirms and designates the differences. With packaged or canned products, the eye cannot see what is there; the trade mark informs the consumer. Even if the eye can see, the purchaser may not be able to evaluate what is viewed (will a machine continue to work; is a medicine effective?); the trade mark helps the consumer answer these questions swiftly.

Brand names became important to cheap goods (soap, razors, candy bars) as well as to expensive ones (cars, clothes washing machines, pianos). They became key not only to consumer products, but to producer goods (from dye-stuffs to harvesters to electrical equipment).[12] For the buyer, the costs of switching to a generic or to an unfamiliar name differ substantially by industry. The costs are extremely high when goods are expensive and bad choices have serious repercussions (vital electrical equipment, for instance). They are low in the case of sweets, for example. Firm-specific names are *not* important to apples or oranges, where the consumer inspects the product in the market, nor to gourmet coffee beans where the reputation of a local shop is sufficient. Likewise, they are not essential to a coal company that sells a homogeneous product. They are, however, vital to the large-scale modern enterprise.

Initially, the trade mark was identified with the maker. As the modern corporation emerged, however, the trade name (which might be the same as the company name, although it need not be) became joined with the goods or services *per se*. By the early twentieth century, an American buyer of Lux soap might not know that the manufacturer was the Lever Brothers Co. Few of us know which company produces Hellmann's Mayonnaise. The manufacturer of the goods sold by Sears is not important to the buyer of the goods (the store name, Sears, is). What the customer is sure of is that no matter who is the maker – that is, even if the buyer is ignorant of the name of the maker – the purchaser will get in the product the anticipated standardised quality; the name carries information. Likewise, today the typical buyer of motel services has no idea who owns a particular Holiday Inn, Days Inn, or Quality Inn. What he (or she) recognizes is that each of these names is linked with a product that evokes certain expectations (and with these motels a reservation service as well). The trade mark defines what is being purchased.

In some ways, the trade name seems even more fundamental than new technology in the emergence of the modern firm, modern products, and the understanding of modern industrial structures. Thus, Sears, Holiday Inn, and McDonald's are not characterised by technological innovation (unless we consider technology in the broadest sense to include the social technology of distributing goods and services). But, these businesses could not prosper without the trade name. The trade mark is indispensable to large firms in the sale of services as well as goods.

In the connections between producer and consumer, the trade mark has a unique role. It is the property of the producer. The trade mark safeguards the producer's 'skill and industry'. But the trade mark also aids the consumer. When the consumer does not know personally the producer, the trade mark becomes the surrogate for the direct access by the buyer to knowledge of the product. Thus, only after the modern giant corporation, with its new products and processes and its multitude of buyers, came into prominence did the trade mark become an essential business asset.

Accordingly, although there has been a long history of trade marks, there has not been a long legal history relating to the defence of the trade mark. In 1925, as the modern managerial firm was emerging, Frank I. Schechter wrote:

> . . . nowhere is the obscurity of the origins and at the same time the 'touching absence of curiosity' concerning these origins more apparent than in the field of the law of the trade-marks. When we consider how great a factor trade-marks and good will represent in commercial life today . . . the comparative brevity of the history of that law . . . is remarkable indeed.[13]

Yet the 'obscurity' is not odd, *because* before the existence of the modern large-scale firm and the separation of producer and consumer, before the rise of the multiplicity of modern product choices, there was no compelling reason for a business to defend this intangible asset in the courts.

The reader will at once counter that long-distance trade is not confined to modern times nor to the modern corporation. Long-distance trade, where producer and consumer are separate, has existed for centuries. Likewise, the internalisation of that trade within a corporation is not unique to the nineteenth and twentieth centuries (the East India companies, the Hudson Bay Co., and similar trading enterprises had sizable transactions within the firm).[14] But, neither the arm's length nor the internalized long-distance trade depended to any great extent on production economies of scale or scope that are characteristic of modern goods and services. The trade mark was thus not crucial, although company names had started to serve an important function (the Hudson Bay traders were known as purchasers of fur and the name attracted Indian sellers of fur).[15] The trade mark becomes a fundamental and absolutely essential property right that requires legal support only when the firm must find means to increase its own sales to lower average unit costs to realise the advantages of economies of scale and/or scope; this is a characteristic of the modern giant enterprise (and the industries that have found giant enterprise appropriate). Subsequently, the established name can be used by the firm – as I will show – for other purposes as well. Likewise, as I will also demonstrate, the trademark has great importance in lowering costs to the buyer, once more serving to increase the quantities of goods sold.[16]

III

Potters' marks, as noted, are known to have existed over 4,000 years ago. They transmitted information on origins. By the middle ages, the trade mark was not an asset but a liability – a means of distinguishing *flawed* merchandise, of identifying culprit craftsmen.[17] Then, trade marks were used by guilds to attest to quality and to control entry into particular trades; they were employed to single out the individual artisan, who manufactured or sold defective products.[18] There is no indication, however, that they received legal protection at that time.

As individuals took pride in their work and mark, the trade mark was transformed into an asset. British silver plate has long been branded, and an antique dealer can tell you the maker. While clearly a mark was a means of identification, Lord Hardwicke in 1742 saw no purpose in enjoining a trader from employing the mark of another firm. He wrote, 'Every particular trader has some particular mark or stamp; but I do not know of any instance of granting an injunction here [in England], to restrain one trader from using the same mark with another and I think it would be of mischievous consequence to do it.'[19] In short, what Hardwicke was saying in the mid-eighteenth century was that the mark had no exclusive rights attached to it, no legal support – a view that would be sternly rejected in the nineteenth (and twentieth) century, when the common law was interpreted as making the mark an exclusive, proprietary asset (under defined circumstances).

When in the eighteenth century, the Principio Co., an early British direct investor in colonial America, exported its iron, it had its name stamped on the bars.[20] Was this essential to the business? Probably not. Was it useful to the buyer? Undoubtedly. The historian Victor S. Clark suggests that in the American colonies laws passed to maintain the quality of manufactured articles came in time to form the basis of the country's subsequent trade mark legislation.[21] Colonial laws requiring the marking of tobacco, flour, pork and so forth before sale or shipment were continued after independence,[22] but not until the 1840s was the first state law passed 'to prevent fraud in the use of false stamps and labels' and it was almost 100 years after independence that the first US federal government trade mark law was enacted; I have never seen a court decision with a reference to the laws in colonial America. Yet, the historical use of trade marks to signify (to identify) product quality persists to the present, although unlike in medieval times or in the colonial era, in the United States the initiative in the adoption of the trade mark is by the manufacturer or the seller rather than by the guild or by a government body.

The US Constitution has a clause on copyrights and patents ('The Congress shall have the power . . . to promote the progress of science and useful arts by securing for limited times to authors and inventors the exclusive right to their respective writings and discoveries'.) The Constitution contains no such statement on trade marks, brand names, trade names, or company names. In the early nineteenth century, American law on trade marks and brand names was common law. Court cases seem to have generally upheld the litigant's rights to exclusive use of a logo if not a specific name.[23]

Interestingly, foreign firms doing business in America were among those most active in defending their trade names.[24] The first case brought before a US federal court (1844), *Taylor v. Carpenter*, was one wherein the plaintiff was 'engaged in manufacturing and selling' in the United States as well as in England a product known as 'Taylor's Persian Thread'; the defendant, in America, had imitated the English firm's names, trade marks, envelopes and labels, and placed them on thread of a different manufacture. The US courts found that the defendant, by seeking to capture a market through imitation of the trade names of this English producer, was engaged in fraud, 'unfair competition'. The defendant, through his imitations, had created confusion in the minds of the consumer.[25]

Scottish thread manufacturers selling in the United States were often in court to protect their names.[26] This was true of J. & P. Coats and also of the Clark companies of Paisley, Scotland.[27] Likewise, a German investor in pencil manufacturing in the United States was a litigant in an early and important trade mark case involving an affiliate of a German multinational enterprise.[28] By the 1860s in the United States the principle was 'firmly established that while a manufacturer has no copyright in a label, he yet may adopt a trade mark, which so far becomes his own property as to entitle him to the protection of courts of law and equity.'[29] But, a party could not be restrained, by injunction, from using his own name, unless he used it to mislead.[30] This later became significant, for if there were two participants in the same business with the same name, could the first bar the second from using the same mark? The courts concluded that, yes, this could occur, *if* there was an attempt to capture the advantages established by the first user's name.

In an 1862 response to a British parliamentary committee hearing, a representative from J. & P. Coats explained that a company with the same name in America copied its wrappers and thus confused buyers. 'The Courts stopped the imitation, but could not prevent the use of the name. The name alone, however, was not sufficient, and as soon as the pirates were prevented from imitating the wrappers, their mere use of the name Coats did but little harm'.[31] Later, as the Coats name became well known in the thread business worldwide (and as Coats production became more mechanised with sizable economies of scale), the company became very concerned over the use of its name and frequently sued to prevent imitators from appropriating it.[32]

The ubiquitous role of foreign firms in the pioneer cases in America would lend support to my contention that the more distant the producer is from the consumer the more the need for legal guarantees of the intangible asset. As the modern enterprise grows, the trade mark becomes known to consumers farther afield and the name cannot be maintained through the personal visits of the buyer to the plant of the producer. The trade mark conveys the information that in prior times could have been obtained through personal contacts.

The first American federal trade mark legislation was finally passed in 1870.[33] Table 1 provides a chronology of US trade mark laws. The 1870 law gave the trade mark holder the exclusive right to use trade marks that had been registered under the provisions of this act. The place of registration was the US Patent Office.[34] This first federal law was entitled, 'An Act to revise, consolidate, and amend the statutes relating to patents and copyrights'; it was based on the assumption that the trade mark was similar to the other property rights (patents and copyrights) and thus guaranteed by the Constitution. For this reason, however, the 1870 law (and the 1876 amendment as well) was held by the US Supreme Court in 1879 to be unconstitutional; the Supreme Court said that the legislation confused the subject matter of trade marks with that of copyrights and patents. The Court asserted that the Constitution had authorised Congress to pass laws on copyrights and patents to encourage original expression and invention, by giving authors and inventors 'the exclusive right to their writings and discoveries'; but trade marks were 'neither an invention, nor a discovery, nor a writing, within the meaning' of that constitutional clause. The decision stated that 'Trademarks are important instrumentalities, aids . . . by which trade, especially in modern time, is conducted. They are the means by which manufacturers and merchants identify their manufacture and merchandise. They are the symbols by which men engaged in trade and manufactures become known in the marts of commerce, by which their reputation and that of their goods are extended and published; and as they become better known, the profits of the business are enhanced'. The trade mark was a distinctive symbol for a product *already in existence*. The 1879 decision continued, 'The ordinary trademark has no necessary relation to invention or discovery. The trademark recognized by the common law is generally the growth of a considerable period of use, rather than a sudden invention. . . . At common law, the exclusive right to it grows out of its use, and not its mere adoption'. It does not depend on 'novelty, invention, discovery or any work of the brain. It requires no fancy or imagination, no genius, no laborious thought. It is simply founded on priority of appropriation'. Thus, the patents and copyrights clause of the Constitution was inapplicable. The decision in the *Trade-mark Cases* suggested the possible relevance of the commerce clause of the Constitution (Congress shall have the power 'to regulate commerce with foreign nations and among the several States, and with the Indian Tribes'.) The 1870 legislation, however, had been based on the clause covering patents and copyrights and this was an error. Of key importance, in the *Trade-mark Cases*, the US Supreme Court defined the trade mark as a property right and indicated that damages might be recovered by an action at law. The Court maintained, moreover, to repeat, that the exclusive right to a mark was established under common law and was based on its *use*. The exclusive right did not depend on an act of Congress, or on registration.[35]

TABLE 1

US TRADE MARK LEGISLATION

The Sequence		The Statutes and their Disposition
1.	1870	16 Stat. 198 (8 July 1870). Amended 19 Stat. 141 (14 Aug. 1876). Found unconstitutional by the US Supreme Court, in *Trade-mark Cases*, 100 US 82 (1879).
2.	1881	21 Stat. 502 (3 March 1881). Amended 22 Stat. 298 (5 Aug. 1882).
3.	1905	33 Stat. 724 (20 Feb. 1905). This continued the registration of trade marks set up under the 1881 legislation. The 1905 act was amended or supplemented on 16 occasions (7 times between 1906 and 1913 and 9 times between 1920 and 1938).
4.	1946	60 Stat. 427 (5 July 1946). The Lanham Act. Between 1947 and 1975, this act was amended 7 times. In 1984, two trade mark acts passed, clarifying further the status of trade marks. The Trademark Law Revision Act of 1988 (PL 100–667, 102 Stat. 3935) that took effect on 16 Nov. 1989 introduced major changes.

Sources: The statutes (as cited above); B. W. Pattishall, 'Two Hundred Years of American Trademark Law,' in American Bar Association, *Two Hundred Years of English and American Patent, Trademark and Copyright Law* (Chicago, IL, 1976), pp.51–79; on the 1984 laws, A. J. Jacobs, *Trademarks Throughout the World* (New York, 1987), p.801; on the importance of the 1988 legislation, *Wall Street Journal*, 15 Nov. 1989.

By the time of this 1879 decision, the trade mark was generally accepted as a property right that was peculiar in that it could not exist apart from the business. It revealed the characteristics of, that is the goodwill embodied in, the product. Likewise, by this time questions on what constituted a legitimate trade mark – when there was a close resemblance, when the use of family names was an infringement, whether geographical designations could be employed, what were merely descriptive terms – were being aired and defined.[36] The courts were confronting what was a legitimate trade mark, a legitimate property right.

After the US Supreme Court rejected the first federal legislation (in the 1879 decision), Congress set out to pass a new act, carefully avoiding basing it on the copyrights and patents clause of the Constitution. As one legal scholar put it, the framers of the 1881 Act, 'no doubt over-reacting to the Supreme Court's decision in the *Trade-mark Cases*, two years earlier, strictly confined the [new] Act's scope to marks used in commerce with foreign nations and the Indian tribes'.[37] The 1881 law provided for the registration of trade marks (still at the Patent Office); an 1882 amendment indicated that nothing prevented registration of any 'lawful trade-mark rightfully used'. Until 1905, with this legislation, only trade marks used in foreign trade (or trade with Indian tribes) could be registered under federal law.[38]

Finally, in 1905, Congress enacted a trade mark law that covered – under the commerce clause – trade between the states (as well as that with foreign countries and Indian tribes). Like the earlier federal laws, it too provided for registration of trade marks at the US Patent Office. Over the years this legislation was amended and supplemented.

Under the 1881 act, registration had been for 30 years; under the 1905 act it was for 20 years. There were renewal provisions. Under a 1920 amendment, registration existed for perpetuity, unless cancelled.[39]

In 1946, Congress passed the Lanham Act, which improved the statutory law in the trade mark field, clarifying the definitions of a trade mark and developing rules of unfair competition.[40] Under the Lanham Act, a person or company sued for trade mark infringement might defend the action by showing that a trade mark had been used in violation of anti-trust laws; if that were the case, the Federal Trade Commission could take steps to cancel the trade mark so used. Trade marks were still registered in the Patent Office, which in 1975 was renamed the Patent and Trademark Office.[41] Under the Lanham Act registration remained in force for two decades, but could be renewed any number of times for additional periods of 20 years. In 1988, there was a major change in the trade mark law. The registration period was reduced to ten years, still with renewal fully available. That was not the major change; until this revision, companies could not register a trade mark without first having a product on the market. The 1988 legislation (which became effective 16 November 1989, a year after its passage) lets companies protect a new trade mark for up to three years – before actually using it.[42] Our essay is historical and deals with the accepted practice of times past.

When foreign multinationals invested in the United States in the late nineteenth and early twentieth centuries, they registered their trade marks, sometimes in particular states, sometimes in Washington, and often under both states' and federal laws.[43] American companies also took advantage of the registration provisions (large US corporations were typically involved in foreign commerce and so could register their marks under the 1881 law). During the 1870 federal law's nine years of existence, about 8,000 trade marks were registered. Under the 1881 and 1905 acts (and their amendments), well in excess of 300,000 trade marks were registered.[44] In the peak year (before the 1920s) of 1906, 10,568 trade marks were registered; during the 1920s, every year registrations were above 10,000 and in 1924 reached 15,727.[45]

The courts were the place, however, where trade marks were defended, definitions clarified, and rights maintained. The courts' role in the history of trade mark law seems far more significant than the statutes. Before 1870, only 62 trade mark cases had been decided by American courts.[46] Subsequently, as companies became larger and the trade mark became an asset ever more important to defend, trade mark cases proliferated. In the *Trade-mark Cases* (1879), the US Supreme Court had stated that exclusive rights to trade marks were accepted under common law and did not require an act of Congress. Registration was not needed to maintain a trade mark (nonetheless, companies registered their trade marks to support the position of the mark should others infringe; the 1881 legislation said that 'registration of a trademark shall be *prima facie* evidence of ownership'.)[47]

In the litigation in defence of trade marks, there continued throughout to be a sizable number of cases with foreign multinationals as plaintiffs. Likewise, many large American companies went to court to protect their intangible asset. The trade mark embodied the goodwill of the enterprise. By the mid-1920s, it was well established by the courts that 'The owner of a trade mark, who expends large sums of money in making his mark known to the public as a symbol and guarantee of the excellence of the quality of his product should receive the same protection from the courts for his investment in advertising his trade-mark that he would undoubtedly be entitled to receive for investment in plant or materials'.[48]

This view had evolved since the late nineteenth century. In 1891, Chief Justice Fuller had put it clearly: 'The jurisdiction to restrain the use of a trademark rests upon the grounds of the plaintiff's property in it, and of the defendant's unlawful use thereof'. This decision established that the doctrine of 'unfair competition' by the infringer was based not only on fraud on the public (confusing the public), but also on the plaintiff.[49] The trade mark manual writer James L. Hopkins quoted Justice Coxe as saying:

No man has a right to use names, symbols, signs or marks, which
are intended . . . to represent that his business is that of another.
No man should in this way be permitted to appropriate the fruits
of another's industry. . . . The money invested in advertising is as
much a part of the business as if invested in buildings, or machinery,
and a rival in business has no more right to use the one than the
other . . . No one should be permitted to step in at the eleventh
hour and appropriate advantages resulting from years of toil on
the part of another.[50]

The courts, however, were ready to qualify this decision and a famous
trade mark case made the point most vividly. Before World War I, all
the principal German chemical companies had affiliated enterprises
in America, to sell and to a lesser extent to manufacture German
products.[51] Of these the German Bayer Co. was pre-eminent. Like
all the German enterprises, it had many patents; it also had trade
marks. Patents are given for a limited time. Trade marks could last
forever. When the patent expired, a way for a firm to hold a market
that had been created was through trade marks. So important were these
intangible assets that the active head of Bayer in the United States was a
patent attorney, Anthony Gref, 'whose chief occupation was to protect
patents and trade-mark rights on dyes and dyestuffs'.[52] Bayer's patent
on aspirin expired on 27 February 1917. But Bayer believed that Aspirin
was a trade mark and hoped to retain its market despite the absence
of patent protection. Several American firms (typically retail druggists)
had made pressed tablets (from Bayer's ingredients) and sold them as
aspirins with their own wrappings. Bayer filed suit against one, the
United Drug Co. After World War I was over, and no doubt influenced
by the anti-German sentiment in the United States, Judge Learned Hand
of the Southern District Court in New York ruled that *for consumers*,
aspirin had become a descriptive name of the product. Prior to 1915,
Bayer had sold principally to physicians and the trade and had promoted
the product through these channels. Judge Hand argued that as a result
of this strategy, the word aspirin for the general consuming public had
passed into the public domain.[53] Clearly, trade mark rights were far
from absolute. Proprietary, exclusive, rights to a trade mark could not
be maintained when the mark had become a general description of the
product.

Businesses recognized how careful they had to be to avoid having
the trade name – a valuable *private* asset – become a generic. Thus,
Coca-Cola regularly engaged in litigation to preserve the firm's rights
to its name; The Kimberly-Clark Corporation has successfully defended

its rights to Kleenex; and later – but similarly – Xerox attorneys kept that name from becoming a general description of the copy-making process.

By the early 1920s, most of the principal aspects of the trade name had been clarified in the courts; managers of most large US enterprises knew its value. One trade mark authority has maintained that 'a free commerce' could hardly exist without trade mark protection. 'Unless one can be assured of some sanctity for his means of commercial identity, thereby to enjoy the fruits of his own labor, free enterprise and the beneficial competition that it engenders is without motivation'.[54]

Nonetheless, in much of the literature, the trade mark has not – in the past – been associated with free enterprise and free competition. Indeed, as we have shown legal protection only became of key importance with the rise of giant enterprises. And, as these large businesses were being perceived as anti-competitive trusts and as 'trust busting' occurred, it was logical that such views would spread over to the issue of how trade marks were used. Could the *trade mark holder* (as distinct from the trade mark infringer) employ the trade mark for anti-competitive purposes?[55] After all, the mark gave exclusive, 'monopoly', privileges to its owner. In 1911, in the same year that the US Supreme Court was breaking up Standard Oil and American Tobacco, the Court ruled that contracts maintaining a resale price of a trademarked good were unlawful under the Sherman Antitrust Act.[56] In a number of anti-trust cases, the strategy of using 'fighting brands' – brands offered to customers at cut-rate prices – was judged a predatory practice.[57] A writer on trade marks in 1917 pointed out that American courts generally ruled in a way that was hostile to monopoly and would encourage competition.[58]

In various instances 'monopolistic practices' linked with trade marks were condemned by the US courts. A series of such decisions came in the immediate post-World War II years, once more associated with the renewed vigour of US courts in anti-trust matters. As Clair Wilcox has noted, 'in a number of cases involving the sharing of markets for trademarked goods by international cartels, decided from 1945 to 1950, the courts found such arrangements to be in violation of the Sherman Act. . . . Trademarks, said the court in the Timken case, cannot be made a tool to circumvent free enterprise'.[59]

In short, as the modern enterprise emerged in the late nineteenth and into the twentieth century, so too there was the passage of legislation and proliferation of court cases dealing with trade marks. The legal history followed two paths, the first concerned the protection of the asset (with court cases usually initiated by the trade mark holder against an infringer) and the second concerned restraint of trade (with court cases generally started by the US government against the trade mark owner). Most large firms came to recognise that the legally-protected trade mark was a necessity.

IV

Trade marks and patents have some similarities, and many differences. A comparison of these two intangible assets helps clarify the role of trade marks in the rise of the modern corporation (and in economic development).[60] Both are 'intellectual property'. Both provide owners with a legally protected monopoly, that is exclusive rights. Often, in the past (and the present) the same attorneys who deal with trade marks handle patents. Many works on the law of patents have a section on the law of trade marks. Frequently, chapters or passages in books read, 'patents, trade marks, and copyrights'. Both patents and trade marks are registered at the same office in Washington, DC. Patents, like trade marks, have interested pursuers of anti-trust violations. Edward Chamberlin studied the two and found that to those who argued that the extent of monopoly power was greater with patents, he pointed to the huge prestige of such names as 'Ivory', 'Kodak', 'Coca-Cola'. He concluded that there was little difference in 'the degree of monopoly' power obtained through the use of patents and trade marks. 'Each [a patent, a trade mark] makes a product unique in certain respects; this is its monopolistic aspect. Each leaves room for other commodities almost but not quite like it; this is its competitive aspect'. For Chamberlin, who was exploring the relationships between monopoly and competition, this combination inherent in both intangible assets had a special interest.[61] Both patents and trade marks are legally protected under the same broad rationale: 'to create incentives that maximize the difference between the value of the intellectual property that is created and used and the social cost of its creation, including the cost of administering the system'.[62] Over the years, the courts have protected both, accepting the advantages of granting exclusive rights.

These similarities accepted, most experts on trade marks argue that it is a mistake to confuse trade marks with patents and that the two are very dissimilar.[63] A patent must be registered to be upheld; a trade mark's validity is confirmed by registration but its *use* is paramount to its legitimacy. The patent protects new inventions, for a temporary period; the trade mark is sustained, to repeat, when it is used[64] and thus has nothing directly to do with new inventions; moreover, the exclusive rights it bestows are without time limits.[65] A patent can be designed around; a trade mark is much harder to copy (legally).[66] On the other hand, patent holders are often accused of using a patent to prevent rivals from making a good and keeping an invention off the market; the trade mark since it is based on use (and on a known product) could never be employed in this manner to preclude others.[67] The trade mark does, indeed, stop others from making Brand X, but it does not prevent them from making or providing a good or service with all the same properties except the name and the trade image (any one can open a motel; they just cannot call it a Holiday Inn). Some writers on trade marks insist that there can be no monopoly at all, because the need *to distinguish* a firm's products from those of other firms implies competition.[68] A patent is specific to a single invention; a trade name can be passed from one product to another; the image created by the name connotes what the enterprise chooses to project.[69]

For the purposes of this paper, it is particularly germane that legal protection for patents existed long before the modern giant enterprise; the importance of this protection did not coincide with the rise of the modern corporation.[70] The trade mark's legal support seems more closely associated with the emergence of the modern firm. A patent, moreover, can be granted to an individual as well as a company; a trade mark, by contrast, is the property of a business.[71]

The trade mark's functions relative to the modern company are entirely separate from those of the patent in other respects. The contract that allows a particular independent firm to bottle Coca-Cola, to sell Exxon gasoline, to distribute Ford cars, or to display the name Intercontinental Hotel provides 'satellite firms', those not owned by the giant enterprise, with the use of a valuable legally-supported intangible asset. The benefits thus accrued from the use of the name go to the owner (the big business that is obtaining further market penetration), to the satellite firm that gains advantage from the owner's past 'skill and industry' and from the latter's promotion of the mark and does not have to replicate that investment, and to the consumer that is attracted by the reputation of the good or service. The patent, even when licensed, does not seem to have this spider-effect.

The specific public policy rationales in granting patent and trade mark protection are also distinct. A patent is given to encourage the 'progress of useful art'. The trade mark not only protects the company that has invested in developing, promoting, and advertising a product, and the satellite firm that uses it, but in addition, and of great significance, protects and gives information to the purchaser. Trade mark protection furnishes incentives for the firm to uphold quality, which serves the buyer. A vital public policy reason for providing the producer exclusive rights over a trade name is that this is a valuable way (there is no other) to inform the consumer.[72] Patent protection has no parallel justification.

V

How, specifically, does the legally-protected trade mark enhance efficiency and aid in the rise and persistence of the modern giant enterprise? The traditional model of perfect competition assumes (*ceteris paribus*) that any exercise of monopoly power results in smaller output and higher price than under competitive conditions. In this spirit, the anti-trust tradition (and at times the American courts) have argued that the trade mark served to reduce efficiency – as all monopoly does. Many economists, however, now accept that large companies (with monopoly power) can be more efficient than smaller ones and that the modern corporation can be viewed as 'an economizing, rather than mainly a monopolizing entity'.[73] This phrase of Oliver Williamson's is part of his general rejection of the 'inhospitable' tradition of anti-trust. It is highly relevant to a consideration of trade names and the emergence of the modern corporation; herein, I will attempt to show the trade mark's important contribution to the rise of such an 'economising' firm.

The trade mark has served the modern corporation by aiding in the increase output and the lowering of price in five specific ways. The first of these reveals efficiency gains at a particular moment. The other four involve efficiency improvements over time. The modern giant enterprise of the late nineteenth and twentieth centuries that sold differentiated (trademarked) products by definition did not face a horizontal demand curve. It could not automatically sell at a single price all it produced. By virtue of its 'monopoly power', it set price or quantity, constrained by the demand curve. When an enterprise – using new technologies – had increasing returns to scale, the quantities sold had to be substantial to obtain the lower unit cost. To sell the sizable quantities – as stated in the introduction to this article – required pulling buyers to the particular firm's products. Products do not sell themselves. Forward integration by manufacturers into distribution was often required, as Chandler has shown. Yet, this remained inadequate, unless the buyer actually selected the particular product. The trade name was, thus, a necessary complement to the enlargement of the firm through forward vertical integration. The promoted, the advertised trade name was the only way to draw buyers to the particular firm. It was impossible to promote or to advertise an abstraction; there had to be a name identification. Thus, the trade mark provided the means to realise the economies of scale and scope. Forward integration, advertising, and promotion, to be sure, entailed added costs, but these costs were more than recovered by the greater volume achieved.

Large modern corporations had histories that established and verified their reputations. Costs were incurred in proving, confirming, and reconfirming their standing. These costs were those of advertising, promotion, and distribution, but also of what was behind the name, that is, of the research and development, quality control, and so forth.[74] By being able to draw customers to the individual firm, by the company's having the sizable market, the trade mark opened the way for added production and the spread of all these costs over more units (reducing unit cost). Accordingly, the use of the trade mark to bring in customers to a single firm resulted in more rather than less output and allowed a firm to capture the advantages of the increased returns to scale. Under conditions of perfect competition with no restrictions on entry, the long-run average cost curves would cross the demand curve at a point where there would be a higher price and lower production; large-scale output, achieved by the presence of a market for the large firm's products, made possible the lower prices.[75] Lower prices made the modern goods accessible to more consumers.

Along the same line, since the trade mark (in Chamberlin's words) 'leaves room for other commodities almost but not exactly like it', since (as others have maintained) the need to trade mark is a need *to distinguish* the product, the presence of the potential for competition and of substitutes – the effect of high cross-elasticities of demand – flattened the demand curve. John M. Clark saw the consequence as mitigating the seriousness of the effects of imperfect competition.[76] The result was to provide for a greater output, so the firm could realise the economies of scale and scope.

Second, economies of scale and scope can be technological; but the trade mark can also directly support other economies. An established firm (with a known name and reputation) has an advantage in borrowing, even without holding the risks of the particular use of the capital constant. A long-established firm with a good credit history – with a 'name' that conveyed financial reliability, could borrow more cheaply than a newcomer. Thus, the firm's name, its reputation, brought down its costs of capital. Its unit costs were reduced. The use of a known name – that carries information on financial viability – over time can provide the basis for a downward shift in the cost curve.

Third, the quality of inputs can be improved through the identification of a corporation as a fine place to work. A familiar company, with a good reputation, is able to attract and retain more talented personnel. This would serve to raise efficiency.[77]

Fourth, sustained profits give the large firm more resources to invest in lowering its entire cost curve (i.e. profits that can be reinvested in research and development). The downward shift in the cost curve over time can often be explained by technological innovations; most economists agree that technological change serves to lower costs, creating efficiencies (this indeed is the main rationale behind patent protection). Does the trade mark encourage invention and in turn, the lower costs? The court cases on trade marks indicate, as noted above, that the legal protection granted this intangible asset was *not* designed to spur invention, but rather to protect the 'skill and industry' devoted to production; in actuality, however, the legal backing of the distinctive trade mark offered incentive for the development of new inventions. Because, as I have pointed out, the substantiated, known trade mark usually served to increase the quantity produced and sold and allocated research and development costs over more units, it appears to have encouraged added research. As it provided for the realisation of economies of scale and scope, it assisted in spreading the risks of innovation in other new products (the reputation of which did not have to be freshly established). Firms invest in research and development when they expect returns on their investments. Since the trade name offered the basis for continuity, this made investment in research and development worthwhile. Thus, cost-reducing research was fostered and aided in the downward shift in the cost curve.[78]

In this context, there is a related efficiency that is not firm-specific. Since the firm can choose to use – to stretch – trade names to the new products developed, the large firm may have the ability to enter related industries at lower costs than other newcomers (taking advantage of economies of scope). This reduces barriers to entry imposed by firms already in a particular industry and creates the possibilities of competition. Markets became 'contestable'. This improves competitive processes. The identical point may be made in relation to national and international markets. Names developed in one or more national markets can be extended to added national markets; the new 'foreign' entrant thus stimulates competitive processes in a domestic market.[79]

A fifth reason for improved efficiency lay in what happened over time to the firm's demand curve. The reputation embodied in the trade mark often results in a shift in the demand curve outward for the firm's particular product (or products). If there were economies of scale or scope, this allows for raised production at the lower unit cost; thus the firm once more is able to take advantage of these economies. Where this differs from my first explanation is that it dealt with any point in time, whereas in this case the *continuing* reputation connected with the trade name actually pushes the demand outward for the firm's output, providing in a dynamic manner for larger production and lower unit costs. This, of course, assumes the existence of increasing returns to scale.

In three other important and associated ways, the trade mark led to (and leads to) efficiencies. For the consumer, 'information is not free. Like any other resource, it is scarce, valuable, and expensive'. The trade mark conveys information. It tells the buyer about the product and its qualities. The purchaser uses the brand name or company name as a means of selecting. As Armen Alchian and William Allen have put it, 'A powerful reducer of the costs of information about the qualities of products is the brand name. Reputations are built and maintained on past reliable performance. . . . Brand names identify goods and services of verified predictable standards of quality'.[80] Trade names also reveal the reliability of the firm offering the product (will delivery be as promised; will service be available if something goes wrong; will there be replacement parts?).

Trade names – as I have shown – are not new, yet, the value of this intangible asset rises as information costs grow. The trade mark substitutes for information that is costly to obtain and difficult to evaluate. It provides the buyer with a 'short-cut', a quick means of appraisal. In the late nineteenth and twentieth centuries, as I have shown, as sellers and buyers increasingly became separated by distance, as sellers with new products (for cost as well as revenue reasons) desired volume sales, the intangible asset (the name) became an ever more valuable property, capitalising on the past history of the firm as well as its present performance. In the modern world, buyers can use their time in many ways. Finding out about a product can be time-consuming and thus costly. The trade name reduces the costs of the transaction. It lowers the cost of searching and exploring alternatives. Neither the seller nor the buyer need open boxes or unwrap packages (to show or to view the product); a mechanic does not have to be hired to inspect a new car. If the trade name has been effectively promoted, it tells the buyer about the product instantly. A warranty on a product depends on a trade name. The trade mark thus created further efficiencies in distribution.[81] It has done so for the industrial buyer as well as for the individual consumer. The name tells an industrial buyer the firm's reputation, whether deliveries will be as promised; whether maintenance will be provided on a complex machine. Modern producer goods from harvesters, to copy machines, to computers require repair services (the reputation of the seller includes the ability to provide aftersale services). The reputation lies in the name. The reduction of search costs for the purchaser is tantamount to a lower price.

A second closely connected source of efficiency is that a trade mark allows for modern packaging. Often, it is cheaper to ship and to sell packaged goods. At the point of sale, goods do not have to be measured, weighed, and wrapped. Time is saved.

A third linked basis for efficiency gains lies in the use in certain industries of independent business networks, 'satellite firms'. Companies can obtain added sales by using the trade name as part of contractual relationships with otherwise independent firms. The owner of the name does not have to incur the governance costs of internal organisation and other costs of extending the giant enterprise. How, however, does the owner of the trade mark assure that its mark is not debased, and its reputation not compromised? If the seller supplies products to the independent, satellite entity, then there is a built-in punishment for that firm not conforming with quality standards, i.e. the products can be withheld. (An independent Coca-Cola bottler that does not conform to the standards set by contract in Atlanta will not get syrup; an independently owned automobile dealer that does not meet showroom standards, do repairs, and so forth, will find that the company will choke off its existence by not supplying automobiles). The trade name provides the basis for a firm's increase in business through its own internalised organisation *and* through independent companies. Free riding by a satellite on a firm's intangible assets is made impossible (or at least very costly) through sanctions that would put the 'independent' out of business and through contracts that are legally enforceable. The consumer comes out ahead as a consequence, obtaining a known product.

What assures the buyer that a firm does not cheat and debase its own name? As Benjamin Klein and Keith B. Leffler point out, reputations and brand names are firm-specific devices that provide incentives to uphold the promises associated with the name. The value of lost repeat purchases 'motivates transactors' to maintain the standards set by the name. 'The value of future exchange' induces the sustaining of the reputation. The firm expects a stream of earnings based on its reputation.[82] Business historians know well cases where corporations have forgotten this lesson. The perils of 'debasement' of a name are especially evident in the recent history of A & P, Grand Union, and Howard Johnson. Each of these firms' managers failed to support the trade name's historically-achieved reputation with devastating consequences.

The trade mark must have and continue to have behind it a defined-quality good or service, or it loses its value. A consumer can switch to alternatives, since a trade mark does *not* preclude competitors from making the same good as long as it does not have the same name.[83] Trade marks stand for a particular company's offerings (they 'fix responsibility')[84] and if the offerings are not up to par, this will mean rejection by the consumer. Thus, the trade mark becomes crucial in requiring a company – *in order to* retain and to expand its market – to hold to its standards, to take responsibility for the standards. There is a built-in enforcement mechanism. Once again, the trade mark improves the workings of the free market and is linked with the continuity of the firm. Moreover, since a firm can use a trade mark as it chooses, it can segment markets – with top-of-the-line products and poorer, cheaper ones. The name communicates information to the customer. And in a 'feed-back' manner, the presence of the name, in turn, influences the producer's behaviour. If it does not do so positively, the firm itself may be in jeopardy.

Typically, products with name recognition are higher priced than generics, or products where the company's trade mark has yet to be established. From a public policy and historical standpoint is this economically inefficient? This paper argues that 'the higher price' is more apparent than real, that the trade mark upholds uniform standards and reduces transaction, specifically, search costs. The quality consistency behind the name alters what is being purchased. The price 'premium' is no premium, since with a generic the consumer bears the costs of uncertainty.[85] In short, in many ways, involving the lowering of costs of production, costs of distribution, and costs to the consumer, the use of the trade mark provides for the efficiency gains of the modern corporation.

VI

In conclusion, in the late nineteenth and early twentieth century, as the modern corporation with its many new products came of age, the US Congress and more particularly the courts provided legal protection to the exclusive use of trade marks, brand names, trade names, company names. The legally-backed trade marks (and the other names) became essential intangible assets, providing the basis for the rise of the modern enterprise. The trade mark had functions entirely different from the patent. The trade mark's fundamental contribution to the modern corporation was that it generated efficiency gains by creating for the firm the opportunity for large sales over long periods. It was the trade mark, as a transmitter of information, that made possible the effective utilisation of patents and new technology. Without the trade mark, the introduction and acceptance by buyers of modern products, produced with economies of scale or scope, and marketed over long distances, would have been impossible. The trade name allowed the firm to persist. Often, it lowered the cost of capital for the giant enterprise. It could provide for attracting quality personnel. Of paramount importance, the trade mark heightened efficiency by saving the buyer's time in transactions, supplying knowledge, and decreasing search costs. The trade mark by reducing the costs of information led to efficiencies in production and distribution. Trade names furnished (and furnish) the intangible cords that supported the existence of thousands of independent satellite businesses with links to the consumer, domestically and internationally. If there were not legal backing for this intangible asset, the trade mark's value would be diluted and it could not serve these functions owing to free-riding and debasing by a company's rivals. It was no accident that the legal history of protection of the trade mark coincided with the rise of modern corporation. By making it feasible to use resources more efficiently, by providing incentive for corporate controls over quality, by saving the buyer time, the trade mark has spurred economic growth and development.

While trade names can be employed by their owners for anti-competitive purposes (I do not deny that), their far more critical and indeed their pivotal role has been in opening the way for large-scale business firms to realise the economies of scale and scope of modern industries by communicating to intermediate buyers and end-users vital information. Trade marks made the very emergence, existence and continuance of giant corporations a reality. They are along with the legal support of them a necessity for modern large businesses. It is no surprise that less developed countries typically do not have nationally or internationally known trademarked products. Trade names represent the translation of ideas, inventions, new technologies, standardised services, into viable, commercial products. They save valuable time for the modern buyer, reducing his costs. Their history, along with how and when they obtained legal protection, adds a significant up to now neglected dimension to American economic and business history.

NOTES

A first rendition of this article was presented at a seminar at the University of California, Los Angeles, in February 1990; I appreciated the comments of Mary Yeager, Ken Sokoloff, Jean-Laurent Rosenthal, Ed Perkins, and Jose de la Torre, as well as all the other seminar participants. Tony Corley has contributed markedly to this paper, as have Geoffrey Jones and Panos Liossatos. I benefited greatly from the comments of one anonymous economist. My thanks also go to Marge Beary and David Feinberg of Florida International University library for their help with LEXIS, the legal information on-line retrieval service, and to Allan Greenberg, Trademark Attorney for Coca-Cola, Atlanta, for his thoughts (17 March 1988) and his providing me access to Coca-Cola's excellent trade mark library. Roughly three decades ago, the sociologist Juan Linz remarked casually, in a conversation, how few Spanish firms had trademarked goods; he asked, was there perhaps a connection between trademarked goods and economic development? That question was the original seed for this long-delayed essay.

1. The best research on trade mark history has been done by legal scholars; there is also much that is valuable on trade marks by economists, albeit most of the work is not historical. Trade mark lawyers have a huge body of writings (often manuals). There exists the large anti-trust and law-and-economics literatures that consider trade marks, typically in a tangential manner. One recent and fine article dedicated to the study of trade marks is W.M. Landes and R.A. Posner, 'Trademark Law: An Economic Perspective', *Journal of Law and Economics*, Vol.30 (1987), pp.265–309. It makes the distinction between anti-trust and trade mark law – and the different rationales behind each. Textbooks by industrial organisation economists usually contain a brief discussion of trade marks in the context of product differentiation and barriers to entry. There is a related, more specialised collection of works on the economics of advertising and the economics of information (the 'signalling literature'). Much earlier, the relationship between trade marks and patents fascinated Edward H. Chamberlin in his Ph.D. thesis (1927) and his *The Theory of Monopolistic Competition* (1933); I have used the eighth edition (Cambridge, MA, 1962). In books and articles on multinational corporations, there has long been an awareness that trade marks or brand names give a firm an advantage. The theoretical approach to multinational enterprise that emphasises intangible asset advantages is an outgrowth of the work by industrial organisation economists. See, for example, C.P. Kindleberger, *American Business Abroad* (New Haven, CT, 1969), p.14; R.E. Caves, *Multinational Enterprise and Economic Analysis* (Cambridge, 1982), p.4; and J.H. Dunning, *Explaining International Production* (1988), p.16. In attempting to understand why a multinational enterprise internalises certain activities (handles them within the firm) and not others, trade marks are often discussed. See, for instance, J.F. Hennart, 'The Transaction Cost Theory of Multinational Enterprise', in C. Pitelis and R. Sugden (eds.), *The Nature of the Transnational Firm* (1991), and his *A Theory of Multinational Enterprise* (Ann Arbor, MI, 1982). The marketing and advertising literatures also deal at length with trade marks and brand names. H. Morgan, *Symbols of America* (New York, 1987), is a recent popular presentation on the history of trade marks in the marketing, advertising genre. US social and cultural historians consider brand names and images, while philosophers, linguists, and anthropologists have studied symbols (I have not explored these writings for the present article). Business historians mention trade marks in their books and articles, but I have not located a single analytic history of trade marks by an economic or business historian. So, too, *historians* who write on law and economics have neglected this subject. For example, in his brilliant exposition, J.W. Hurst, *Law and Markets in United States History* (Madison, WI, 1982) omits entirely – aside from a brief reference to fighting brands – the crucial role of trademarks *vis-à-vis* law and markets.

2. D.C. North and B.R. Weingast, 'Constitutions and Commitment', *Journal of Economic History*, Vol.XLIX (1989), p.803.

3. When travelling to Japan in the last three decades, I have noted how widespread is the use of trade marks by Japanese companies. See, also, Akio Morita's account of how SONY became his firm's name. In *Made in Japan* (New York, 1986), pp.69–73, he wrote, 'I have always believed that a trademark is the life of an enterprise and that it must be protected boldly. A trademark and a company name are not just clever gimmicks – they carry responsibility and guarantee the quality of the product.' He explained how the trade mark was essential if SONY was to become a major enterprise. On various occasions, Morita reported, SONY has turned to the courts to attack infringers on its trade name. This statement by the leader of

one of Japan's most innovative companies coincides with and, indeed, iterates for another developed nation, for Japan, the theme of this paper.

4. A.D. Chandler, 'The Beginnings of "Big Business" in American Industry', *Business History Review*, Vol.XXXIII (1959), pp.1–31; *idem*, *Strategy and Structure* (Cambridge, MA, 1962); *idem*, *The Visible Hand* (Cambridge, MA, 1977); *idem*, *Scale and Scope* (Cambridge, MA, 1990); and *idem*, 'Technological and Organizational Underpinnings of Modern Industrial Multinational Enterprise', in A. Teichova, M. Lévy–Leboyer and H. Nussbaum (eds.), *Multinational Enterprise in Historical Perspective* (Cambridge, 1986), pp.30–54.

5. The phrase economies of scale has over the years taken on different, although related, meanings. Chandler has argued for the technological efficiency of the modern corporation (economies of scale – lower unit costs as output rises, based on large throughput of oil and other such products); in his newer work, he has stressed production and distribution economies of scope – lower unit costs as output rises, based on the complementarities of products and functions; and throughout his writings, in his emphasis on organisational efficiencies, he has maintained that the large multifunctional, multiproduct, multiplant, multiregional, multinational enterprise can achieve scale economies – lower unit costs as output rises, based on administrative co-ordination.

6. H. Demsetz, *Efficiency, Competition, and Policy: The Organization of Economic Activity, Volume II* (Oxford, 1989), p.30; *idem*, 'The Theory of the Firm Revisited', in *Ownership, Control, and the Firm: The Organization of Economic Activity, Volume I* (Oxford, 1988), pp.157–62.

7. D. Yergin, *The Prize* (New York, 1991), p.40.

8. See M. Wilkins, *The Emergence of Multinational Enterprise: American Business Abroad from the Colonial Era to 1914* (Cambridge, MA, 1970); *idem*, *The Maturing of Multinational Enterprise: American Business Abroad from 1914 to 1970* (Cambridge, MA, 1974); and *idem*, *The History of Foreign Investment in the United States to 1914* (Cambridge, MA, 1989).

9. F.I. Schechter, *The Historical Foundations of the Law Relating to Trade-Marks* (New York, 1925), p.20. If the dating is correct this is well before the Greeks appear as a people. A fine discussion of the early history of trade marks is in E.S. Rogers, 'Some Historical Matter Concerning Trade Marks,' *Michigan Law Review*, Vol.XI (1910), esp. pp.29–39.

10. Landes and Posner, 'Trademark Law', pp.266, 271–3, point out that the goal of language (and symbols) is communication that minimises 'the costs of avoiding misunderstanding and the costs of communicating'. Language, however, has 'attained a reasonable decree of efficiency' without 'a legally enforceable power to exclude others'.

11. The criteria for a patent are given in F.M. Scherer, *Industrial Market Structure and Economic Performance* (Boston, MA, 2d ed. 1980), pp.439–40.

12. Most industrial organisation economists consider the brand name as highly important in sales to the final consumer. They take the view, however, that profit-motivated firms are wiser than individuals, so trade marks are not needed to convey information to producers. Scherer, *Industrial Market Structure*, pp. 378, for example, writes that trademarking is usually not required for industrial goods, since industrial buyers are skilled at evaluating the products they receive. I argue that when there is a close relationship between the industrial buyer and the seller, an established trade mark may not be necessary since the intimate relationship between buyer and seller suffices. On the other hand, many companies that sold industrial goods – especially in international business – used trade names (or company names) to promote their goods. The name – often a company name – has been as important as an information communicator in producer and intermediate goods, as in consumer ones. Repeatedly, for example, German dye makers, in the United States before World War I, sought to use their German names, Hoechst, Badische, etc., in order to take advantage of their international reputation. Wilkins, *History of Foreign Investment*, Ch.12. As

another case, prescription drug companies have been among the heaviest users of trade marks; they sell to hospitals and market through doctors. For companies such as the German Siemens and the American General Electric that sell producer goods on a large scale, the trade name is crucial in expressing the reputation of the firm – and has been since the nineteenth century.

13. Schechter, *Historical Foundations*, p.4.
14. A. Carlos and S. Nicholas, '"Giants of an Earlier Capitalism": The Chartered Trading Companies as Modern Multinationals', *Business History Review*, Vol.LXII (1988), pp.398–419.
15. This turns the coin over with the firm as buyer rather than seller, yet the universality of the argument lies in the point that I will be making as this paper progresses, i.e. that the name incorporates information and that this information content is the basis for the value of the intangible asset.
16. In general, a lower price increases the quantities sold.
17. Schechter, *Historical Foundations*, pp.38ff.
18. A. Hoogvelt, *Multinational Enterprise* (New York, 1987), p.211.
19. E.S. Rogers, *Good Will, Trade-Marks and Unfair Trading* (Chicago, IL, 1914), p.272, and *idem*, Some Historical Matter', p.40 n.30.
20. Wilkins, *History of Foreign Investment*, p.21.
21. V.S. Clark, *The History of Manufactures in the United States* (New York, 1949), Vol.I, pp.64–5.
22. Rogers, 'Some Historical Matter', p.41.
23. R. Cox, *American Trade Mark Cases* (Cincinnati, 1871).
24. T.A.B. Corley found in the Harvard Law Library a pamphlet on an 1834 case before the NY State Superior Court, involving as plaintiff, a British drug maker (James Morison); the judge, in charging the jury, stated that the defendants had manufactured a 'spurious imitation of these [Morison's] pills, and falsely represented that they were the same as those made by the plaintiffs; using their labels, and in every way wishing to deceive the public that theirs were the genuine pills'. The defendants had, in short, 'practised a fraud on the public and on the plaintiffs'. The jury awarded $400 in damages.
25. *Taylor v. Carpenter*, Circuit Court, US District of Massachusetts (1844), in Cox, *American Trade Mark Cases*, pp.14–20; see also *Taylor v. Carpenter*, Circuit Court, US District of Massachusetts (1846), in ibid., pp.32–44; and ibid., pp.45–67, and Wilkins, *History of Foreign Investment*, p.73. The Morison case (in a state court), cited in the prior note, was not referred to in *Taylor v. Carpenter*.
26. Taylor was an *English* maker, who was not important in the American market. The case, however, was often cited as the pioneer federal case in America. The *Scottish* thread makers *were* significant in their US business and the cases involving them were crucial to their success.
27. See, for example, *Coats v. Holbrook* (1845) in Cox, *American Trade Mark Cases*, pp.20–33. Another pre-1860 case, not reprinted in Cox, which is mentioned in ibid., p.259, was *Coats v. Piatte*, 19 Leg. Int. 213. A third one is *Clark v. Clark* (1857) in Cox, *American Trade Mark Cases*, pp.206–10. The historian of J. & P. Coats, J.B.K. Hunter, wrote to inform me (27 April 1986) that the firm faced numerous cases of counterfeiting of its product in the United States in the 1840s and 1850s and often obtained injunctions.
28. *Faber v. Faber* (1867) in Cox, *American Trade Mark Cases*, pp.401–3. See also Cox, *A Manual of Trade-Mark Cases* (Boston, MA, 2nd ed. 1892), pp.158–9.
29. *Colladay v. Baird* (1860), in Cox, *American Trade Mark Cases*, p.258 (quotation). See also *Faber v. Faber* (1867), in Cox, *A Manual*, p.158.
30. *Clark v. Clark* (1857), in Cox, *American Trade Mark Cases*, p.206.
31. Wilkins, *History of Foreign Investment*, p.690.
32. In *J. & P. Coats v. John Coates Thread Co.*, 135 Fed Reg 177, 179 (1905), the court ruled that while any person has the right to use his own name in the conduct of his business in describing articles of his manufacture, and which he is dealing

in, he has not the right to use the name of any other dealer. A corporation did not have the right to use the name of one of its incorporators for the purpose of unfair competition with an older dealer, where it was likely to do injury. The court ruled in favour of J. & P. Coats.

33. There was earlier state legislation. New York had passed in 1845 an Act 'to prevent fraud in the use of false stamps and labels', and by the time of the enactment of the federal legislation in 1870, 11 other states had similar laws. B. W. Pattishall, 'Two Hundred Years of American Trademark Law', in American Bar Association, *Two Hundred Years of English and American Patent, Trademark and Copyright Law* (Chicago, IL, 1976), p.58. See also Rogers, 'Some Historical Matter', pp.41–2, on the state legislation and D. Robert, *The New Trade-Mark Manual* (Washington, 1947), Ch.12. On whether states could adequately protect trade marks, see Schechter, *The Historical Foundations*, p.141 n.2. All the lawyers' trade mark histories agree that the first federal legislation was in 1870. Yet, according to Morgan, *Symbols*, p.10, in the 1840s, 1850s, and 1860s, the possibility existed of registering trade marks at US district courts. Indeed, Morgan's book (pp.10, 46, 66, 79, and 104) prints pictures of trade marks registered at the Southern District Court in New York, and at district courts in Connecticut, Illinois, and Pennsylvania (in 1846, 1849, two in 1867, and one in 1868); each picture has the phrase, 'Entered according to Act of Congress' and most have the next three words 'in the year'; then there follows the date (1846, 1849, 1867, 1868). Nothing I have read (including Morgan), however, indicates that any law was passed by the US Congress on trade marks prior to 1870. Rogers, 'Some Historical Matter', p.41, and Pattishall, 'Two Hundred Years', pp.52–3, cite (as does Morgan) a 9 December 1791 *recommendation* by Thomas Jefferson that an owner of a trade mark should be permitted to register it at the 'court of the district' wherein the manufacturer was present, 'rendering it penal to others to put the same mark on any other wares'; yet Rogers, Pattishall, and Morgan then concur that the first federal trade mark law was passed in 1870. The early trade marks (the pictures of which are in Morgan as cited above) that were registered at the district courts were for patent medicines (in the 1840s), tobacco and cigars (in 1867, 1868), and canned oysters (1867). I hypothesised that there might have been private laws of Congress authorising such registrations, but a scrutiny of private laws did not come up with any relating to trade marks. It, thus, remains a mystery how and why these pictures show the words 'entered according to Act of Congress'. Jefferson made his recommendation in 1791 after a Boston sail cloth maker, Samuel Breck, petitioned Congress to be allowed to register his trade mark. Rogers, 'Some Historical Matter', p.41.

34. Statistical series on numbers of trade marks registered thus begins in 1870. See US Department of Commerce, Bureau of the Census, *Historical Statistics of the United States* (Washington, 1975), p.959. Note that the series does *not* include the registrations at the district courts (see prior note).

35. 100 US 82 (1879).

36. Pattishall, 'Two Hundred Years', pp.60–1.

37. Ibid., p.61.

38. It is not clear why interstate commerce was not included in the 1881 law. Recall, however, that 1881 was six years before the Interstate Commerce Commission Act and nine years before the Sherman Antitrust Act were passed, the first of which put the federal government directly in the regulation of railroads and the second of which dealt specifically with interstate commerce. In the period 1881–1905, as in earlier and in subsequent times, state governments provided opportunities for trade mark registration. By 1905 most states had a statute allowing the registration of trade marks at the office of the secretaries of state and protecting such marks from infringement. Rogers, 'Some Historical Matter', p.42, and J. L. Hopkins, *The Law of Trademarks, Tradenames and Unfair Competition* (Cincinnati, 3rd ed. 1917), p.384, and his Appendix F.

39. The first renewals of registered trade marks in the series on trade mark registrations

in *Historical Statistics*, p.959, were in 1914, 33 years after the passage of the 1881 legislation.

40. Pattishall, 'Two Hundred Years', pp.61–7.
41. A. J. Jacobs, *Trademarks throughout the World* (New York, 4th ed. 1987), p.801.
42. *Wall Street Journal*, 15 Nov. 1989; see also R. J. Posch Jr., 'The New Trademark Law', *Direct Marketing* (Aug. 1989), pp.80–1. (Posch is the author of *The Complete Guide to Marketing and the Law* (Englewood, NJ, 1988)).
43. Wilkins, *History of Foreign Investment*, p.177.
44. Pattishall, 'Two Hundred Years', p.61; and *Historical Statistics*, p.959.
45. *Historical Statistics*, p.959.
46. Schechter, *Historical Foundations*, p.134.
47. See discussion of this in Hopkins, *The Law of Trademarks*, p.545.
48. Schechter, *Historical Foundations*, p.171.
49. *Lawrence Manufacturing Co. v. Tennessee Manufacturing Co.*, 138 US 537. See Hopkins, *The Law of Trademarks*, pp.42–3, on this case. Yet, as early as 1834 this point had been made in the Morison case, see above.
50. Hopkins, *The Law of Trademarks*, pp.42–3. Coxe made this statement in *Hilson Co. v. Foster*, 80 Fed. Rep. 896–7.
51. Wilkins, *History of Foreign Investment*, Ch.11.
52. W. Haynes, *American Chemical Industry* (New York, 1945), Vol.III, p.312.
53. *Bayer v. United Drug Co.*, 272 Fed. 505 (SDNY 1921). The ownership of Bayer's assets in America had after World War I passed to American hands; the American owners (Sterling Products) had pursued the pre-war trade mark suit.
54. Pattishall, 'Two Hundred Years', p.51.
55. In the trade mark literature the phrase 'unfair competition' is used in the context of the behaviour of the trade mark *infringer*, who fraudulently captured another's trade. In the anti-trust literature, it is the trade mark owner, who is subject to accusations of anti-competitive acts.
56. In *Dr Miles Medical Co. v. John D. Park & Sons Co.*, 220 US 373 (1911). See C. Wilcox, *Public Policies toward Business* (Homewood, IL, 3rd ed. 1966), pp.191, 706–18. Until the 1930s, resale price maintenance was condemned by the courts as violating the Sherman Antitrust Act. Ibid., p.706. This viewpoint changed. For details see ibid., pp.706–18. What is important for our purposes is the use of the trade mark as an essential concomitant to resale price maintenance.
57. For an example, see Wilkins, *History of Foreign Investment*, p.367.
58. Hopkins, *The Law of Trademarks*, p.2.
59. Wilcox, *Public Policies toward Business*, p.191; *US v. Timken Roller Bearings Co.*, 83 F. Supp. 294 (1949); Wilkins, *Maturing of Multinational Enterprise*, pp.292–9, on the *Timken* case and other 1945–1950 anti-trust cases involving international business.
60. Economic historians have paid a great deal of attention to patents and economic growth.
61. Chamberlin, *Theory*, p.62.
62. S. M. Besen and L. J. Raskind, 'An Introduction to the Law and Economics of Intellectual Property', *Journal of Economic Perspectives*, Vol.V (1991), p.5.
63. Pattishall, 'Two Hundred Years', pp.58–59.
64. Even the 1988 legislation does not change this; if the trade mark is not used after three years, it will not be upheld.
65. Renewal provisions in trade mark legislation along with continued use provide perpetuity to the property right. The 'inapplicable-to-trade marks' patents and copyright clause of the Constitution offers protection only 'for limited times'.
66. This is the view of most trade mark manuals.
67. Scherer, *Industrial Market Structure*, p.452, for use of patents to foreclose entry and leave an invention undeveloped. Under the 1988 trade mark law, the trade mark could be used for a similar purpose but then only for three years and the

consequences would seem not to be material and, in fact, to be incidental (since no unique invention was behind the mark registered).

68. Rogers, *Good-will*, p.41. Mary Yeager tells me that with meat products, the eye sees them as alike. Only with long-distance trade *and competition* did meatpackers in the late nineteenth century start using brand names. Swift and Armour are included among Chandler's modern corporations.

69. In the industrial organisation literature this is called 'multibrand' interaction. It exists for General Electric toasters and General Electric generators, for example. I sit here looking at my computer: Zenith data systems (I know Zenith is reliable; I had a Zenith radio for many years; the name is familiar).

70. See for example, K. L. Sokoloff, 'Inventive Activity in Early Industrial America: Evidence from Patent Records, 1790–1846', *Journal of Economic History*, Vol.XLVIII (1988), pp.813–47.

71. Patents can be registered by individuals or by companies, and the US Patent Office statistical series separate the two. With trade marks there were never two series; the trade mark has always been identified with (registered by) a firm.

72. R. A. Posner, *Economic Analysis of the Law* (Boston, MA, 3rd ed. 1986), pp.37–8.

73. O. Williamson, 'The Modern Corporation: Origins, Evolution, Attributes', *Journal of Economic Literature*, Vol.XIX (1981), p.1542. Williamson is not alone in this argument; this is, of course, Chandler's view. See also, for example, Demsetz, *Efficiency*, pp.ix, 222. I share with these authors, and many others, the belief that optimal size does not have to be small; that concentration is industry-related and can arise by reasons of efficiency; and that the rise of the modern corporation can be identified with the superior rather than inferior use of resources.

74. This insight was suggested by Demsetz, *Efficiency*, p.29.

75. For a demonstration, Scherer, *Industrial Market Structure*, p.22.

76. See J. M. Clark, 'Toward a Concept of Workable Competition', *American Economic Review*, Vol.XXX (1940), pp.246–7. See also, W. F. Mueller, 'Du Pont: A Study in Firm Growth', (unpublished Ph.D. thesis, Vanderbilt University, 1955) pp.207–8.

77. Companies do institutional advertising – emphasising their name – to attract and retain quality personnel; surely this explains in part the recent Dow Chemical Company advertisements: 'Dow Lets You Do Great Things'.

78. Lest my reader find this too abstract, consider the innovators in US industrial research: General Electric, Bell Labs, and Du Pont. All of these firms had well-known *trade names* that gave continuity to their reputations.

79. The literature on multinational corporations has discussed international oligopolies, arguing that 'market failure' exists when these large companies are able to enter host country national markets. Yet, perhaps the coin should be reversed and the presence of large firms in international markets should be viewed as encouraging competitive vigour rather than discouraging it.

80. A. Alchian and W. R. Allen, *Exchange and Production* (Belmont, CA, 1977), pp.192, 294. Landes and Posner, 'Trademark Law', p.275, argue that the reduction of consumer search cost is 'the essential economic function of trademarks'. See their formal model in ibid., pp.275–80.

81. Scherer, *Industrial Market Structure*, p.378.

82. B. Klein and K. B. Leffler, 'The Role of Market Forces in Assuring Contractual Performance', *Journal of Political Economy*, Vol.LXXXIX (1981), pp.616–7.

83. If the reader counters that the barriers to entry – because of the costs of name promotion – are often too high for the consumer to have choices, one has only to point to the case of the US automobile industry. Honda, Toyota and Nissan were able to provide new product options when consumers became unhappy with the product quality of existing name brands.

84. J. T. McCarthy, *Trademarks and Unfair Competition* (New York, 2nd ed. 1984),

Vol.I, p.45, argues that the 'quality encouragement function' is the most important economic function of the trade mark.

85.   I agree with Landes and Posner, 'Trademark Law', p.274, in rejecting the view that the trade mark provides its owner monopoly rents because it creates false images and deflects the consumer from lower-price substitutes of equal or higher quality and allows the firm to 'bamboozle' the public. All the historical evidence indicates otherwise.

Marketing in the Second Industrial Revolution: A Case Study of the Ferranti Computer Group, 1949–63

GEOFFREY TWEEDALE

University of Sheffield

It is 40 years since the first commercial electronic digital computer was delivered – a comment on an astonishing rate of technological advance, and an event which a few insightful individuals at the time predicted would launch a second industrial revolution.[1] Yet such has been the American dominance of the world computer industry since the 1960s that few care to remember that this was a revolution in which Britain initially led the way; that British scientists at Cambridge and Manchester Universities and the National Physical Laboratory built the world's first practical electronic digital computers; and that UK firms pioneered their commercial development.

It was Ferranti Ltd., the Manchester-based electronics firm, which built and installed the first commercial computer in 1951. Subsequently, Ferranti became one of the leading computer manufacturers in the 1950s (for a time it was *the* leader), establishing its dominant position with a blend of innovative technology and Government support. After not much more than decade, however, Ferranti sold its computer business to International Computers & Tabulators Ltd. (ICT). Against a background of increasing competition in the British market from American manufacturers, Ferranti had found mainstream computer activity unprofitable.

Finding the reasons for this remarkable and precipitous fall from such a commanding position has already exercised business historians, either as case studies of individual firms, such as ICL, or as examinations of the computer industry as a prime example of the 'British disease' – the chronic inability of UK manufacturers to exploit their competitive advantage.[2] This paper examines the selling and marketing function of Ferranti and attempts to discover whether failures in this direction were responsible for the company's lack of success. Marketing is a subject which remains relatively neglected amongst business historians, despite some recent attempts to reach a historical consensus on the subject.[3] What has been written so far has tended to reinforce an image of British business failure – lack of adaptability, obsession with technological considerations, excessive individualism, condescension to foreigners – that has been found in other areas of British business organisation and production. A few dissenting studies, however, have drawn attention to British marketing achievements, though this has been for the period before 1914.[4] More studies, it has been said, are needed. This is not least because most historical studies of British marketing have only examined nineteenth- and early twentieth-century industries.

Even amongst computer historians, marketing has attracted relatively little attention.[5] Computer historiography remains heavily oriented towards the machines and the people who built them. Thus the technical details of Ferranti's early machines are relatively well known.[6] Yet the importance of marketing should hardly need stressing. The most successful computer manufacturer of the twentieth century, International Business Machines (IBM) Ltd., has always regarded marketing as of paramount important. It was no coincidence that its first chairman, Thomas J. Watson (1874–1956), made his reputation in selling; and always regarded IBM salesmen as the stars of the firm. With his slogans, factory sing-songs and sales conventions, Watson endowed marketing with an almost spiritual significance. As his son and successor has remarked: 'technology turned out to be less important than sales and distribution methods . . . [and] we consistently outsold people who had better technology because we knew how to put the story before the customer, how to install the machines successfully, and how to hang on to customers once we had them'.[7] IBM still retains much of Watson Snr.'s sales-driven philosophy and (some would say) cut-throat methods.[8] That philosophy has proved eminently suitable in recent times, when computers have become a commodity and skilful marketing has become indispensable. Even such individualistic firms as Apple Computers Inc. have not been immune from these developments. According to a recent study: 'People at Apple focused their attention inward – on their leaders [Steve Jobs and Stephen Wozniak], on their myth, on their technology, on everything except their customers'.[9] This helped Apple become the fastest growing firm in American history, but it was John Sculley – a marketing executive at Pepsi-Cola, credited with reviving the 'Pepsi-Generation' campaign – who usurped Jobs as the head of the company and made it much more market-oriented.[10] In Britain the crucial importance of marketing can be seen in the fortunes of Amstrad, which under its founder Alan Sugar has been above all propelled by marketing rather than production considerations; and in the eclipse of the more technologically-inclined Sinclair Research and Apricot Computers. While Amstrad has regularly topped the league tables of best performing companies (absorbing Sinclair in the process), Apricot has moved out of computer manufacture entirely and into software by selling its interest to Mitsubishi of Japan.[11]

The development and exploitation of the computer after 1951, therefore, presents an opportunity to extend the historical debate to a 'new' industry, which has rapidly become as important as the 'old' industrial revolution giants of steel, coal and cotton. The sources for such a study are unusually rich, comprising internal Ferranti documentation (including a detailed typescript history of the Ferranti Computer Department by its sales manager), the papers of computer scientists at Ferranti and Manchester University and the correspondence of government organisations, such as the National Research Development Corporation.[12]

I

Early Marketing

The computer business of Ferranti Ltd. had evolved naturally from its war-time interests in electronic control systems and radar. It was above all the war and its nuclear aftermath that had, in the words of one electronics expert: 'converted a mass of radar experts with endless problems for which they were seeking solutions, into a mass of experts with endless solutions and no problems'.[13] In other words, the Second World War had built up a large pool of specialised knowledge within Ferranti that demanded a commercial outlet. In 1948 Ferranti sent a technical representative, Dr Dietrich G. Prinz, to study computer developments in the USA.[14] In the event, Ferranti were to find enough technical expertise closer to home. In June 1948, a team at Manchester University led by Professor Sir F.C. Williams (1911–77) and (Professor) Tom Kilburn, had run the world's first stored-program on a small prototype computer. This was the practical realisation of a long-term technical and theoretical problem that had occupied the minds of the best mathematicians and electronics engineers, mostly British and American, for a decade or more: how to build a calculating machine with an internal memory, that could store both programs and data. The Manchester device was thus the practical embodiment of Dr Alan Turing's idea for a *universal* machine, that could solve any problem capable of solution by mathematical means once an appropriate program had been inserted.[15] Government support from the Ministry of Supply for a commercial version of the Manchester computer followed soon after, bringing together the Ferranti and Manchester University teams in the first of a series of collaborative projects.

A Ferranti Computer Group was thus set up in 1949 at Ferranti's factory in Moston, under Jim Carter, the manager of the Instrument Department. Its first product was the Ferranti Mark I, which in February 1951 became arguably the first computer to be delivered commercially (though two American computer scientists, J. Presper Eckert and John Mauchly, had already been exploring the market in the USA and their UNIVAC I appeared on the scene only a few months later).

The Manchester University Computer (the first Ferranti Mark I) was formally opened at the University's Machine Computing Laboratory on 9 July 1951. Since Ferranti regarded this as an announcement to the world that they were ready to make and sell computers, the company ensured that the ceremony was suitably lavish. Well over 150 scientists, Government officials and interested businessmen were invited to the launch – a virtual who's who of the British computing community – which was also marked by a four-day computer conference. The firm made the most of this opportunity, producing a glossy booklet for the inaugural conference, which proved a great success.[16] Many seminal ideas, such as Professor Maurice Wilkes' ideas on micro-programming, were propounded at the conference and the event firmly placed Ferranti in the vanguard of the emerging computer industry.

A coherent computer sales policy at that time, however, was slow to emerge at Ferranti. Initially its efforts were diffuse, partly a reflection of the enviable fact that Ferranti had no UK competitors in 1951. All that needed to be overcome was the inertia of customers, which proved to be a formidable obstacle in itself. (Lord) Vivian Bowden (1919–89) became the chief salesman from 1951 to 1953, though as he himself admitted there was no formal sales position. Bowden himself had no experience in marketing, though his wartime career in radar work at the Telecommunications Research Establishment and his energetic personality probably counted for more in the early 1950s, when the computer fraternity was a small one.[17] Bowden provided personal links to both F.C. Williams and (Lord) Patrick Blackett (1897–1974), the Professor of Physics at Manchester University. Bowden was also enthusiastic about computers, recognised their potential, and did what he could to publicise them. He edited a classic collection of essays, *Faster Than Thought* (1953), which was a pioneering attempt to provide a popular introduction to computers and which Bowden initially began writing, as he put it, 'as a hand-out' to help sales. Ferranti earmarked about £20,000 a year for Bowden and his sales team, at a time when a Ferranti computer cost about £85,000. Ferranti's sales strategy consisted of Bowden going 'on the road' in search of orders, while the Ferranti board did its best to effect sales though its not inconsiderable contacts in the government and military spheres. These contacts had been widened by Ferranti's partnership with the NRDC (National Research Development Corporation), a linkage which also brought with it considerable financial support. In 1951 the NRDC agreed to place a contract with Ferranti for four computers on the basis of cost plus $7^1/2$ per cent profit, and in addition the firm was to receive $2^1/2$ per cent of the price as selling commission as a reward for success in 'using their best endeavours to find customers'. The NRDC connection was to be an important factor in the development of the Ferranti Computer Group.

Bowden recalled his early adventures in trying to sell computers with fond nostalgia, even though he found it a 'terribly uphill' task.[18] The problems were, after all, immense. The potential for computers was unknown, with expert opinion advising that the demand would be limited. Professor Douglas Hartree at Cambridge University, one of the foremost mathematicians of his day with a wide experience in mechanical and electro-mechanical methods of computation, reportedly told a Ferranti salesman that they were wasting their time. Hartree said: 'We have a computer in Cambridge, there is one in Manchester and at the NPL. I suppose there ought to be one in Scotland, but that's about all'.[19] The fact that there would be a shortage of skilled operators, which nearly everyone assumed had to be trained mathematicians, added weight to Hartree's pronouncements. Moreover, computers had not yet been adapted to customary procedures, though it was soon evident that this would be a crucial consideration. The NRDC's expert programmer and computer consultant, Christopher Strachey (1916–75), perceptively summarised the situation in 1952. He remarked that already:

> the first phase of the development of large digital computers is now virtually over. There are now more than a dozen large machines already operating in America, and rather more than a hundred more (mostly copies of these) are either in the course of production or projected. These machines are all characterised by being primarily the child of the engineer. Their logical design was laid down before there had been any opportunity to get experience in using a computer of this type. The main problem in this phase has been to get a machine which worked at all and as a result features which appeared desirable from a programming point of view have often been sacrificed to simplify the engineering problems. Now that these machines are coming into use in fair numbers there has been a very marked shift of emphasis. The major problem now seems to be to use the machines properly.[20]

The Manchester machine used paper tape, and no work had been done in adapting it to the office environment where punched cards were in use. Bowden certainly appreciated the potential of using the computer in commercial work, proposing in November 1950 'to make a more detailed study of this important application of digital computing machines'.[21] But the complexities of the problems involved and the pressing nature of the scientific calculations that were waiting to be run on the Manchester machine inevitably meant that such work had to be temporarily postponed. Above all, the Manchester machine was an unreliable beast. In May 1952, for example, it was reported that the Mark I had operated routinely for 75 hours: 57 hours of these had been usefully employed in computation, but 18 hours had been lost due to a faulty cathode ray tube (10 hours) – 'as this happened to be the B-tube, which plays a key part in the logical design of the machine, it was extremely troublesome' – and eight hours were lost in minor faults.[22] This was regarded as a creditable performance, though obviously it would not have been a very positive selling point either for the buyer or Ferranti, especially if the machine was located a great distance from the works.

Thus, as both Bowden and his successor Bernard Swann remarked, selling was 'interesting and often exciting, but unrewarding. Time and again we could only report that, after customer visits, that they were showing a keen interest, but no order'.[23] Prospective purchasers were unconvinced of the advantages of the machines, or were put off by their price and unreliability. The purchasing controller of ICI, for example, stated that his firm would never pay more than £50,000 for any one instrument. Many preferred to 'wait and see', allowing others to make the early running. Typical was the response of Short Brothers & Harland, which in 1953 was reported to be:

> cooling off because they said that they could not carry the whole cost of the machine by themselves and indeed they doubted whether they could employ it full time or on an economic basis. They had said . . . that, if there were a possibility that one or two other substantial bodies in Northern Ireland might be prepared to pay fees to use the machine, the firm might take a different view of the matter and they would be prepared to give consideration to joining some kind of consortium interested in installing the machine in Northern Ireland.[24]

The Metal Box Co. provided another example of the patience that was required to sell a computer in Britain in the 1950s. A representative of that firm attended the launch of the Mark 1, but it took twelve years of selling effort before Ferranti sold them a computer.

Nevertheless, there were enough successes for the Ferranti team to believe that they were making progress. Apart from the sale to Manchester University, Bowden's personal approach scored a coup when he sold a Mark I computer to Toronto University (this machine is discussed in greater detail below). In 1952 the Shell Co. had become interested and after visiting Manchester ordered a machine in the following year at a cost of about £95,000. The managing director of the NRDC, Lord Halsbury, wrote: 'Shell have definitely bought a computer at the price asked. This is our first firm sale and needless to say I am very pleased'.[25] But it was also clear that the Mark I (and its successor the Mark I*), which needed elaborate installation procedures and expensive maintenance staff, would only be suitable for a small class of customers. As will be evident from Ferranti's sales of the Mark I (see Appendix), the firm relied mainly on a solid but limited customer base – the government and the military – which had purchased the computers for scientific calculations.

Clearly, Ferranti needed a smaller and cheaper computer aimed at the commercial market if it was to sell large numbers of machines. Here, though progress was slow. Professor Blackett was interested in the commercial application of computers and at a meeting with Bowden and Swann in 1952 he outlined his ideas for a PAYE computer. It had been found after experiments on the Mark I that the cost of preparing a payroll was very much the same as when done manually, but computers could also use the wages data for building up cost accounts and statistics. But the experiment also highlighted one of the problems of commercial work – each type of task was full of rules unique to that problem. In fact, Ferranti at this time would usually tell potential customers that initially the numbers of staff would have to be *increased* – a fact which astonished the representative of one punched-card firm, who wondered how Ferranti ever sold a computer. The problems with the commercial market, and the fact that Ferranti were slow to design a suitable magnetic tape/card interface, meant that the firm concentrated on its strengths – the use of the computer for scientific rather than accountancy problems.

II

The Search for a Winner

In the early 1950s Ferranti possessed a number of clear advantages over both their domestic and international rivals. Their technical knowledge, boosted by the Williams-Kilburn partnership at Manchester

University, placed them in the forefront. The Ferranti name itself provided an important selling point. And the company's selling expertise, under a team headed by Bernard Swann (Bowden had left in 1953 to pursue a career at Manchester College of Science & Technology), was growing in strength. Why then did Ferranti not sweep all before it?

The first reason was that computers were only *one* of Ferranti's products. Its main business was in the marketing and production of transformers and there seemed no good reason, at least in the early 1950s, why computers should take precedence. They were, after all, a highly speculative product. Ferranti was also a family firm – a simple fact which does much to explain its subsequent conservative approach to computers.[26] Sir Vincent de Ferranti (1893–1980) owned the major shareholding and liked to run the business on personal lines. (Bowden recalled how matters were discussed over 'high-table' with fellow directors, with each one daily taking turns to carve the joint of meat.) This family set-up was to cause frustrations to those, such as Lord Halsbury at the NRDC, who were keen to push British firms into the computer age. Halsbury neatly summed up the Ferranti attitude when he wrote in 1954:

Manchester University Mk I control desk, July 1952 (Source: National Archive for the History of Computing, Manchester University)

The Ferranti family own the whole of the equity capital in Ferranti Ltd.; [they] have all the money they need for personal purposes and money is not an object of interest to them; they are in business for fun and will therefore under no circumstances agree to any proposition whatever that is from their point of view not so funny; in particular they will not open one crack, cranny or crevice whereby any third party could gain a permanent toehold inside the Ferranti group of enterprises; if Sir Vincent were looking for a new enterprise to invest Ferranti money in, he would not himself pick computers. He has, however, no objection to a Government agency picking computers for him provided that he is fully compensated for the use of Ferranti facilities.[27]

This hard-headed attitude enabled Vincent de Ferranti to expand his firm so that by 1963 it was among the first three British companies (by sales) in electronics and aircraft instrumentation. But it also meant, as Halsbury was wont to highlight, that the Ferranti computer group lacked direction and was a 'cackle of competing voices'.[28] Halsbury told F.C. Williams: 'I am frankly distressed at the lack of leadership in Ferranti. There seems to be no one there with a capacity for clear-cut strategical thinking who is at the same time prepared to give his mind to the subject. No one at their higher levels has taken over the leadership of the team, and no leader has emerged from the working levels of the business'.[29] In these circumstances it proved difficult, for example, even to cost computer production accurately. Complained Halsbury in 1953: 'Ferranti base their quotations on a notional cost price without any proper attempt to cost out. It became clear that they had no proper notion of costs and did not very much care, for if, in the present case, for example, the prime cost rose from £50,000 to £55,000, our profit would suffer a corresponding reduction and Ferranti would fold their hands and look smug'.[30] Such slipshod accountancy probably led to significant undercosting for Ferranti computers and a loss in profits.

Moreover, Ferranti's technical lead was not easily translated into orders. Crucially, the original techniques that had brought the Ferranti Mark I into being could not be used to make the more moderately priced and more easily maintained machines that the times were to require – at least, not without a great deal of commitment and finance. Ferranti needed a winner – a popular, moderately priced machine – but given Ferranti's attitude to the business this could only happen through an alliance with another firm. Since Ferranti knew it would need to use punched cards, an agreement with the two British firms in this area – the British Tabulating Machine Co. (BTM) and Powers Samas – seemed logical. Each had a good deal of commercial systems knowledge and a large customer base which would be tied to them for some time.

Powers emerged as the likeliest candidate and in 1952 negotiations began, which were based on two principles: the two companies should collaborate in designing a small computer for the commercial market; and the Powers Samas sales team would take over the selling of Ferranti computers. The latter seemed to have particular attractions for Vincent de Ferranti, who felt that the firm's problems lay in marketing (whereas the Ferranti sales team felt that production and prompt deliveries held the key). The negotiations were to extend many years, but were not counted a success by Ferranti. The protracted discussions failed to produce a new computer, though a Powers card input/output system was to be added to the Pegasus computer in 1958 under the name of Pluto. The only significant project – the Perseus computer, which had been developed specifically for insurance work – resulted in only two orders after its arrival had been delayed by possible conflict with Powers' projects. The plans for the collaboration in sales did not work well, due to inevitable conflicts of interest. Powers produced no new orders in five years, though its intervention frustrated the efforts of the Ferranti sales team and resulted in lost business. Sir Vincent de Ferranti later said that the only thing he got out of the Powers negotiations was a fancy nutcracker for Christmas!

Not surprisingly, Ferranti's commitment to collaboration was less than wholehearted. Meanwhile, other opportunities soon presented themselves. In 1953 there had been a break up of the Elliott Bros. computer team at Borehamwood, which resulted in (Professor) W.S. Elliott joining Ferranti. He brought with him the modular packaging technology that was to be used to such good effect in the Elliott 400 computer series. Here the design emphasis was on the use of standard, interchangeable circuit modules, instead of the laborious 'hand-built' methods employed in such computers as the Manchester Mark I. Ferranti soon embraced this design philosophy, which had been heavily influenced by Christopher Strachey. Under Elliott, and with financial support from the NRDC, they began building the so-called Ferranti Packaged Computer No. 1 (FPC1), later renamed the Ferranti Pegasus.

III

Pegasus and the Competitive Scene

The Pegasus proved popular and gave Ferranti a relative 'best-seller'. It has been described as the most elegant British machine of its generation, with a reputation as a trusty work-horse, well-suited to a large number of programs, inexpensive to maintain, and through long-service even inspiring affection in its users. Thirty-eight were made (see Appendix). Half were sold for research work in government and industrial establishments; seven were sold for aircraft calculations; and four were sold for commercial work. However, the Ferranti salesman felt that more than double this number should have been sold.

Ferranti was certainly as well placed as any of its competitors when Pegasus 1 appeared on the scene in 1956. The sales force, managed by Bernard Swann, numbered 18, all except one being graduates. There were also 11 graduates in the Ferranti Programming Research Group, which included (Professor) Stan Gill from Cambridge and four women. The latter provided the link between technical developments and customer problems, which surfaced at Ferranti's London showroom at 21 Portland Place. The London computer centre, which was operational by 1955, was a direct initiative of the Ferranti sales team, and a highly successful one. Here visitors came to learn programming and try out solutions to their problems, thus not only generating income but also (as Ferranti knew) familiarising themselves with Ferranti machines for

Tape editing equipment, Ferranti Mark I Computer at Manchester University, 1951 (© Ferranti Archives)

which they would be likely purchasers. Ferranti printed and distributed a considerable number of typescript memoranda (the CS Lists) describing problems that had been run on Ferranti machines.[31] These had a wide distribution. The sterling work of Ferranti's programmers, such as George Felton, ensured that a wide range of programmes were available for the Pegasus, which naturally increased its saleability. The Pegasus programming system itself, demonstrating the virtuosity of Christopher Strachey, has been described as 'a high point in programming in Britain during the 1950s and had great influence'.[32] Ferranti's experience in commercial work had been growing rapidly and by 1956 included wages calculations, index numbers, transportation problems, linear programming, inventory control investigation and airline seat reservation problems. Selling obviously involved educating the customer, and by 1956 Ferranti had already run three courses on computing, each of which lasted about two weeks.

No other English computer manufacturer was so well placed to attack the market.[33] BTM had only slowly developed an effective selling operation in the early twentieth century; indeed, it has been said that this failure was the main reason for the relative disparity in performance between BTM and IBM in the inter-war period.[34] By the 1950s BTM had an impressively large regional sales force, including a staff of 12 at BTM headquarters to publicise digital computer applications. However, BTM lagged behind Ferranti in digital computer technology and the firm admitted that it was only slowly seeking orders for data-processing. English Electric employed a staff of 20 programmers on the DEUCE computer, which functioned as the service division of the company, but developments were still in their early stages. On the technical sales side, English Electric only employed two men, neither highly qualified as programmers; and training courses had still to be developed. As a comparison, Elliott Bros. and LEO Computers Ltd. both had sales teams of about 15, and both were running training courses (Elliotts was running one on the 'Application of Computing Machines to Business Organisation'). As for IBM UK Ltd., it hardly featured at this time. Only one IBM 650 had been installed in the UK by this date and the British operations were only beginning. This was reflected in the sales and programming staff, which numbered ten, with only two or three with any appreciable experience.

Ferranti, however, was unable to turn this situation to its competitive advantage. On occasions, it is true, the sales team and engineers worked smoothly and a customer was hooked. The Royal Aircraft Establishment, for example, had virtually decided to buy an Elliott computer. But C.A. Wass, who was in charge of the mathematical section of the RAE, telephoned Swann to say that as a good civil servant he should check on what Ferranti was offering. Ferranti arranged to receive him and Elliott organised a team, nominating one of each group designing the parts of the computer – circuitry, magnetic drum, magnetic tape system, input/output equipment – while Felton from the sales department demonstrated the programming facilities, so that all the questions could be dealt with. The RAE was impressed and Ferranti won the order.[35]

Generally, however, the peculiar situation of the Ferranti computer group provided a great stumbling block. Ferranti salesmen were unable to seek orders openly for commercial work because of an agreement with Powers that they could only negotiate with purchasers who approached them directly. So Ferranti gained a reputation for 'selling from the shop' at Portland Place, a policy which suited a Ferranti management who were concerned to keep sales costs to a minimum. Ferranti had 50–80 visitors weekly at its London office; naturally, a much larger staff would be required to visit customers at their own offices. The limitations of such a policy are obvious. They were to be compounded by production difficulties that brought Ferranti another reputation – for late deliveries. Plans for the development and production of the Pegasus became awkwardly split between Manchester and London, reflecting the differing ideas and personalities of W.S. Elliott and Brian Pollard, the head of Ferranti computer production in Manchester. Elliott (and Swann) recognised the opening for a saleable product, such as the FPC1, while Pollard's energies were directed towards the powerful, but expensive, Manchester Mark II computer (eventually marketed as the Mercury). Finally, Ferranti allowed Elliott to concentrate his activities in London, though he remained nominally responsible to Pollard, under whom production of the FPC1 went ahead. It was not a happy arrangement. According to one study: 'The main practical outcome of all this during the first year of the project seems to have been that Bill Elliott spent much of his time planning to enlarge his London laboratories so as to establish his independence from Pollard, while Pollard did what he could to frustrate this, largely by refusing to transfer much-needed staff to London'.[36] The Pegasus project suffered. Production was slow to begin and costs were so uncertain that for a period of nine months in the middle of the sales drive Swann and his men were unable to give quotations. Costs of the Manchester and London operations escalated rapidly, to the consternation of the NRDC, which was left wiser but poorer after the affair.

IV

Scientific Computers Again

As Pollard's stance demonstrated, Ferranti had by no means abandoned the market for big scientific computers. Indeed, given the input of the Manchester University team, with its strong bias towards technological innovation rather than user convenience, and Ferranti's own interest in the defence market, this was inevitable.

By 1952 the Manchester University engineers were ready to utilise their expertise gained with the Mark I in constructing a faster, more reliable and more easily programmed machine. This was nicknamed MEG (Megacycle engine), which later entered production as the Ferranti Mercury. Twenty times faster than the Mark I (though more compact), Mercury pioneered the use of floating-point arithmetic, and had a provision for a magnetic core store instead of the old cathode ray tubes of the Mark I.

Mercury was aimed at large-scale scientific users, such as government establishments, which could make use of its undoubted speed – the Mercury's chief selling point. Compared to American machines Mercury was also relatively good value. Technically, it was a major achievement:

The Atlas Laboratory at Harwell (Chilton) about 1968 (Source: National archive for the History of Computing, Manchester University)

it proved that big computers could be made reliable enough, and the greater speed increased the throughput of jobs and opened up bigger markets, such as in aircraft design. But the greater complexity of Mercury stretched Ferranti's production team to the limit and soon the firm had difficulty once more in meeting orders. The lack of better input/output facilities, particularly for using punched cards, also proved a problem. Here again the Powers link did not produce the goods, with the result that Ferranti had to provide its own elaborate and costly punched card units for oil company buyers. By the time these units were supplied they were already outdated.

Mercury in some ways reflected the Ferranti production team's obsession with technological advance to the detriment of commercial considerations. According to Swann: 'In Manchester there was always something of an "anti-sales" attitude: Manchester University always felt that so remarkable a product as a computer should sell itself, and were impatient of "sales points", if they interrupted the research work'.[37] This was perhaps also reflected in the fact that Ferranti never advertised in the press or produced large quantities of glossy brochures (though it did produce a few). This neglect of promotional literature became important later, when it brought forth at least one complaint. A.V. Roe, one of the early Ferranti customers, requested information on computers for production control. When Swann said that Ferranti would like a close look at the job first, the managing director replied: 'that was the trouble with the English companies; they all wanted to look at the job, whereas IBM gave [me] a booklet which showed [me] how to do [my] production control'. Recorded Swann: 'He waved a slim and colourful pamphlet and installed IBM equipment'.[38]

The Ferranti salesman, of course, took a broader view: they wanted a computer they could go out and sell – such as the Pegasus – and remained sceptical of the market for the Mercury. Nevertheless, Mercury sold reasonably well, mainly because a promising (and unpredicted) demand emerged from the atomic energy industry. Eighteen Mercurys were sold and the technical approach had, to some extent, been vindicated. But with its next major project – the Atlas – Ferranti was not to be so lucky.

It was the Americans who indirectly provided the stimulus for the Atlas computer. By 1956 there was concern amongst leading British computer scientists and government officials, especially the NRDC, at the USA's increasing technological superiority in computer manufacture. In particular, the Remington Rand LARC and the IBM Stretch projects, raised the spectre of future American dominance. To counter the threat Lord Halsbury and the NRDC attempted to convince British manufacturers and government establishments of the necessity of some kind of national fast computer project. In the absence of a satisfactory consensus, however, Halsbury's efforts had largely foundered by the end of the 1950s.[39] But Ferranti, one of the early bidders for the project, had pressed on regardless with the development of its Atlas computer.

Atlas followed the usual Ferranti pattern: collaboration with Manchester University and a measure of financial support from the NRDC, with Ferranti providing the production and sales know-how. Again, the result was a technical success. Designed specifically to meet the needs of the large-scale computing and data-processing centre, the Atlas became one of the most influential computers ever built. On its official inauguration in December 1962 it was considered to be the world's most powerful computer, into which Tom Kilburn and his team had built a number of enduring innovations. Particularly notable was the use of 'virtual memory', a paging system which expanded the effective fast memory by automatically transferring blocks of material between it and the backing store. There was even a pioneering provision for time-sharing terminals, though rising production costs meant that this could not be implemented in the final model.[40]

This technical triumph, however, was not rewarded in the market. After the experience with Mercury, the Ferranti sales team had their eyes on the universities and the nuclear energy centres, and also (as will be described below) intended to explore the overseas market. But two things blunted their efforts – cost and time – both of which reflected the tremendous burden that the Atlas project had placed on Ferranti's limited resources. When Atlas went on sale the price tag for the cheapest machine was over £1 million. The long development period also allowed US manufacturers to step into the field, such as the Control Data Corporation. CDC actually benefited from the early publication of some of the ideas behind Atlas (a classic example of a British manufacturer paying the penalty for an early start) and this helped the American firm overtake Ferranti.[41] CDC's 6600, designed by Seymour Cray, had improved time sharing and better peripheral equipment than the Atlas and so was able to take its place in the scientific computer market. The result was that only two Atlas computers were sold: one to the UK Atomic Energy Authority (for £3½ million) and the other to London University. A subsequent exchange of hardware and design know-how with Cambridge University resulted in Atlas 2: but only one of these was sold, again to the UKAEA. Finally, any chance that the Ferranti salesman had to secure a market for the Atlas was effectively ended in 1963 when the Ferranti computer interests were sold to ICT.

The latter decided to concentrate on the 1900 series computers and Atlas was scrapped.

V

International Marketing

Ferranti had some hopes that its computers would sell well abroad. Indeed, the first Mark I computer that was sold was bought by the University of Toronto, as a result of Bowden's salesmanship. Professor Watson of that university wanted the distinction that his university should be among one of the first establishments in the world to have a computer; and, more importantly, the university wished to help the Canadian Government in its share of the design and cutting of the St Lawrence Seaway. Installing the FERUT (as it came to be known), which was not far beyond the prototype stage, thousands of miles from Manchester was a considerable challenge to Ferranti. On the whole it was met successfully, though inevitably there were considerable teething problems. The project provided another opportunity for the talents of Christopher Strachey, who developed the programme for calculating the effects of the new seaway on the water flow of the river past the Thousand Islands. According to Bowden the performance of FERUT gave the Americans 'the fright of their lives' and a 'giant inferiority complex', with the Canadians scoring some political advantage over the Americans when they were able to insist that their designs has some priority.

Canada was to provide Ferranti with an important springboard for a subsidiary venture, Ferranti Electric Ltd. (later Ferranti-Packard), based in Toronto. Here engineers, led by the Manchester University-trained technologist Dr Arthur Porter, were responsible for important pioneering designs in the mid-1950s. They built a naval data acquisition and target tracking system that included the first computer network in which three physically separate processing systems were interconnected through radio channels and operated as a single system. This was copied by the Americans. Ferranti-Packard also built the FP6000, the world's first time-sharing, multi-tasking machine, which in the mid-1960s was used in the UK as the basis for ICL's 1900 series.[42]

In terms of sales, however, Ferranti were unable to capitalise on this success. It did bring the firm useful publicity, but the reliability problems of the FERUT (which were reflected in the fact that the chief maintenance engineer was working over 60 hours per week) did not prove a good advertisement, especially since it was obvious to the Americans that they would soon have machines of their own that would be more efficient. The input/output facilities of the FERUT were also limited, due to the fact that customer requirements in this area had never been properly studied. Strachey had strong reservations about the applications of the Mark I to commercial use. 'To put it bluntly', he wrote after his North American trip in 1952, 'I think it is a waste of time to try to sell the present Ferranti machine to large commercial firms . . . as an all-purpose machine'.[43]

Evidently, Ferranti did not entirely agree with Strachey's assessment. A member of the Ferranti board had also visited the USA in 1952 and 'came back convinced that we now have the best machine available. We ought to be able to sell lots of them'.[44] Another Ferranti man believed that 'so long as our price is right, the US market is not closed to us'.[45] This belief seems to have been fostered by some early enquiries from American firms and Ferranti's initial assessment of US computer prices, which it believed it could easily better. In 1953, for example, Ferranti was approached by the Sandia Air Base in New Mexico, part of the American Atomic Energy Commission. A Ferranti sales representative wrote: 'our main competitor seems to be the Remington Rand Company. [They] have offered to allow the customer to pay for the machine over a period of three years from the date of delivery and the head of the Sandia Corporation has told our manager that he prefers such an arrangement to an outright purchase on normal terms. In the event of our being able to offer something similar we may stand a chance of getting the order since our price is substantially lower than that quoted by Remington Rand'.[46] Other enquiries were from the Tennessee Valley Authority and A.C Nielsen, which specialised in market research for advertising. Bowden had met the manager of Nielsens in Chicago as early as December 1950, when he reported that the firm was 'very anxious to get a machine from somewhere. They would obviously prefer to buy it in America, but are prepared to consider buying one here if need be'.[47]

Bowden set off on a tour of possible American customers to clinch such prospective deals but he had no success. The firm's technical lead and its slightly lower price were little recommendation to US buyers who happily awaited their own firms' entry into the market. American purchasers' hesitation to buy British, whether from conservatism, patriotism, or shrewd assesssment of Ferranti's ability to supply the goods, gave US makers the chance to make up lost ground. Ferranti's lead proved more apparent than real, especially in view of the work that was required in providing software and peripherals for the new machines. As Bowden admitted, despite the early interest of A.C. Nielsen, 'a complete solution to [their needs] will await our construction of more elaborate input-output equipment'.[48]

This situation was to recur when Ferranti again established a technical lead with the Atlas. In about 1961 Ferranti scouted the potential American demand by sending John Fotheringham to spend some months there. In 1962 Ferranti followed this up by engaging a Plessey man, Dr David G. White, to launch a sales campaign in America. There seemed to be considerable possibilities amongst the atomic energy authorities, the aerospace industry and government departments. But after an early flicker of interest the Americans proved reluctant to buy British. The Atlas was only slowly coming into production, CDC was about to enter the market, and none of the potential American purchasers wished to be the only buyers of Atlas. With Ferranti's reputation for late deliveries it was certain that the Americans would demand penalty clauses in the contracts, thus forcing the British firm to put huge capital sums at risk. Atlas was thus unable to improve Ferranti's sales performance in the USA: in over a decade the firm never sold a single computer there – a remarkable contrast to the performance of Ferranti's transformer department, which during the period 1945–60 had sales of £3 million in America. In fact, foreign sales (shown in Tables 1 and 2) of Ferranti computers were poor. Only a handful of countries – Canada, Australia and Sweden – purchased more than one Ferranti computer. This was not because Ferranti ignored these markets. In Italy, for example, Bowden was especially energetic in pursuing the early interest shown by the Italian Government. Bowden was given to understand that 'negotiations of this kind are conducted in Italy in a rather unusual way which involves a fair amount of what one had perhaps best describe as "rather delicate personal negotiations"'.[49] Even after much negotiation, however, the Italians only bought one machine.

The Australian market, which Ferranti had earmarked for special attention, also showed how the company had difficulty in translating its hard sales effort into potential orders. The firm already had contacts in Australia through its transformer business; government organisations there, such as the Commonwealth Scientific and Industrial Research Organisation (CSIRO), were preparing to install large computers; former Ferranti men (such as Professor John Bennett) were active in Australia and were likely to look on the firm with a friendly eye; and the Atlas might have a large potential in a country as large as Australia. In 1961 Ferranti decided to open a sales office in Melbourne under Barry de Ferranti to press home this advantage. A Ferranti Sirius computer – a spin-off from the Orion computer, that had been developed at about the same time as the Atlas – was sent out and a successful sales and service centre was created. Again the sales prospects looked promising: CSIRO had over £1 million to spend, possibly on an Atlas; while the universities seemed ready to order the medium-to-large computers of the Orion type. Production difficulties, however, dogged the Orion so that Barry de Ferranti had only the Sirius to sell (eventually he sold four). As regards the Atlas, it was a familiar story: though keen to buy British, the CSIRO eventually bought a CDC 6600, which was at a more fully commissioned stage than the Atlas and cheaper.

TABLE 1

FERRANTI COMPUTERS SOLD, 1949–63

Computer	Date Launched	Total sold	Overseas sales
Mark I	1951	2	1
Mark I*	1953	7	2
Pegasus 1	1956	26	3
Pegasus 2	1959	12	1
Mercury	1957	19	6
Perseus	1959	2	2
Orion	1963	13	1
Sirius	1960	16	6
Atlas	1963	3	0

Source: see Appendix.

TABLE 2

FERRANTI COMPUTERS: OVERSEAS SALES

Country	Sales	Country	Sales
Sweden	5	Germany	1
Australia	4	Holland	1
Canada	2	Italy	1
Argentina	1	Norway	1
Belgium	1	South Africa	1
Czechoslovakia	1	Spain	1
France	1	Switzerland	1

Source: see Appendix.

VI

Conclusion

By the end of the 1950s the Ferranti computer department was clearly losing money. By 1963 the firm had sold 99 computers, which had generated nearly £25 million, but this was nowhere near enough to cover production and development costs. The result was a loss of £4 million. At the end of 1962 Ferranti began negotiating with ICT for the sale of the computer department, which duly took place in December 1963. According to one source, this was due to the fact that Ferranti had realised that 'successes in the computer business depended on a marketing operation and a base of data-processing users that Ferranti did not have and ICT did'.[50]

The subsequent story – the merger of British firms into a national flagship, ICL, against the backdrop of growing American dominance – is well known and has been described elsewhere. Here an assessment is confined to the selling and marketing aspects of Ferranti's operations. To what extent was failure in this sphere responsible for Ferranti's disappointing performance?

It is often said that the British are excellent innovators and manufacturers, but poor salesmen. This paper certainly provides some evidence for such a view. Amateurish marketing techniques, muddled costing procedures, inappropriate sales strategies and poor co-ordination between R & D and marketing characterised Ferranti's rise as a computer manufacturer. However, it must be remembered that these deficiencies occurred in a period of intense and unparalleled technical advance. Moreover, they were by no means unique to Ferranti.

Similar problems were also evident in Ferranti's rivals. LEO Computers Ltd. became carried away with pioneering a new technology and failed to consider the needs of the ordinary customer. At LEO it was said that marketing was almost unknown.[51] The office machinery firms in the UK were slow to realise the implications of the new technology, while the electronics companies such as Elliott and English Electric were, like Ferranti, attracted to the scientific and military markets. In the 1960s when business computing went into high gear, the military electronics producers continued to focus on the small and specialised defence and scientific market, while the Americans took over the business sector. By March 1965, British computer manufacturers had sold less than 600 machines worldwide, whereas the Americans had installed over 20,000. By that date US penetration of the British computer market was reaching 50 per cent.

Yet even in America the pioneering computer entrepreneurs found it difficult to assess and market the new technology effectively. Two of the leading technologists, J. Presper Eckert and John Mauchly, formed a business partnership in 1946 to exploit the experience gained during the war. By 1950, although they were well on the way to developing and marketing a commercial computer (the UNIVAC) ahead of the competition, their company was bankrupt and had been sold to Remington-Rand. They had seriously underestimated development costs and failed to contract with the government on a cost-plus-fixed-fee basis; they had allowed technical staff to determine business policy; and directed too much of their efforts at perfecting devices, sometimes at the expense of bringing them to fruition.[52] A.C. Nielsen, the marketing research firm that had approached Ferranti, for example, had started negotiations with the Eckert–Mauchly Computer Corporation in 1946. An order for a computer was placed at $150,000, to be delivered within a year. But Eckert and Mauchly were unable to complete the contract and Nielsens, after toying with the idea of acquiring a controlling interest in the EMCC, finally turned to the competition – IBM – which put a computer on the market in April 1953. IBM itself had been extremely conservative in the face of the new technology, refusing to move out of its traditional office machinery market without government backing.[53] Studies of some of the smaller US office machine and calculator companies, such as Remington-Rand, National Cash Register, and Underwood paint a similarly conservative picture: firms kept a watchful eye on the emerging technology, but were reluctant, like Ferranti, to make large-scale commitments.[54]

On these terms, Ferranti's performance was a creditable one. What faults there were do not appear to have been primarily the result of sales and marketing deficiencies. Bernard Swann appears to have built up a vigorous sales team, which, when it had the right product, performed well. In fact, in view of Ferranti's production problems, it may well have been that the only result of even more efficient selling techniques would have been a longer backlog of orders. Even Lord Halsbury, in his more detached moments, expressed satisfaction with the Ferranti sales department, telling Vincent de Ferranti that he 'considered there was no complaint on the score of their selling effort'.[55] Two things, however, blunted that effort: one was the nature of the British market; the other was the peculiar position of the computer department within the Ferranti firm.

Ferranti, like other British computer manufacturers, eventually found itself competing with American firms which were underwritten massively by the resources of the US government. As Lord Halsbury noted, in the USA the government fully supported the rise of the data-processing industry and came forward with orders in a way that was not evident in the UK. America ploughed enormous resources into computer development, especially for military applications.[56] It was no coincidence that the take-off in the American computer industry occurred during the Cold War. During the 1950s IBM alone was awarded contracts totalling nearly $400 million; while Halsbury's NRDC had a total budget of only £5 million for the whole of the UK industry, and was, moreover, expected to be self-financing. In the 1960s the results of such policies were apparent: by 1964 it was estimated that there were almost 22,000 computers installed in the US, including approximately

1,767 in civil government, 2,000 in the Department of Defense, and another 2,000 or so used by government contractors at the state's expense. In contrast, less than 1,000 computers had been installed in the UK by the same date, of which only 56 were in civil government departments.[57] The implications of this in America for the development of core computer technologies, commercial spin-offs and the training of personnel can hardly be over-estimated. IBM employed something like 300 graduates on the Stretch supercomputer programme; while Ferranti never had more than 25 programmers working on the Atlas. Although this represented an exemplary use of manpower, eventually the greater American resources told against Ferranti, leading to late deliveries and the loss of the Atlas's dominant position. American industry was also more enthusiastic. Halsbury's criticisms of Ferranti were tempered by his concession 'that the enthusiasm of the American user was a big factor in determining the rate at which progress can be made by a manufacturing and development centre. In England potential users are not enthusiastic'.[58] The 'conspicuous lack of initiative and enterprise' of British managements was also criticised in the contemporary press.[59]

If Ferranti had been fully committed to computer development it might have held its technical lead long enough to secure a commercial niche in the market. But this was not the case. The Ferranti family refused to commit greater resources to both production and marketing and its position, despite its pioneering stance, remained basically conservative. Significantly, as the computer industry began to take off, the Ferrantis placed their money where it was safest – in small defence computing systems or in control systems computers that were spin-offs from military contracts. In 1962 Ferranti sold the first of nearly 100 Argus process control computers, and thereafter the Automation Systems Department at Ferranti grew steadily. Other Ferranti defence computers included the Poseidon, Hermes and F1600 (also sold as a commercial product). Ferranti's military computing department at Bracknell also began to grow rapidly in the 1960s and appears to have been consistently profitable. This defence work had the advantage that it could also be applied to non-military applications. When Ferranti sold off its computer interests to ICT, the defence computing section of the company was retained. By the mid-1980s Ferranti Computer Systems Ltd. had emerged amongst the top ten UK computer manufacturers.[60] In retrospect, it appears that Ferranti got the computer business it wanted – a profitable niche in the defence market; unfortunately for the British computer industry, this was not a strategy which allowed it to remain amongst the leaders of the world computer industry.

NOTES

A preliminary draft of this article was read at the Deuxième Colloque sur l'Histoire de l'Informatique en France, Conservatoire National des Arts et Métiers, 26 April 1990.

1. In the preface to *Faster than Thought: A Symposium on Digital Computing Machines* (1953), B.V. Bowden wrote: 'It seems probable that we shall have a second Industrial Revolution on our hands before long'. On Bowden, see below.
2. M. Campbell-Kelly, *ICL: A Technical and Business History* (Oxford, 1990); J. Hendry, *Innovating for Failure: Government Policy and the Early British Computer Industry* (Cambridge, MA, 1990).
3. R.P.T. Davenport-Hines, *Markets and Bagmen: Studies in the History of Marketing and British Industrial Performance, 1830–1939* (Aldershot, 1986). For a comparison, see R.S. Tedlow, *New and Improved: The Story of Mass Marketing in America* (1990).
4. See S. J. Nicholas, 'The Overseas Marketing Performance of British Industry, 1870–1914', *Economic History Review*, 2nd series, Vol.37 (1984), pp.489–506.
5. W. Aspray, 'Marketing the Monster: Advertising Computer Technology', *Annals of the History of Computing*, Vol.8 (1986), pp.127–43.
6. S. H. Lavington, *History of Manchester Computers* (Manchester, 1975); idem, *Early British Computers: The Story of Vintage Computers and the People Who Built Them* (Manchester, 1980).
7. T. J. Watson Jr. and P. Petre, *Father, Son & Co: My Life at IBM and Beyond* (1990), p.242. See also W. Rodgers, *THINK: A Biography of the Watsons and IBM* (1970). The following books (only a selection of the most recent and informative) provide further information on IBM's history and marketing policies: S. Engelbourg, *International Business Machines: A Business History* (New York, 1976); F.M. Fisher et al., *IBM and the US Data Processing Industry* (New York, 1983); Michael Killen, *IBM: The Making of the Common View* (Boston, 1988); W.W. Simmons, *Inside IBM: The Watson Years, A Personal Memoir* (Bryn Mawr, PA, 1988); R. Sobel, *IBM: Colossus in Transition* (New York, 1981)
8. For a critical view of IBM's sale tactics, see R.T Delamarter, *Big Blue: IBM's Use and Abuse of Power* (New York, 1986).
9. F. Rose, *West of Eden: The End of Innocence at Apple Computer* (1989), p.38.
10. J. Sculley (with J.A. Byrne), *Odyssey: Pepsi to Apple* (1989). There are a number of popular accounts of Apple and its founders, such as: J. S. Young, *Steve Jobs: The Journey is the Reward* (Barnet, Herts, 1988); L. Butcher, *The Rise and Fall of Steve Jobs at Apple Computer* (New York, 1988).
11. Sugar's philosophy was expounded to the City University Business School in 1987 as: 'Pan Am takes good care of you; Marks and Spencers loves you; IBM says the customer is king . . .; at Amstrad – We want your money'. Quoted in D. Thomas, *Alan Sugar: The Amstrad Story* (1990), p.249. On Sinclair see R. Dale, *The Sinclair Story* (1985). Interesting details on Apricot are presented in J. Harvey-Jones (with A. Masey), *Troubleshooter* (1990), pp.71–98.
12. The main source for this study has been the National Archive for the History of Computing (hereinafter NAHC), Manchester University, which holds the papers of the National Research Development Corporation (NRDC), Manchester University Department of Computer Science and of Dr D.G. Prinz. It also has manuscript material relating to the Ferranti Computer Group, including an unpublished typescript history by its sales manager Bernard Swann, and an extensive collection of Ferranti trade catalogues and manuals. A catalogue of this material is now available. At time of writing (September 1990) Ferranti's own archive at Moston, which includes much relevant material, is scheduled for closure.
13. F.C. Williams, 'Early Computers at Manchester University', *Radio and Electronic Engineer* Vol.45 (July 1975), pp.327–31, 327.
14. NAHC/PRI/Cla, D.G. Prinz, Report of a Visit Made to the USA in September 1948, on behalf of Ferranti.

15. Modern computers are often said to have originated with the ideas and designs of the English mathematician Charles Babbage, though the question as to who 'invented' the first computer is a vexed one. For the best consensus view, see: S. Augarten, *Bit by Bit: An Illustrated History of Computers* (New York, 1984); M.R. Williams, *A History of Computing Technology* (Englewood Cliffs, N J, 1985).

16. *Manchester University Computer Inaugural Conference* (July 1951), booklet reproduced in M. Campbell-Kelly and M.R. Williams (eds.), *The Early British Computer Conferences* (Cambridge, MA, 1988).

17. G. Tweedale, 'Eloge: Bertram Vivian Bowden (1919–1989)', *Annals of the History of Computing*, Vol.12 (1990), pp.138–40.

18. Lord Bowden, interview with the author, 1 Nov. 1988. Subsequent uncited Bowden quotations in the text are from this source.

19. B. Swann, 'The Ferranti Computer Department' (1975), p.13. Hartree did no more than voice the common view of many other mathematicians, who regarded the computer as a scientific device. Even the great American mathematician and computer theorist John von Neumann regarded computers as the tool of applied scientists – quite exclusively!

20. NAHC/NRD/86/4, Christopher Strachey, 'General Conclusions from American Trip: September-November 1952', p.1.

21. NAHC/NRD/86/7, Bowden, 'Ferranti High Speed Digital Computer' (Nov. 1950), p.21.

22. NAHC/NRD/86/9, Halsbury memo, 27 May 1952.

23. Swann, 'Ferranti Computer Department', p.15.

24. NAHC/NRD/86/4, John Crawley to Professor P.M.S. Blackett, 23 Sept. 1953.

25. NAHC/NRD/86/4, Halsbury to J.F. Lockwood, 13 March 1953.

26. For background on Ferranti, see J.F. Wilson, *Ferranti and the British Electrical Industry, 1864–1930* (Manchester, 1988); idem, 'Sir Gerard Vincent Sebastian de Ferranti', in D.J. Jeremy and C. Shaw (eds.), *Dictionary of Business Biography* (1984–6) Vol.2.

27. NAHC/NRD/86/29, Halsbury's notes on a meeting with Ferranti, 23 March 1954.

28. NAHC/NRD/86/9, Halsbury to Blackett, 19 June 1952.

29. NAHC/NRD/86/29, Halsbury to Williams, 8 July 1954.

30. NAHC/NRD/86/4, Patents manager to Crawley, 16 Jan. 1953.

31. The NAHC has a fairly complete collection of CS listed programming literature.

32. M. Campbell-Kelly, 'Christopher Strachey: A Biographical Note', *Annals of the History of Computing*, Vol.7 (June 1985), pp.19–42, 27. See also idem, 'Foundations of Computer Programming in Britain, 1945–1955' (Unpublished Ph. D. thesis, Sunderland, 1980).

33. The following section is based on a NRDC 'Survey of Computer Availability', typescript, c. 1957, in NAHC/NRD/86/4.

34. Campbell-Kelly *ICL*, p.52. For comments on Powers Samas marketing, see p.74.

35. Swann, 'Ferranti Computer Department', p.41.

36. Hendry *Innovating for Failure*, p.101.

37. Swann, 'Ferranti Computer Department', p.39.

38. Ibid., p.82.

39. P. Drath, M. Gibbons, and R. Johnston, 'The Super-Computer Project: A Case Study of the Interaction of Science, Government and Industry in the UK', *Research Policy*, Vol.6 (1977), pp.2–34; J. Hendry, 'Prolonged Negotiations: The British Fast Computer Project and the Early History of the British Computer Industry', *Business History*, Vol.26 (November 1984), pp.280–306.

40. S.H. Lavington, 'The Manchester Mark I and Atlas: A Historical Perspective', *Communications of the ACM*, Vol.21 (Jan. 1978), pp.4–12; Williams, *History of Computing Technology*, p.401. On CDC, see David E. Lundstrom, *A Few Good Men from Univac* (Cambridge, MA, 1987).

41. Paul Drath, 'The Relationship between Science and Technology: University Research and the Computer Industry, 1945-1962' (Unpublished Ph. D. thesis, University of Manchester, 1973), Ch. 7, p.14.
42. B. J. Bleakely and J. LaPrairie, *Entering the Computer Age: The Computer Industry in Canada: The First Thirty Years* (Agincourt, 1982), pp.10-12, 51-2; G. Tweedale, 'Aspects of the Anglo-American Transfer of Computer Technology: The Formative Years, c. 1930s to 1960s', in D.J. Jeremy (ed.), *Studies in the International Transfer of Technology* (Aldershot, in press).
43. NAHC/NRD/86/4, Christopher Strachey, 'General Conclusions from American Trip: September–November 1952', p.2.
44. NAHC/NRD/86/9, Ferranti managing director's report to board, 26 March 1952.
45. NAHC/NRD/86/9, M.E. Sions to D. Hennessy, 24 April 1952.
46. NAHC/NRD/86/4, A. Ridding to NRDC, 28 May 1953.
47. NAHC/NRD/86/7, Bowden to Halsbury, 7 May 1951.
48. Ibid.
49. NAHC/NRD/86/4, Bowden to Halsbury, 21 April 1953.
50. Drath, 'Relationship between Science and Technology', quoting Peter Hall of Ferranti.
51. J. Hendry, 'The Teashop Computer Manufacturer: J. Lyons, LEO and the Potential and Limits of High-tech Diversification', *Business History*, Vol.29 (Jan. 1987), pp.73–102.
52. See N. Stern, *From ENIAC to UNIVAC: An Appraisal of the Eckert-Mauchly Computers* (Bedford, MA, 1981).
53. According to Thomas J. Watson Jr.: 'My father initially thought the electronic computer would have no impact on the way IBM did business, because to him punch-card machines and giant computers belonged in totally separate realms. A computer revolution might sweep across the scientific world, but in the accounting room the punch card was going to stay on top.' See Watson, *Father, Son & Co.*, p.189. Even in more recent times, IBM has been slow in following the market trends. See, for example, J. Chposky and T. Leonsis, *Blue Magic: The People, The Power and the Politics Behind the IBM Personal Computer* (1989). Even less conservative firms such as Digital Equipment Corporation (DEC) have found the market difficult to predict. Its founder Ken Olsen, who had a distaste for advertising, failed to appreciate the growing importance of the personal computer market. See G. Rifkin and G. Harrar, *The Ultimate Entrepreneur: Ken Olsen and Digital Equipment Corporation* (Chicago, 1989).
54. C. Burke, 'The Remington-Rand Computer of 1946 and the Development of the American Computer Industry', unpublished typescript (1990), kindly loaned to me by the author.
55. NAHC/NRD/86/9, Halsbury's notes on a meeting with Sir Vincent de Ferranti, 11 March 1953.
56. Halsbury, 'Ten Years of Computer Development', *Computer Journal*, Vol.1 (Jan. 1959), pp.153–9. According to Halsbury, such was the American advantage in this area that: 'the wonder is not that the US industry is some ways ahead of our own, but that our own industry can exist at all in competition with it'. For a fuller treatment of the impact of defence see I. B. Cohen, 'The Computer: A Case Study of the Support by Government, Especially the Military, of a New Science and Technology', in E. Mendelsohn, M. Roe Smith and P. Weingart (eds.), *Science, Technology and the Military* (Dordrecht, 1988); K. Flamm, *Creating the Computer: Government, Industry and High Technology* (Washington, DC, 1988).
57. B. White, 'State Intervention in Technology in the Post-War Years: Case Studies in Technology Policy' (Unpublished Ph.D. thesis, University of Aston, 1985), p.124.

58. NAHC/NRD/86/9, Halsbury's notes on a meeting with Sir Vincent de Ferranti, 11 March 1953.
59. R.H. Williams, 'Britain and the World Market for Computers', *The Times*, 11 April 1962.
60. T. Kelly, *The British Computer Industry* (1987), p.214. Ferranti's involvement in the defence market has not had a happy ending, due to an ill-fated link-up with the American entrepreneur James H. Guerin's International Signal & Control.

FERRANTI COMPUTER SALES, 1951–ca.1963

Customer	Delivery Date	Scientific Applications	Commercial Applications
MARK I			
Manchester University	1951	Mathematical research	
Toronto University	1952	Mathematical research	
MARK I*			
Ministry of Supply	1953	Classified work	
Royal Dutch/Shell Laboratories, Amsterdam	1954	Oil refining studies	
Atomic Weapons Research Establishment, Aldermaston	1954	Research Work	
A.V. Roe & Co. Ltd., Manchester	1954	Aircraft design	
National Institute of Application of Mathematics, Rome	1955	Research work	
Ministry of Supply, Fort Halstead	1955	Research work	
Armstrong Siddeley Motors Ltd., Coventry	1957	Research work	
PEGASUS 1			
Ferranti Ltd., Portland Place, London	1956	Computing service	Computing service
Hawker Aircraft Co. Ltd., Kingston-upon-Thames	1956	Aircraft design	
Armstrong Whitworth Aircraft Ltd., Coventry	1956	Aircraft design	
Admiralty Research Laboratory, Teddington	1957	Research Work	Payroll
Royal Aircraft Establishment, Farnborough	1957	Research calculations	
Vickers-Armstrong (Aircraft) Ltd., Weybridge	1957	Aviation design	
ICI Dyestuffs Division, Manchester	1957	Research work	Sales analysis, stock control
NRDC, Northampton Polytechnic, London	1957	Research and training	
De Haviland Aircraft Co. Ltd., Hatfield	1957	Research work	Payroll, budgeting
British Thomson-Houston Co. Ltd., Rugby	1957	Turbine design	Costing
British Iron & Steel Research Association	1957	Operational research	
Leeds University	1957	Research, service work	University registration

Customer	Delivery Date	Scientific Applications	Commercial Applications
Durham University	1957	Research, service work	University registration
Southampton University	1958	Research, service	University registration
Babcock & Wilcox Ltd., London	1958	Research work	Stock control, accountancy
United Steel Co. Ltd., Sheffield	1958	Operational work	Production control research
Blackburn Aircraft Ltd., Brough	1958	Research work	Production control
Svenska Flygmotor A/B, Trollhatten, Sweden	1958	Research work	
Stuttgart University	1958	Research, service work	
Ministry of Supply, Military Survey, London	1959	Survey calculations	
Ferranti Ltd., Hollinwood, Lancashire	1959	Transformer design	Production, wages, service work
C.A. Parsons & Co. Ltd., Newcastle	1959	Transformer design	
Ferranti Packard Electric Ltd., Toronto	1959	Transformer design	
Steel Co of Wales Ltd., Port Talbot	1960	Operational research	
College of Aeronautics, Cranfield	1960	Aircraft design	
Aircraft Armament Experimental Establishment, Boscombe Down PEGASUS 2	1961	Aircraft design	Data analysis
De Havilland Propellors Ltd., Stevenage	1959	Aircraft design	
Skandia Insurance Co., Stockholm, Sweden	1959		Actuarial work
Ferranti Ltd., Newman Street, London	1960	Computing service	Computing service
Bruce Peebles & Co. Ltd., Edinburgh	1960	Transformer design	Production control
London & Manchester Assurance Co., London	1960		Insurance/investment
DSIR, Road Research Laboratory, Harmondsworth	1961	Research calculations	
Shell Research Ltd., Thornton	1961	Technological work	Accident record analysis
Vickers-Armstrong (Aircraft) Ltd., Weybridge	1961	Aircraft design	
Martins Bank Ltd., Liverpool	1961		Bookkeeping

Customer	Delivery Date	Scientific Applications	Commercial Applications
Scottish Widows Fund & Standard Life Assurance Society, Edinburgh	1962		Pensions, valuations
Westminster Bank Ltd., London	1962		Bookkeeping
MERCURY			
Norwegian Defence Research Establishment, Kjeller	1957	Atomic energy	
Manchester University	1957	Research, service work	
French Atomic Energy Authority, Saclay	1957	Atomic energy	
UK Atomic Energy Authority, Harwell	1958	Atomic energy	
RAF Meteorological Office, Dunstable	1958	Weather forecasting	
Council for European Nuclear Research, Geneva	1958	Atomic energy	
London University	1958	Research, service work	
UK Atomic Energy Authority, Risley	1958	Atomic energy	
Oxford University	1958	Research, service work	
Shell International Petroleum Co. Ltd.,	1959	Linear programming	Sales analysis
Royal Aircraft Establishment, Farnborough	1959	Aircraft design	
ICI Central Instruments Division, Reading	1959	Chemical analysis	
Swedish Atomic Energy Authority, Stockholm	1959	Atomic energy	
Belgian Atomic Energy Authority, Mol	1959	Atomic energy	
General Electric Co. Ltd., Erith	1959	Atomic energy/design	
Metropolitan-Vickers Electrical Co. Ltd. (AEI), Manchester	1960	Transformer design	
UK Atomic Energy Authority, Winfrith Heath	1960	Atomic energy	
Buenos Aires University	1960	Atomic energy work	
British Petroleum Co. Ltd., London	1961	Linear programming	Sales analysis
PERSEUS			
AB Datacentralen (Trygg & Fylgia Insurance Companies), Stockholm	1959		Insurance policies

Customer	Delivery Date	Scientific Applications	Commercial Applications
South African Mutual Life Assurance Association, Cape Town	1959		Insurance policies
ORION			
Ferranti Ltd., Manchester	1963	Computing service	Computing service
Ferranti Ltd., Newman Street, London	1963	Computing service	Computing service
AB Turitz Co., Gothenburg, Sweden	1963		Stock control/sales
National Provincial Bank Ltd., London	1963		Bookkeeping
Prudential Assurance Co. Ltd., London (Orion 2 replaced Orion 1)	1964		Insurance work
Norwich Union Life Insurance Society	1964		Insurance
Beecham Group, Brentford	1964		Stock control, sales, accounts
Metal Box Co. Ltd., Worcester	1964		Payroll, statistics
Cadbury Brothers	1964		Statistics
Vickers-Armstrong	1965	Design	
SIRIUS			
Ferranti Ltd., Newman Street, London	1960	Computing service	Computing service
Ferranti Ltd., Newman Street, London	1961	Computing service	Computing service
Yarrow & Co. Ltd., Glasgow	1961	Pipe stressing	Technical/external service
Ferranti Ltd., Melbourne, Australia	1961	Computer service	
Cement & Concrete Association, Slough	1962	Frame stressing	
KOVO, Czechoslovakia	1962	Technical work	
ICI, Melbourne, Australia	1962	Scientific/technical	
Ferranti Ltd., Melbourne, Australia	1962	Computing service	
Davy Ashmore	1962	Still making design	
Heriot-Watt University	1962	Teaching	
Admiralty, Bath	1963	Ship design	
British Railways	1963	Technical work	Bonus calculations
Trumpy y Sirvent, Madrid	1963	Computing service	Computing service
	1963	Research	

Customer	Delivery Date	Scientific Applications	Commercial Applications
ATLAS			
Manchester University	1963	Research/service	University registration
London University	1963	Computing service	
UK Atomic Energy Authority	1964	Atomic energy	

Sources: This is reproduced in 'Ferranti Computers Installed' (Ferranti CS List 286 A, Jan. 1962) and in B.B. Swann, The Ferranti Computer Department', unpublished typescript, 1975, in the National Archive for the History of Computing, Manchester University. The details have been checked, where possible, in various surveys, such as *The British Commercial Computer Digest* (Computer Consultants Ltd., 1962).

Industry Structure as a Competitive Advantage: The History of Japan's Post-war Steel Industry

PATRICIA A. O'BRIEN

Harvard Business School

The rapid growth of the Japanese economy in the post-World War II decades revived a controversial debate concerning the role of the state in economic development.[1] On one extreme are those who attribute much of the growth of the Japanese economy to its developmental state.[2] According to these researchers, the Japanese government, through institutions such as the Ministry of International Trade and Industry (MITI), adopted sectoral policies that supported and developed particular industries for trade. On the other extreme are those who argue that Japan's success resulted largely from the natural response of industrialists to market incentives.[3] These researchers assert that competition in a growing domestic market challenged managers to innovate and increase productivity, thereby fueling steady industrial growth. Implicit in this perspective is the assertion that government policies were, at best, inconsequential.

To advance our understanding of the role of the state in economic development, it is useful to isolate and examine specific sectoral policies. This article contributes to the debate by examining the role of the Japanese government in the development of one industry, steel. The steel industry provides a vivid example through which to analyse Japan's sectoral intervention. Government policies targeting steel for growth began as early as 1947 and continued through the high-growth decades of the 1950s and 1960s. The policies ranged from protectionism, via tariffs and import restrictions, to preferential financing and coordinated capacity expansion. Then too, steel was one of Japan's earliest and possibly most dramatic industrial successes and, as such, became the archetype of Japan's post-war economic success.[4] The industry was rebuilt in the early 1950s, and, by 1953, was producing 7.7 million tons of steel, equal to its peak output a decade earlier during World War II. For the next two decades, Japan's steel output grew at an average annual rate of 15 per cent. By 1976, the industry was capable of producing nearly 150 million tons of steel yearly and was responsible for 16 per cent of the world's steel market share. Even in the mid-1980s, by which time Japan had lost its superiority in steel to Korean companies, Japan produced over 20 per cent of the world's total steel exports.[5]

Of course, simply observing that, on one hand, the Japanese government adopted policies targeted at steel and, on the other hand, that the industry grew rapidly and achieved the government's desired objective, proves little about the effectiveness of state intervention.[6] Consequently, this study goes beyond these observations and isolates and analyses the effect of Japan's industrial policies in steel.[7] It examines how the government intervened, for what purposes, and the actual behaviour of firms in the industry.

The central question of this article is: did Japan's government policies in steel help, hinder, or leave unchanged the industry's development? My main argument is that Japan's policies in steel helped the industry develop a competitive advantage by shaping the industry's structure. Through sectoral-specific policies, the Japanese government intervened in the market to organise the factors of production in steel. MITI understood the economics of capital-intensive industries and used its power to ensure that the industry's resources were employed efficiently. In the early post-war years, the government, through MITI, constrained supply and channelled resources into a few large manufacturing units, enabling steel firms to realise the economies of scale fundamental to efficient steel manufacturing. Later, the government allowed the steel industry to manage and co-ordinate its capacity expansion decisions. In this way, the Japanese government influenced the structure of the Japanese steel industry and helped it develop a manufacturing cost advantage. While the government's policies alone were not sufficient to guarantee the industry's success, they contributed to it by accelerating the formation of Japan's steel oligopoly.

I

The Economics of Steelmaking

To understand the evolution of Japan's post-war steel industry, one must first understand the fundamental economics of steelmaking. This study is concerned with the basic carbon steel industry which, through the 1970s, accounted for over 85 per cent of all steel produced.[8] Basic carbon steel is made into products which are sold to producers of capital and consumer goods either as finished products – plates, bars, shapes, wire and pipe

– or as semifinished products – blooms, billets and slabs. The industry manufactures hot-rolled sheets for automobile and household appliance makers, beams used in bridgework and construction, and plates used in shipbuilding. Carbon steel is a commodity: its products have to meet general physical and chemical tests after which all companies' products are virtually identical. Unlike specialty or alloy steels which have to meet a host of other product requirements, basic carbon steel has almost no brand differentiation. Consequently, price and, to a lesser extent, service are the key factors in determining sales. Thus, competition in the world steel market depends on price which depends largely on costs.

The steel manufacturing process is generally composed of three discrete steps: the blast furnace, in which raw materials are heated and reduced to liquid pig iron; the steel furnace in which pig iron is oxidised and converted to raw steel; and the rolling process in which the raw steel is moulded and rolled into finished or semifinished products. From the late nineteenth century, efficient steel production required that companies engage in all three stages of this process.[9] By integrating backwards into iron production and forward into rolling, steelmakers could assure themselves an adequate and steady supply of affordable inputs and a continuous flow of materials through their plants.

The most salient fact about steel manufacturing is its extreme capital intensity.[10] Every stage of the steelmaking process requires companies to commit huge amounts of capital exclusively to the manufacturing of steel. Moreover, unlike labour-intensive industries in which an increase in output requires a corresponding increase in labour, capital-intensive industries enable producers to increase output with a one-time investment in capital. Capital intensity, which obviously translates into a large fixed cost component, provides producers with the opportunity to achieve greater economies of scale. Because of the large fixed costs, as the volume of materials being processed increases the cost per unit drops quickly.

In the 1950s, the minimum efficient scale – the scale of operation necessary to reach the lowest cost per unit – for an integrated steel plant was estimated to be approximately 1–2.5 million tons of steel capacity.[11] Technological improvements during the 1960s and 1970s increased the minimum efficient scale of blast furnaces and rolling mills and, in turn, of entire steel plants. The optimal capacity of a blast furnace increased from 300,000 tons of pig iron a year in 1950, to over 3 million tons by the 1970s. By then, a modern hot strip mill, which is used to roll slabs into sheets, could produce 3–4 million tons a year when used continually. Given the minimum efficient scale of blast furnaces and the logistical problems of balancing the output of blast furnaces, basic oxygen furnaces, rolling mills, and finishing mills, the efficient scale of a steel plant was upwards of 6–7 million tons of crude steel by the 1970s. If built in the United States, a new steel plant of this size would have cost more than three billion dollars.[12]

To minimise the unit fixed cost, however, a steel plant has to operate at or near full capacity; operating below capacity wreaks havoc on unit costs. Consequently, a steel plant's overall efficiency depends on it operating 'full and steady', around the clock, throughout the year.[13] Thus, the capital intensity of steel manufacturing dictates that plant size and capacity utilisation are primary cost determinants.

Additionally, although the basic chemical process for manufacturing steel barely changed during the twentieth century, several technological innovations improved manufacturing efficiencies and reduced the time, labour, and raw materials required to produce a ton of steel. The primary technological breakthrough was in the steelmaking furnace. Starting in the late 1950s, the basic oxygen furnace replaced the open hearth furnace as the most efficient method of oxidising pig iron to produce raw steel. Continuous casting technology, developed in the 1960s, eliminated several steps in the manufacturing process, thereby minimising steel waste and reducing energy consumption and labour usage. Computer controlled technology also yielded significant costs savings and further accelerated the upward trend in the size of steel plants and equipments.

II

The Industry's History: Pre-1950

Japan's modern iron and steel industry started in 1897 when the government built the integrated Yawata Iron Works. By 1920, the industry boasted more than 100 private steel mills, yet the industry remained small, fragmented and struggling. In 1929, Japan produced only 2.3 million tons of steel or two per cent of the world's total.[14]

When Japan invaded Manchuria in 1931, the government feared that the country's weak steel industry could not meet Japan's military demand. From then until the end of the Pacific War in 1945, Japan's steel industry was co-ordinated by the Japanese government. In Japan's 14 years of war, the Ministry of Commerce and Industry (which became the Munitions Ministry from 1943–45) planned steel capacity, production, raw material procurement, distribution and prices. National resources were poured into heavy industries, more than doubling capacity in steel, aluminum, and machine tools between 1937 and 1944. Steel output rose from 2.4 million tons in 1932 to nearly 7 million tons in 1939 and, finally, to 7.7 million tons in 1943, the industry's highest level of output up to that point in history.

When Japan's military offensive ended, its economy was in ruins and its industries were barely functioning. With a mere half a million tons of output in 1945, Japan's steel industry had collapsed. Due to a combination of economic and political factors, less than 30 per cent of the iron and steel facilities were in operation. At the war's end, the future of Japan's steel industry was doubtful.[15]

The industry faced four serious problems. First, the Supreme Commander of the Allied Powers (SCAP), charged with demilitarising Japan for the Allies, had prohibited over one-half of Japan's steel mills from operating. In attempting to ensure that Japan could never again wage an aggressive military offensive, the early Occupation policy restricted operations in all munitions industries, in which group it classified steel. The Pauley Plan, a well-known SCAP document named after its author, the US ambassador Edwin W. Pauley, charged Japan with permanently reducing its steel capacity to its pre-war level of 2 million tons.

Second, peace ended the heavy war-related demand for Japanese steel. Crippled by severe shortages of food, energy, raw materials, and foreign exchange, Japan's first priority was to avoid the mass starvation which in 1946 seemed imminent. The country's post-war civilian economy simply could not generate enough activity to replace the military demand for steel.

Third, severe shortages combined with Japan's post-war inflation raised Japan's production costs. The departure of forced Korean and Chinese labourers at the end of the war crippled the nation's coal industry which, in turn, threatened manufacturing industries like steel and increased the country's dependence on imports. Moreover, Japan's chief sources of raw materials – China, Manchuria and Korea – were closed to Japanese trade at the end of the war. With no alternative suppliers in Southeast Asia, Japan turned to Western supplies which, in being further away, were more costly to transport. A shortage of foreign exchange severely limited Japan's ability to import supplies. Manufacturing costs were also affected by Japan's rampant inflation. Soon after the war the Japanese government repaid its huge wartime obligations to the private sector and flooded the unproductive economy with yen. In the first six months after the war, Japan's price levels rose by a factor of ten.

Finally, although at the end of the war Japan had over 40 steel companies, the vast majority of iron and steel facilities were too debilitated to operate. The war had destroyed 20 per cent of the industry's plants and, of the plants and equipment remaining, much was obsolete, debilitated or both. For 14 years, the industry had primarily manufactured shapes for munitions. After the war, the companies needed to shift output from military goods to sheets, strips, and hoops necessary for capital-goods industries. For this, firms needed new rolling mills. Moreover, during the war, the companies' equipment had been used unremittingly and maintained minimally so that even equipment that was not obsolete needed to be repaired or replaced. As Japan's equipment manufacturers were also not operating, new steel equipment would have to be imported from Europe or the United States. This in turn required a supply of foreign exchange that Japan lacked.

These economic factors – low demand, input shortages, domestic inflation, and obsolete facilities – ensured that Japan's steel companies had among the highest manufacturing costs in the world. Despite very low wage rates, Japanese steel costs were 50–100 per cent higher than those of comparable products manufactured in the US, France, and Great Britain.[16] High manufacturing costs, of course, precluded Japanese steelmakers from exporting except for periods of extreme shortages.

III

A Strategy for Steel

By 1948, SCAP, responding to the Cold War, had modified its reparations policy for Japan and instituted a modest recovery programme. To encourage economic development and independence, the SCAP allowed heavy industries like steel to reopen and, in addition, transferred to the Japanese government authority over the allocation of scarce resources and economic policy. Japan already had a tradition of central economic planning from its decade and a half at war. Moreover, since the government had directed Japan's industrial production during mobilisation, the country had agencies and bureaucrats experienced in developing and implementing industrialisation policies. After some reshuffling – during which the Ministry of Commerce and Industry, which supervised war mobilisation, and the Board of Trade, which oversaw exports, imports, and foreign exchange, were abolished and the functions of these two former institutions were combined in one new ministry called the Ministry of International Trade and Industry (MITI) – Japan's post-war developmental state was in place.[17]

In 1950, the objective of the Japanese government was to rebuild the country's devastated economy. One priority, of course, was to earn foreign exchange with which Japan could pay for necessary imports of food, raw materials, technology, and heavy machinery. To earn the foreign exchange, Japan needed a correspondingly large volume of exports, preferably of the high-value-added variety. At the time, textiles – a low-value-added commodity – were Japan's primary exports. Consequently, it was necessary for Japan to change the particular mix of industries that comprised the nation's economy.

MITI targeted several industries for potential export growth. One of these was steel.[18] Considered the 'rice of industry' in Japan, steel had long enjoyed a privileged position in the Japanese economy. In the aftermath of war, the Japanese government renewed its commitment to the steel industry for three reasons. First, steel was perceived to be a potential export commodity because world steel demand was strong and was expected to become even stronger as national economies recovered and converted to peacetime production. Second, because of their high value added, steel exports would contribute more foreign exchange to Japan's national income than other low-value-added commodities such as textiles. Third, as a basic material used in key industries such as shipbuilding, automobiles, and machinery, steel would be essential to Japan's economic development.

For Japan to compete successfully in the world steel market, the industry required a comparative cost advantage. Given the fundamental economics of steelmaking, the industry needed large, modern, integrated facilities that operated at or near their full capacity. The small size of Japan's market dictated that the country could accommodate only a limited number of plants. In 1950, for example, the Japanese steel industry shipped nearly 5 million tons of steel – 4.1 million tons domestically and 0.7 million tons abroad. With the optimal plant size of approximately 2 million tons, an efficient industry – one that fully exploited the economies of scale – could meet this demand with two or three large, modern plants. This ideal industry structure would enable plants to run full and steady thereby minimising production costs by fully exploiting the economies of scale.

Japan's steel industry structure, however, was a far cry from this ideal. In 1950, the country's steel capacity was spread over 44 iron and steel companies: four integrated makers, 15 open hearth furnace makers, and 25 small, highly specialised rolling mill or pig iron companies. Like steel industries in all major steel-producing countries, Japan's was dominated by a few large firms. The six major companies, which were privately owned and operated, produced about 65 per cent of the industry's output. Yet only one integrated plant – the Yawata works – even approached the minimum efficient scale in steelmaking. Japan's remaining five integrated plants possessed far too little capacity to exploit the economies of scale in steel production (see Table 1).

TABLE 1

JAPAN'S INTEGRATED STEEL PLANTS, 1950

Company	Works	Steel Capacity (million tons)
Yawata Steel Co.	Yawata	1.80
Fuji Steel Co.	Mororan	.50
	Kamaishi	.69
	Hirohata	.60
NKK	Kawasaki	.34
	Tsurumi	.34

Source: Annual Reports.

The three largest companies – Yawata, Fuji, and Nippon Kokan Kabushiki (NKK) – were integrated steelmakers and, on average, were twice as large as the next three companies. Yawata and Fuji were established in 1950 when the Occupation forces dissolved the country's largest and only government-owned steel firm, the Japan Iron & Steel Co. Yawata Steel, Japan's largest steel maker, operated two plants, Yawata and Tobata, in Japan's southwest Kyushu area. Of these two plants, only Yawata was integrated. With 1.8 million tons of capacity, Yawata was the largest steel plant in Japan. The Fuji Steel Co. operated three integrated plants – Hirohata, Kamaishi and Muroran – each of which had fewer than one million tons of steel capacity. Japan's third integrated producer, NKK, operated the integrated Tsurumi and Kawasaki works. NKK's two integrated plants, which were both situated in the Yokohama area near Tokyo, each possessed a mere 0.34 million tons of steel capacity.[19]

The next three companies in order of market share were Kawasaki Steel, Sumitomo Metal Industries and Kobe Steel Works. Each had at one time planned to build blast furnaces and integrate backwards into pig iron production but all had been forced to postpone these investments during Japan's decade and a half at war. Consequently, Kawasaki Steel, Sumitomo Metal and Kobe Steel were 'open hearth furnace makers'; they bought pig iron, converted it into molten steel in steel furnaces, and then moulded and shaped the steel into products.

Formerly the Steelmaking Division of the huge Kawasaki Heavy Industries Co. Ltd., Kawasaki Steel became an independent legal entity in 1950 after the Occupation authorities ordered the dissolution of Kawasaki Heavy Industries.[20] Kawasaki Steel inherited seven small, non-integrated plants which together manufactured a wide variety of products including sheets, plates, tubes, and wire ropes. Sumitomo Metal Industries was also formed when the Occupation Authorities dissolved the *zaibatsu* and other large industrial groups. Separated from the Sumitomo group, one of the most powerful combines in pre-war Japan, Sumitomo Metal operated three small, non-integrated works: a new plant in Wakayama, in south-eastern Japan; a castings and forgings plant in Osaka; and a tube mill in Amagasaki, across the river from Osaka. Finally, Kobe Steel, which became a private steelmaker in 1911, possessed several small, specialised plants, none of which was integrated at the end of World War II.

Thus, in 1950, when the Japanese government targeted steel as a potential export product, Japan's steel facilities were not competitive in the world market. While the vast majority of steel capacity in America and Europe was in integrated plants of more than one million tons, over 75 per cent of Japan's capacity was in plants far smaller than the minimum efficient scale in steelmaking. Moreover, every integrated plant, except Hirohata (of Fuji Steel), had been constructed before 1920 and operated old, worn-out equipment. Yawata, Japan's largest plant, was built in 1897 and consisted of 12 small blast furnaces – eight of which were in such disrepair that they were not functioning – and 29 small open-hearth furnaces. The layout and transportation systems through the Yawata works was also intricate and technologically obsolete.

Bureaucrats at MITI recognised that to win global market share, the steel industry had to be transformed from this fragmented agglomeration of small-scale plants into an oligopoly with large, modern facilities. This fact brought the Japanese government face-to-face with perhaps the central dilemma of industrial policy: was government intervention necessary – or even desirable – to effectively organise an industry's resources? If left to the invisible hand of the market, would resources be drawn to steel? Would too many or not enough factors of production enter the industry? More to the point, if left to market forces, would the factors of production be organised in the most productively efficient structure?[21] Conversely, could government policies facilitate a superior industrial organisation?

The Japanese government approached these questions with assumptions that differed from those that prevailed in the west. To begin with, most Japanese policymakers had never subscribed to Adam Smith's notion that the market was the optimal way to achieve economic objectives. Influenced by the German school of economics, especially the ideas of neo-mercantilism, Japanese policymakers assumed that the government had a vital role to play in fostering industrial development.[22] Moreover, the government had experimented with questions like these as far back as the Meiji Restoration, and in the 1920s and 1930s, when Japan had faced economic problems comparable in kind and severity to those of the 1950s. While these experiments resulted in only mixed success, the prevailing ideology in the post-war bureaucracy assumed that government leadership was needed to guide private sector economic activity.

To determine how the government could intervene, MITI bureaucrats turned to the economics of steel manufacturing. The government, through MITI, intended to build a sustainable cost advantage to ensure that steel companies were competitive in the global market. Thus, the over-riding principle guiding MITI's policies was that to succeed internationally, the industry had to minimise its manufacturing costs. To do this the industry required large scale plants, high throughput, and modern technology. MITI reasoned that industrial policies could facilitate the development of these structural characteristics.

Consequently, the primary objective of MITI's policies in steel was to co-ordinate the factors of production in a way that enabled producers to fully exploit the economies of scale in steelmaking. The first structural requirement then was that the industry maximise the number of units produced – or throughput – at each plant. To ensure that plants operated full and steady around the clock, required that capacity – or supply – remain relatively balanced with (domestic and export) demand. Therefore, throughout the post-war decades, MITI's policies were aimed at creating an equilibrium between supply and demand.[23]

Second, since large steel plants are more economical than small, MITI's second guiding principle was that each plant be as large as the minimum efficient scale in steelmaking. Conversely, the maximum number of plants the industry could accommodate was determined by the size of the market. The optimal number of plants was equal to the quotient of estimated total demand divided by the minimum efficient scale in the industry. Third, to ensure that companies maintained modern technology and efficient methods of production, MITI intended to preserve interfirm rivalry.

To manage these structural requirements, MITI controlled capacity and entry. MITI ensured that Japanese steel was manufactured in large-scale facilities that exploited the economies of scale in steelmaking by controlling the supply of steel in Japan's market. By limiting the amount of total steel capacity and the number of plants in the market, MITI restrained the Japanese steel industry. This restraint ensured that steel would be manufactured in large plants with high capacity utilisation. Other short-term policies, such as price and production cartels, were used to help companies through periods of temporary market instability. But the government's overwhelming policy choice was to intervene systematically in the market to constrain the industry's structure. By limiting the resources invested in new steel capacity and concentrating those in the hands of a few large companies, the government concentrated volume in a few plants and accelerated the development of a steel oligopoly.

The striking aspect of these industrial policies was not the economics of steelmaking, for these were not unique to Japan, but that the objective of Japan's public policy intervention was to exploit the economics of capital-intensive industries to develop a world-class steel industry. MITI understood the essential requirements of capital-intensive industries and used its policies to co-ordinate the industry's resources in a way that facilitated a competitive industry structure. Because these policies furthered MITI's objective – developing steel into a successful export industry – these policies were perceived to be an improvement on the competitive market outcome. As in the decision to regulate in all market systems, the government's intention was never to break completely with the market but rather to improve on what it perceived as an inevitable market failure.

IV

Capacity Limits Through Protectionism

The first, and easiest, way for the Japanese government to limit steel capacity was to close the domestic market to steel imports. From the beginning of the Occupation until the mid-1960s, foreign steelmakers were generally prohibited from selling in Japan. Protectionism gave the industry the time, volume, and experience to rebuild its manufacturing competence. When the Korean War broke out in June 1950, the prosperous world economy was already suffering from a steel shortage. As a result, demand for Japanese steel was boosted by 45 per cent in 1950 and 28 per cent in 1951. By 1953, the steel industry had recovered from its war-time damage. With national income growing at more than 10 per cent a year, domestic steel demand revived and matched its prior wartime peak. According to developmental economics, continued protectionism at this time would have had a deleterious long-run effect on steel firms by reducing their exposure to international competition.[24]

But Japan maintained import barriers in steel until the mid-1960s because they yielded more than the benefits of time and experience. Rather, the fundamental advantage of protectionism was that it limited the supply of steel in the market and thereby maximised the throughput of domestic plants. As companies used their capacity more fully, unit costs were reduced, enabling Japanese producers to begin exporting steel. Protectionism guaranteed that the supply of steel in Japan's domestic market would be limited to what domestic producers collectively produced. Japanese steel producers were thus assured a larger volume and therefore lower unit costs than if there had been free market entry. A critical fact seldom realised is that Japan's trade barriers were a strategic tool for limiting capacity and enabling firms to maintain close to maximum throughput.

Japan's use of protectionism as a means of balancing supply and demand is further indicated by the government's policies during domestic steel shortages. On two occasions when Japan found itself suffering from a severe steel shortage, the country temporarily suspended its prohibitions on steel imports. Faced with a domestic shortage and rising prices in 1953 and 1956–57, MITI first allocated foreign exchange to steel users, thereby enabling them to import foreign-produced iron and steel. As demand continued to grow, however, MITI opened Japan's market further by suspending all steel tariffs. Foreign steel streamed into Japan, accounting for 12 per cent of consumption in 1957, a level that imports never again attained.

MITI's decision to suspend Japan's protectionist policies in the face of domestic shortages makes it vividly clear that the government's overriding objective was to balance supply with demand in order to build a globally competitive steel industry. If the government's objective had been exclusively to protect or develop the domestic steel industry, it might have allowed the shortage and resulting high prices to prevail as both an incentive and a method of financing more capital investment. If, instead, the government had been following an import substitution strategy, it would have simply prohibited exports. But, as reflected in Table 3, when Japan's trade restrictions in steel were relaxed in 1957, Japan's companies exported 1.3 million tons of steel while domestic buyers simultaneously imported 1.6 million tons. Japan's policy of allowing foreign steel to enter the market during periods of domestic shortages was logical because the overarching objective of Japan's trade policy was to equilibrate supply and demand to assure effective capacity utilisation.

V

Capacity Limits Through Government Fiat: 1951–60

Though protectionism was necessary, it was not sufficient to ensure that Japanese steel was manufactured in large modern plants with high capacity utilisation. According to MITI, the industry faced two potential problems. First, as more resources were drawn to steel, supply could outstrip demand, forcing the industry to suffer from overcapacity. The industry could then fall into a cycle of low capacity utilisation, low margins, and large losses. By 1951, Japan's environment had changed propitiously for steel. By targeting steel as a priority, the government had publicly renewed its commitment to the industry and drawn resources to it. While the government offered no guarantees and only modest financial assistance, through targeting it had announced that steel was a cornerstone of national economic development and, given steel's strategic importance, the government would try to ensure its survival. Not surprisingly, in 1950, many of Japan's top university graduates entered the steel industry. In this propitious environment, MITI feared a stampede of entry and bold strategies of investment.

Second, MITI feared that, if left to market forces, new steel capacity could be spread over the industry's many small-scale plants. Yawata, Fuji and NKK – the three largest producers – intended to add capacity to their existing works. In addition, Kawasaki Steel, Sumitomo Metal and Kobe Steel were likely to revive their plans to integrate backwards into pig iron production and become integrated producers. MITI feared that new capacity would be spread over an excessive number of plants, and Japanese steel would continue to be produced in uneconomically small plants. Alternatively, if too many companies invested in plants of minimum efficient scale, the plants would be unable to utilise fully their capacity given the small size of Japan's market. In either case – the proliferation of small-scale plants or sheer overcapacity – market forces would yield an industry structure that prohibited efficient steel manufacturing.

To avoid these conditions – which the government deemed 'excessive competition' – MITI intervened.[25] Through a series of *ad hoc* measures that were eventually transferred to the industry, the government limited the amount of new steel capacity built in Japan. With the industry's assistance, the government also co-ordinated which firms built new capacity. The government managed the industry's structure by regulating the quantity of capacity that entered the market and which companies were allowed to build. This ensured that supply remained balanced with estimated demand and that capacity was concentrated in a few large plants that could begin to exploit the economies of scale.

In general, MITI had little legal authority and few sanctions through which to control private sector capacity decisions. During the early 1950s, however, MITI had a commanding influence because of its control over scarce resources. The government agency had full authority over the allocation of Japan's foreign exchange and, through that, came to control imports and all joint venture licences. Additionally, either explicitly or implicitly through relationships, MITI had the ability to approve credit or authorise the expenditures of the Japan Development Bank, the Electric Power Development Co., the Export-Import Bank, the Smaller Business Finance Corporation, the Bank for Commerce & Industrial Co-operatives, the Japan Petroleum Development Corporation and the Productivity Headquarters.[26]

In 1951, when MITI's influence over the industry was strongest, steel companies in need of capital submitted expansion plans to MITI's Heavy Industries Bureau for review. If MITI approved the plan, the company was granted loans from Japanese banks. If MITI found a company's plans inconsistent with its plan for the industry, government officials met with company management to negotiate a mutually acceptable level of investment. Likewise, MITI earmarked foreign exchange for coal, iron ore, scrap steel and technology imports to companies as their plans were approved.

MITI used its influence to concentrate resources in a tiny handful of large steelmakers. Rather than allocate funds to many firms and create what western theory would consider a 'competitive market structure', MITI channelled capital exclusively to Japan's largest companies. From 1951–56, the three largest integrated steelmakers – Yawata, Fuji and NKK – received 58 per cent of the funding with Yawata, Japan's largest steelmaker, individually absorbing more than 25 per cent of the loans. The four largest companies received 72 per cent of the capital targeted for steel, equal to $227 million. The remaining 40 steel companies received 28 per cent of MITI's modernisation funds, an amount approximately equal to what was spent by Yawata Steel alone.[27] (Table 2.)

While it is difficult to prove MITI's intention in promoting concentration, subsequent events suggest that it was a deliberate strategy to organise the factors of production in steel in a way that capitalised on the inherent economic characteristics of steelmaking. Under the espoused objective of 'renovation, not expansion', MITI refused to authorise most new construction and continued to constrain the amount of overall capacity in the industry. No new blast furnaces and only those open hearth furnaces that were absolutely necessary to balance existing iron or rolling mill capacity were approved for construction. The vast majority of funds went toward repairs to existing equipment and replacements for old dysfunctional equipment.[28]

Yawata, Fuji and NKK invested in renovating – or 'rounding-out' – their six integrated plants. No greenfield plants or new blast furnaces were built in these companies.[29] Rather, these steelmakers invested in the conventional technology of the time to improve the equipment

TABLE 2

JAPANESE STEEL COMPANY FINANCE, 1951–56

Company	Funds (millions of)	(000$)	% of Total	Market Share % Crude Steel Production
Yawata	28,166	80,474	25	30
Fuji	20,791	59,403	19	18
NKK	15,006	42,874	14	14
Kawasaki	15,658	44,737	14	8
Sumitomo	7,005	20,014	6	4
Kobe	4,380	12,514	4	5
26 Companies	19,623	56,000	18 }	19
11 Companies	0	0	0 }	
Total	110,629	316,000	100	100

Source: Compiled from *Japan's Iron and Steel Industry, 1953–54* and annual reports.

and layout of their pre-war plants. Round-outs included repairing 13 blast furnaces, refurbishing all open hearth furnaces and installing 12 new open hearth furnaces to balance the production flow through the plants. In the renovations, however, each company also increased the scale of its plants. Yawata Steel, for example, increased its crude steel capacity from 1.82 million tons to 2.32 million tons, while Fuji Steel increased capacity from 1.6 million tons to 2.1 million tons, and NKK from 0.68 million tons to 0.88 million tons. From 1951 to 1955, Japan's capital was directed primarily at upgrading facilities, increasing the scale, and ensuring a steady, coordinated flow of material through a limited number of integrated steel plants.

The Kawasaki Steel Co., the fourth firm that received government funding, was the exception to this pattern.[30] The company's strategy, and its difficulty in implementing it, illustrates the objectives and limits of MITI's power. Japan's fourth largest company and largest open hearth furnace maker, Kawasaki Steel opposed MITI's capital allocation plan and fought to enter the integrated sector. With pig iron and scrap steel prices high and sources unreliable, Kawasaki Steel applied to MITI for capital to build a new, integrated steelwork in 1951. The proposed new works was eventually to have 4.5 million tons of capacity, a plant scale almost unheard of at the time. MITI, however, had other ideas. Kawasaki's proposal met with vehement opposition from government officials and bankers and MITI refused to authorise funds for the greenfield construction project. There ensued a one and a half year battle between MITI and Kawasaki Steel. The government argued that added capacity was unnecessary at the time and would result in 'excess competition'. Fear of overcapacity became the central issue and, as the Kawasaki Steel question began to attract national attention, steel capacity problems were debated in Japanese newspapers and radio programmes.

In an abrupt reversal of policy, however, MITI approved Kawasaki's proposal in late 1952. Explanations for MITI's action vary. One view contends that MITI yielded because of the persistence of Kawasaki Steel's outstanding entrepreneurial leader, Yataro Nishiyama. Some believe that MITI had essentially lost the battle and, to prevent the incident from undermining the Ministry's power, merely condoned Kawasaki's strategy after the fact. Others claim that MITI approved the proposal because the president of Yawata Steel publicly attested to the technical superiority of the proposed work.[31] Whatever the reason for MITI's reversal, the entire incident illustrates both the government's attempt to regulate capacity and entry and, at the same time, the limits of its power.

By restricting companies' access to capital, MITI constrained the growth of small and medium-sized steel companies. Although the three largest open hearth furnace makers had attempted to build blast furnaces before the war, two of these companies were compelled by lack of funds to wait until the integrated firms modernised before they could integrate backwards into pig iron production. The third company, Kawasaki Steel, expanded, but only in defiance of MITI's industrial policy. Several of Japan's small and medium-sized companies challenged the government's policy, charging MITI with 'attaching undue importance to big makers'.[32] Despite these protests, however, the overwhelming majority of Japanese steel companies came to accept MITI's concept of a rationalised industry structure. Although MITI's strategy constrained the growth of these companies in the short-run, managers of these firms generally accepted that it was in their firms' long-run interest to postpone expansion. The government gambled that the industry's concentrated structure would yield a comparative cost advantage which, in turn, would stimulate demand for more Japanese steel. With additional demand, small and medium-sized makers could eventually expand. In the meantime, Japan's resources were concentrated in a few large, updated plants that fully utilised their capacity.

From 1951 to 1955, Japan's crude steel capacity nearly doubled from almost 5 million tons to 9.4 million tons. Helped by a rapidly growing world steel demand and declining production and shipping costs, Japan's steel exports more than tripled, from 0.7 million tons in 1950 – an amount which was possibly inflated by the Korean War – to over 2.3 million tons in 1955. In all likelihood, steel firms were motivated to expand and modernise facilities by market conditions. Yet, the way in which the industry developed during these years cannot be explained simply by market forces. Rather, through protectionism and capacity controls, the government ensured that Japan's steel was produced in plants with higher throughput than what would have resulted from market forces alone. Although capacity doubled, virtually all the new capacity was concentrated in Japan's six pre-war integrated plants. The seventh integrated plant, Kawasaki Steel's new Chiba works, had a mere 0.50 million tons of capacity by 1955. And each of these six plants was larger than it had been five years earlier. Moreover, as MITI strictly controlled the amount of capacity that entered Japan's market, supply was relatively well balanced against domestic and export demand. In 1955, Japan's steel industry reported 9.42 million tons of capacity and 9.41 million tons of crude steel output.[33] Consequently, the companies operated at or near full capacity.

Although MITI's power to direct company investment decisions declined after the early 1950s, MITI continued to use its power over scarce resources to restrain and co-ordinate companies' growth strategies. To prevent overcapacity in steel, MITI rotated capacity investments among the leading steelmakers, and matched the industry's overall capacity growth with the prevailing business cycles. The government assumed the role of co-ordinator, or 'traffic cop' and replaced the 'confusion' of the market with steady, 'orderly growth'.[34] In the slow growth market of 1954, for example, MITI cancelled all new construction loans and capacity increases in steel. In 1956, when the prosperous world economy combined with Japan's rapidly growing domestic market to cause demand for Japanese steel to exceed supply, MITI asked companies to resubmit expansion plans for government approval. To ensure that Japanese steel companies continued to increase their manufacturing competitiveness rather than simply build new capacity, MITI recommended that companies 'scrap and build' existing outdated capacity. MITI advocated that all old steelmaking equipment be removed and replaced with a small number of modern, state-of-the-art machines.[35] Constrained from building new capacity except during approved rotations, Japanese steel firms adopted scrap-and-build as the basis for competing with each other.

Kawasaki Steel Company, Japan's most aggressive firm in the early 1950s, was conspicuously absent from the expansions of the late 1950s.

Until the end of 1958, Kawasaki added no capacity to Chiba or any other facility. Kawasaki not only missed a market opportunity that was recognised by other companies, Kawasaki deliberately cancelled the second phase of construction at Chiba in a boom market. While at least one Japanese researcher speculates that the government disqualified Kawasaki from the industry's construction programme, Kawasaki's own explanation at least confirms the importance of the business-government capacity plan:

> We plan to build more blast furnaces and open hearth furnaces. . . . All these works the Corporation intends to carry out gradually, keeping pace with the progress of the Government's plan of industrial production.[36]

There is no record of what transpired between the government and Kawasaki or the rest of the industry but Kawasaki's behaviour suggests that it postponed construction plans until other companies had built.

Throughout the 1950s, the Japanese steel industry grew in this stable, orderly manner. By the end of the decade, the country's steel capacity had surged to 22 million tons, nearly four time its level ten years earlier. But instead of the stampede of entry that MITI had feared, the industry had grown primarily through incremental expansions and rationalisations of the existing facilities at a few leading companies. Yawata, Fuji and NKK increased capacity by upgrading the blast furnaces and open hearth furnaces at their existing plants. This strategy required all three companies to scrap some existing furnaces and replace them with larger, more efficient equipment. The two major open hearth furnace makers, Sumitomo Metal and Kobe Steel, integrated backwards into pig iron production by acquiring iron producers and, eventually, by building blast furnaces at their open hearth furnace plants. Although by 1960 plans for five greenfield plants had been announced, no greenfield construction (except for Kawasaki Steel's Chiba) had begun.

VI

Capacity Limits Through Self-Regulation: Post-60

By 1960, MITI's control over company investment decisions was significantly reduced from what it had been ten years earlier. Although MITI could still influence the allocation of some capital through the World Bank and the Export-Import Bank, steel companies could obtain capital from equity markets and banks without the government's endorsement purely on the basis of their potential earning power. Moreover, like managers all over the world, Japanese steel company managers were opposed to relinquishing their autonomy over critical business decisions to the government. Consequently, MITI's role changed from one of direct supervision and control to one of hortatory guidance.

In this second phase of development, steel capacity decisions continued to be coordinated but the industry now managed the process. Encouraged by its success in gaining global market share during the 1950s when MITI strictly controlled capacity expansion and entry, the industry came to share the government's concern regarding the dangers of overcapacity. While, on one hand, domestic companies were in a fierce race for capacity and market share, at the same time, managers were acutely aware that the industry was engaged in a far bigger global contest that depended on each firm maintaining a competitive cost advantage. If the industry could maintain a cost advantage by co-ordinating the factors of production within Japan's domestic market, every Japanese steel company would benefit in the long-run. Thus, the domestic market became a greenhouse in which the essential factors of steel production – throughput and scale – were controlled and adjusted to build a globally competitive industry.[37]

By the early 1960s, a new system for controlling capacity investments emerged in steel. The system was known as *Jishu Chosei* which means voluntary or self-regulation.[38] Under this system, managers of the leading steel companies met monthly at the Japan Iron & Steel Federation to coordinate capacity investment plans. While the government did not require that its officials – from either MITI or Japan's Fair Trade Commission – be present, the industry occasionally invited MITI officials to attend to arbitrate disagreements. Industry representatives also met MITI official regularly to co-ordinate the industry's *Jishu Chosei* agreement with the plans of the Japanese government.

The *Jishu Chosei* system institutionalised MITI's earlier capacity co-ordination. With MITI's help, the leading steel company managers assumed the task of co-ordinating capacity increases to protect firms from overcapacity, low operating rates, and rising unit costs. An important aspect of the *Jishu Chosei* system was establishing the criteria for deciding which companies could build. The industry devised a system that allocated expansion rights according to a combination of market share and technical efficiency or productivity. For a company to win the right to build a new plant or add significant new capacity, it first had to demonstrate that it had the most modern and efficient equipment available. This encouraged companies to scrap and build equipment, actually tearing out or razing functioning facilities and replacing them with more modern technology. Under the *Jishu Chosei* system, steel company executives negotiated capacity expansions on the basis of past market share, proven efficiency of existing capacity, and expected future world demand. The process of allocating national capacity according to productivity drove managers decisively away from the marginal-cost analyses typical of most business planning; instead they entered a frenzied race for the right to construct giant modern facilities.

Of course, while the firms agreed that a common solution was desirable, negotiating an agreement was far from orderly or harmonious. *Jishu Chosei* meetings were intensely heated, described by some participants as 'boxing matches' among the companies.[39] The largest companies, particularly Yawata and Fuji, argued most strongly for cartels and restricted expansion. The smaller firms tended to advocate more free market competition. Nevertheless, the six major firms attended the meetings regularly and generally abided by the industry's agreements.

Persistent negotiations were called for on at least four fronts: between large and small companies; MITI and the companies; steel and other industries; and between MITI and other government agencies. At every turn, each side's particular interest had to be placated and, for every decision, there were winners as well as losers. Moreover, the government and industry were far from omniscient in estimating future global steel demand. Nor was it easy for the industry to decide which firm should build. Finally, as in most cartels, the level of commitment to the industry's agreements varied among participants.

The limits of the self-regulatory system were revealed in 1965 when Sumitomo Metal challenged the industry and MITI in a public dispute over the industry's capacity co-ordination. Intent on expanding despite a recession in the domestic market, Japan's fifth largest steelmaker, Sumitomo Metal, refused to abide by the industry's capacity investment limit. Trouble began in 1962–63 when, contrary to the industry's agreement, Sumitomo continued to expand its new Wakayama works in flagrant disregard for the industry's constraint on new capacity. Tension over Sumitomo Metal's rapid expansion mounted throughout the early 1960s until it finally came to a head in the recession of 1965. Sumitomo fought to continue its expansion while the industry argued that the company should abide by the moratorium on new capacity. As the industry tried to strike a bargain agreeable to all, MITI stepped out of its usual role of arbiter and ordered Sumitomo Metal's compliance. MITI's heavy-handed intervention, however, sparked fear of excessive government intervention and, thus, provoked strong opposition from Japanese industry and the press. In the end, the economy improved and Sumitomo Metal was allowed to continue its construction programme.

Although, after 1960, steel capacity was managed collectively by the industry through the informal *Jishu Chosei* system, the government remained influential. But MITI became less the industry's regulator and more just another governing member of the steel oligopoly. Of course, compared to western economies, where capacity co-ordination violated national competition policies, the Japanese government was influential simply by allowing firms to negotiate capacity limits. Then too, throughout the negotiations, MITI tried to persuade the industry of its estimates of future domestic and export demand. MITI repeatedly warned the industry against 'excessive investment', by which it meant investment in redundant capacity.[40] In the early 1960s, MITI formed a 50-person Industry Structure Investigation Council to compare the industrial structure of Japan's leading industries with the structure of industries in leading industrialised nations. The Council analysed the number and size of firms in an industry as well as the prevailing economies of scale, capitalisation, and export ratios in the other countries' industries.

During the 1960s, Japan's steel capacity again quadrupled, surpassing 100 million tons by 1970 (see Table 3). With capacity coordinated by the *Jishu Chosei* system, supply continued to grow in an orderly pattern. Instead of *focusing* their investments on additional tonnage, the leading steelmakers scrapped old facilities and replaced them with new ones to rationalise the industry. For example, from 1950 to 1960, Japanese steel companies, like steel companies everywhere in the world, had invested heavily in open hearth furnace capacity. But during the 1950s, Japanese steel companies aggressively experimented with the new, unproven basic oxygen furnace. As it became clear that the basis oxygen furnace was the superior technology, MITI intervened and compelled the industry to share the oxygen furnace licensing agreement. MITI's intervention both reduced the cost of innovation and dissipated the rivalry in the domestic market. From 1961 to 1966, Japanese steelmakers shut 56 functioning open hearth furances, or 40 per cent of the industry's open hearth furnace capacity.[41] By the late 1970s, every open hearth furnace operating in Japan had been replaced with the more efficient basic oxygen furnace.

Of course, no industry can grow from 5 million tons of capacity to 150 million tons without significant greenfield construction. Indeed, by 1976, nearly two-thirds of Japan's steel capacity was in greenfield plants. But plant construction was constrained and staggered among the six major steelmakers. Only one new plant – the infamous Kawasaki Steel's Chiba works – was built during the 1950s, and this in opposition to MITI's plans. Partly to accommodate the new basic oxygen furnace technology, two new plants – Sakai (Yawata) and Nagoya (Fuji) – were constructed during the early 1960s. Three other new plants – Mizushima (Kawasaki), Fukuyama (NKK), and Kimitsu (Yawata) – were opened between 1965 and 1970. Two more plants – Kashima (Fuji) and Kakogawa (Kobe) – were constructed during the 1970s. By 1975, over 90 per cent of Japan's steelmaking capacity was concentrated in 17 plants.

TABLE 3

JAPAN'S STEEL PRODUCTION, EXPORTS AND IMPORTS
(thousands of metric tons)

	Production	Exports	Imports
1943*	7,650	125	159
1950	4,839	727	3
1953	7,662	1,465	106
1957	12,570	1,261	1,590
1960	22,138	3,144	308
1965	41,161	12,705	32
1970	93,322	23,666	132
1975	102,313	37,927	124

Note: *Peak year of war production.
Source: *Japan's Iron and Steel Industry*, selected years.

The two notorious steel disputes – Kawasaki Steel and Sumitomo Metal – suggest that, like regulation in America, industrial policy in Japan was largely a political art.[42] And, as elsewhere, this constant negotiation yielded imperfect results; on occasion, smaller firms – like Kawasaki Steel and Sumitomo Metal – built capacity despite the government and industry's entreaties to the contrary. Although growth was controlled and equalised among firms, small companies seemed to break the agreements more frequently, and therefore grew more quickly, than large companies. But these inequalities seemed to matter only slightly in the long run since all six firms agreed on the importance of co-ordinating resources in steel. Imperfect as this system undoubtedly was, it enabled the Japanese steel industry to exploit the fundamental economics of steelmaking more fully than any other steel industry in the world at that time.

VII

Industry Performance

From 1950 to 1975, the Japanese steel industry grew by more than 3,000 per cent, yet the industry's structure changed minimally. In 1950, over

65 per cent of Japan's steel was produced by five companies; in 1976, over 82 per cent was produced by the same five companies.[43] More importantly, although annual steel output rose from 5 million tons to nearly 150 million tons, the number of integrated plants barely tripled, rising from six to 17. With this staggering level of growth, it is not surprising that two-thirds of Japan's integrated plants were new. But the unusual way in which this growth occurred, involving a government-co-ordinated system of capacity limits, is critical to a real understanding of the development of the industry. Through MITI, the government helped the industry structure its capacity to ensure that plants would fully exploit the economies of scale in steel manufacturing. As Japanese steelmakers minimised their unit costs of production, demand for Japanese steel surged, increasing the demand for additional capacity in Japan's market.

TABLE 4

CRUDE STEEL CAPACITY: TEN LARGEST STEEL PLANTS IN JAPAN AND THE UNITED STATES, 1977–78
(millions of metric tons)

Japan		United States	
Fukuyama (NKK)	16.0	Indiana (Inland)	7.7
Mizushima (Kawasaki)	12.0	Gary, IN (USS)	7.2
Chiba (Kawasaki)	8.5	Sparrows Pt, MD (Bethlehem)	6.3
Kimitsu (Nippon Steel)	10.0	Great Lakes, MI (National)	5.9
Wakayama (Sumitomo)	9.0	E. Chicago, IN (Youngstown)	5.0
Kashima (Sumitomo)	7.5	Burns Harbor, IN (Bethlehem)	4.8
Yawata (Nippon Steel)	9.8	S. Chicago, IL (USS)	4.7
Oita (Nippon Steel)	8.0	Fairless, PA (USS)	4.0
Nagoya (Nipon Steel)	7.5	Cleveland, OH (Republic)	4.0
Kakogawa (Kobe)	6.4	Wierton, WV (National)	3.6
Total (10)	94.7		53.2

Source: Japan data from IISS, *Steel Industry in Brief: Japan (1977)*; US data from IISS Commentary: *Steel Plants: USA, 1960–80*.

During the post-war decades, changes in technology increased the minimum efficient scale in steelmaking, prompting Japanese steel managers to expand their plants to an unprecedented size. By the mid-1970s, the average capacity of an integrated Japanese plant was 7.4 million tons; in comparison, the average capacity of an American steel plant was 2.9 million tons – less than half as large. As shown in Table 4, Japan's five largest plants were capable of producing 56 million tons of crude steel while the US's five largest plants could produce only 32 million tons. Japan's largest plant, Fukuyama, was more than twice the size of America's two largest plants. No less than 71 per cent of Japan's entire national capacity was in ten plants, compared to 37 per cent of America's.

Japan's steelmaking equipment also exploited the economies of scale in production. By 1975, 37 of Japan's 69 blast furnaces measured over 2,000 cubic metres. A handful of Japan's furnaces measured in excess of 4,500 cubic metres and could produce over 4 million tons of pig iron a year. In comparison, the US possessed only five furnaces that measured more than 2,000 cubic metres and no blast furnaces in excess of 3,000 cubic metres. European steelmakers fared as poorly with merely 17 furnaces measuring more than 2,000 cubic metres.[44]

Capacity co-ordination enabled Japanese companies to keep overall supply balanced with domestic and export demand. As a result, Japanese companies operated their plants at or relatively near full capacity. Operating rates for the Japanese steel industry as a whole demonstrate the success of this system. (Table 5.) In comparison, US steel firms under-utilised their capacity.[45]

TABLE 5

AVERAGE STEEL CAPACITY UTILISATION: JAPAN AND THE UNITED STATES, 1960–70

Year	Japan (%)	US(%)
1960	88.0	66.8
1961	94.2	65.4
1962	80.3	65.3
1963	82.7	72.4
1964	92.1	83.7
1965	83.5	86.1
1966	84.4	87.4
1967	92.5	82.5
1968	86.3	84.8
1969	91.7	90.8
1970	90.0	84.6

Source: Council on Wage and Price Stability, *Prices and Costs in the American Steel Industry* (Washington, 1977), p.145.

Finally, Japanese steel companies also adopted new technology more rapidly than American or European steel firms. By the mid-1970s, 83 per cent of Japan's crude steel was produced in basic oxygen furnaces compared to 62 per cent of America's and 63 per cent of Europe's. More revealing still, in 1976, no Japanese steel was produced in open hearth furnaces whereas the US still produced nearly one-fifth of its steel in the obsolete open hearth furnace. Likewise, Japan's large integrated steelmakers installed continuous casting machines long before comparable producers in America or Europe. By 1976, 35 per cent of Japan's crude steel was continually cast, compared to only 11 per cent of steel in America and 22 per cent of steel in Europe.[46]

These two factors – the companies' full exploitation of economies of scale and their extremely modern facilities – ensured that Japanese steel producers had a sizable cost advantage. By the mid-1970s, Japanese steelmakers had attained an estimated cost advantage of between $61 and $120 per ton over American and European steel producers. Interindustry cost comparisons are difficult to interpret since they depend on a range of assumptions about operating rates, the cost of capital, and exchange rates. Moreover, some calculations consider only integrated producers while others include minimills and specialty steel companies. Nevertheless, the major comparative studies of the steel industry concur that, during the 1970s, Japanese steel companies were the world's low-cost producers.[47]

Japan's sizable cost advantage in steel manufacturing enabled the industry to secure a significant world market share. By the mid-1970s, Japan was responsible for more than 20 per cent of all world steel exports, making it the world's leading steel-exporting nation. Japanese firms shipped steel to over 20 countries, with the largest shipment, by far, going to the United States. Faced with competition from Japan's low-cost producers, the American and European steel industries' production fell from 50 per cent and 25 per cent of the world total in 1950, to 17 per cent and 20 per cent in 1976. If one included indirect exports – that is, Japanese steel purchased domestically for use in export products, such as autos and machinery – Japan's share of the export market was even larger. In less than two decades, the Japanese steel industry was transformed from one that required import protection just to secure domestic market share, into Japan's leading export industry.

Of course, as any student of political economy knows, economic outcomes seldom result from single factors alone, governmental or otherwise. Japan's steel industry was, undoubtedly, also influenced by Japan's situational imperatives and coherent national strategy. Other factors, too – such as low wage rates, an explosively growing GNP, and a possibly favourable exchange rate – also contributed to the development of Japan's steel industry. Japan's trading companies, the *sogo shosha*, facilitated the industry's growth by procuring raw material from overseas and distributing the finished steel products to the domestic and export markets. Likewise, an intense spirit of rivalry always prevailed among Japanese steel firms.[48] But these factors, which are not unique to Japan, do not fully account for the industry's low-cost position.

The argument of this article is that the Japanese government's industrial policies helped the steel industry develop its unique competitive advantage: large-scale plants, full exploitation of economies of scale and modern facilities. The industry's low-cost position did not result from market forces alone. Rather, by constraining capacity expansion and channelling new capacity into a small number of existing facilities, MITI enabled the industry to exploit more fully the economics of steel manufacturing. These fundamental structural characteristics yielded a unique competitive advantage. In later years, as MITI's power was reduced, it relied on hortatory guidance to encourage steel firms to coordinate their capacity expansion decisions. As a result, Japan's steel capacity was concentrated in fewer, larger plants, and was used more thoroughly, and therefore more economically, than any in the world.

In its endorsement of co-operative, non-arm's-length transactions, Japan's capacity co-ordination may challenge some of the fundamental tenets of western economic theory. But in doing so, it also raises difficult questions about the equity, equality, and social welfare of Japan's system. Although much has been written about the costs and benefits of intervening in the market's allocation of resources, there is no general agreement on this subject. Some observers have pointed out that the Japanese steel industry appears to have performed worse financially than the US steel industry.[49] Yet the highly leveraged financial structure of Japanese companies may change the relevant measure of profitability. Likewise, in Japan's economic system it may be entirely spurious to assess rates of return in steel independent of the rest of the economy. Steel was developed partly as a building block to national industrial development. The relevant social welfare benefit – or loss – then may not be in steel *per se* but in Japan's overall economy. The system in steel which, on first glance, may appear inefficient or inequitable, may have provided higher indirect returns in final goods industries such as automobiles, ships and machine tools.[50]

Then too, because Japan's capital controls limited investment alternatives, steel managers may have invested in some projects with lower rates of return than what was justifiable by global market rates. Nevertheless, while the return to individual projects may have been less than optimal, to the country as a whole the returns appear to have been very high. The implication, of course, is that the burden of these investments was borne by Japanese consumers who, through Japan's tax and social security systems, were motivated to save more and consume less than westerners. But the wisdom of this tradeoff between consumption and investment is far from settled, for Japan as well as the rest of the world.

These considerations serve as a reminder that the Japanese system was, above all, a national strategy. Thus, the question of social welfare gain is not intrinsic to steel or to any one of Japan's other global industries. Whether or not Japan's economic strategy was optimal, the central fact remains that the Japanese government achieved its objective of building a globally competitive steel industry by intervening in the market and shaping the industry's structure to enable firms to fully exploit the economies of scale in steelmaking.

VIII

Conclusion

This article examines the effect of Japan's industrial policies on the evolution of the steel industry. It argues that the government and industry together deliberately organised the industry's resources to yield a competitive advantage in the world market. Through government and industry-wide coordination of capacity, the Japanese steel industry was structured fully to exploit the economies of scale in steel manufacturing.

The history of the Japanese steel industry suggests two important lessons. First, industry structure can yield a competitive advantage. Japan's low-cost position in steel resulted, in part, from its uniquely large-scale plants and full exploitation of economies of scale. While other factors were also necessary, the industry's deliberate management of its structure allowed it to exploit the fundamental economics of capital-intensive industries which contributed towards its competitive cost position. Second, the Japanese government assisted the industry in developing this unique competitive advantage. In the Japanese steel industry's early post-war history, the government, through MITI, directly facilitated the industry's full utilisation of its capacity by co-ordinating capacity investment decisions and concentrating capital in a few large steelmakers. In later years, the industry itself regulated capacity expansion to ensure that its factors of production were used efficiently.

No overall government policies compelled Japanese steel companies' strategies. But the investment decisions that transformed Japan's small, backward steel industry into the strongest in the world were made in an economic environment in which firms were sheltered from the inherent risks attending the huge investments typical of the steel industry. MITI intervened with deliberate policies that were grounded in the fundamental economics of capital-intensive industries. These policies aimed at ensuring that, from the start, the industry was an oligopoly with high, stable throughput, and competitive costs. This suggests that by concentrating capacity in a few large plants and constraining redundant capacity, the Japanese government, operating through MITI, facilitated the emergence of a globally competitive Japanese steel oligopoly.

These lessons raise profound challenges for companies in global industries. Can companies from conventional market environments - those that, for example, allow free and easy entry - compete with firms from markets that allow them to manage and shape their industry structures? If history is any guide, MITI may help other Japanese industries exploit structural opportunities. Other industries could circumvent market forces and accelerate the development of efficient industry structures, ones that yield a competitive advantage in the global market.

Of course, the Japanese government has not always succeeded. In some industries, such as energy, MITI's policies seem to have produced results that were less efficient and effective than what the market would have yielded.[51] Other industries, such as automobiles, declined MITI's structural assistance and succeeded anyway. In addition, in many industries, the underlying economics or optimal industry structure may be more ambiguous than in steel, for which the logic of economies of scale were formidable. Nevertheless, the steel industry's history makes clear that the Japanese government is willing to experiment with new and, as yet, untried methods of industrial organisation. These experiments, which appear to have succeeded more often than they failed, challenge companies, industries and, most of all, governments in foreign markets to change their established ways of doing business.

NOTES

I would like to thank Alfred D. Chandler, Jr., Steven W. Tolliday, and two anonymous referees for comments on an earlier draft of this article.

1. There is a vast literature on Japan's economic miracle including; W.W. Lockwood (ed.), *The State and Economic Enterprise in Japan: Essays in the Political Economy of Growth* (Princeton, NJ, 1965); H. Patrick and H. Rosovsky (eds.), *Asia's New Giant: How the Japanese Economy Works* (Washington, 1976); M. Shinohara, *Industrial Growth, Trade, and Dynamic Patterns in the Japanese Economy* (Tokyo, 1982); K. Yamamura, *Economic Policy in Postwar Japan: Growth versus Economic Democracy* (Berkeley, CA, 1967). For a comprehensive discussion of the industrial policy debate, see D. Friedman, *The Misunderstood Miracle: Industrial Development and Political Change in Japan* (Ithaca, NY, 1988), pp.3–14; C. Johnson, *MITI and the Japanese Miracle: The Growth of Industrial Policy, 1925–75* (Stanford, CA, 1982), pp.6–34; and D.I. Okomoto, *Between MITI and the Market: Japanese Industrial Policy for High Technology* (Stanford, CA, 1989).
2. Examples of this school of thought include: Johnson, *MITI*; E.F. Vogel, *Japan as Number One: Lessons for America* (Cambridge, MA, 1979); and J. Zysman, *Governments, Markets and Growth: Financial Systems and the Politics of Industrial Change* (Ithaca, NY, 1983).

3. R.E. Caves and M. Uekusa, *Industrial Organization in Japan* (Washington, 1976); H. Patrick, 'The Future of the Japanese Economy: Output and Labor Productivity', *Journal of Japanese Studies*, Vol.3 (Summer 1977); P. Trezise and Y. Suzuki, 'Politics, Government, and Economic Growth in Japan', in Patrick and Rosovsky (eds.), *Asia's New Giant.*

4. For the view that steel is the archetypical example of the Japanese system, see I. Magaziner and T.M. Hout, *Japanese Industrial Policy* (Berkeley, CA, 1980); I. C. Magaziner and R.B. Reich, *Minding America's Business: The Decline and Rise of the American Economy* (New York, 1982); 'Japanese Government Promotion of the Steel Industry: Three Decades of Industrial Policy', prepared by Verner, Liipfert, Bernard and McPherson, Chartered, for the Bethlehem Steel Corporation and United States Steel Corporation, (Washington, DC, July 1983); and Testimony of Kiyoshi Kawahito before the United States International Trade Commission, No.332–162, 'A Critique of the "Bethlehem Steel Report" on Japanese Government Promotion of the Steel Industry', 16 Aug. 1983.

5. *Japan's Iron and Steel Industry 1987*, p.216.

6. This is a common criticism of research on the role of the state in Japan's economic growth. For a summary, see D. Friedman, *The Misunderstood Miracle*, pp.4–5. There is, however, also a good deal of excellent research that avoids this problem. See, for example, M. Anchordoguy, *Computers Inc.: Japan's Challenge to IBM* (Cambridge, MA, 1989).

7. The study of which this article is one part is P.A. O'Brien, 'Coordinating Market Forces: The Anatomy of Investment Decisions in the Japanese Steel Industry 1945–1975' (unpublished doctoral dissertation, Harvard Graduate School of Business Administration, Boston, MA, 1985).

8. The remaining approximately 15 per cent is stainless and heat-resisting steel, and non-stainless alloy steel.

9. During the 1970s, a new segment of producers emerged, called 'minimills', which operate without blast furnaces. Responsible for about 15 per cent of the American steel market by the mid-1980s, the minimills manufacture primarily light structural rods, bars and shapes, traditionally low-end-of-the-market products. With virtually no investment in raw materials and transportation facilities and with a limited range of products, minimills are unencumbered by high capital costs and, consequently, can operate efficiently with as little as 250,000 tons of capacity per year. Although minimills are responsible for an increasing share of the market, they do not have the technical capability to replace the integrated sector in sheets and other flat-rolled products. D.F. Barnett and R.W. Crandall, *Up From The Ashes: The Rise of the Steel Minimill in the United States* (Washington, 1986), esp. Ch. 6; and J.R. Miller, 'Steel Minimills', *Scientific American*, 250:9 (May 1984), pp.32–9.

10. This discussion of capital intensity and its implications for the economics of steel manufacturing owes a great deal to the theory and concepts of Alfred D. Chandler, Jr. See especially, A.D. Chandler, Jr., *Scale and Scope: The Dynamics of Industrial Capitalism* (Cambridge, MA, 1990), pp.21–8; and *The Visible Hand: The Managerial Revolution in American Business* (Cambridge, MA, 1977), pp.258–69. Economists in the field of industrial organization have also developed extensive literature on the subject. For a brief summary, see F.M. Scherer, 'Economies of Scale and Industrial Concentration', in H.J. Goldschmid *et al.* (eds.), *Industrial Concentration: The New Learning* (Boston, 1974), pp.16–54.

11. S. Bain, *Barriers to New Competition: Their Character and Consequences in Manufacturing Industries* (Cambridge, MA, 1956), p.236.

12. Estimates of the optimal size of a blast furnace are from M.G. Boylan, Jr., *Economic Effects of Scale Increases in the Steel Industry: The Case of US Blast Furnaces* (New York, 1975), esp. p.138; and US Federal Trade Commission, *The United States Steel Industry and Its International Rivals: Trends and Factors Determining International Competitiveness* (Washington, 1978), esp. Ch. 7. Estimates of the minimum efficient scale of steel plants and the cost of construction are from R.W. Crandall, *The*

US Steel Industry in Recurrent Crisis: Policy Options in a Competitive World (Washington, 1981), pp.11 and 76; and H. Mueller and K. Kawahito, *Steel Industry Economics: A Comparative Analysis of Structure, Conduct and Performance* (new York, 1978), p.6.

13. Chandler, *Scale and Scope*, p.128.

14. By comparison, UK steel production in 1929 was 9.79 million tons. US steel production was 57.34 million tons (or 63 million net tons). Unless otherwise indicated, all steel output is in metric tons.

15. E.M. Hadley, 'Industrial Policy for Competitiveness', *Journal of Japanese Trade and Industry* (Sept. 1982), p.48; and E.W. Zimmerman, *World Resources and Industries: A Functional Appraisal of the Availability of Agricultural and Industrial Materials* (New York, revised ed. 1951), pp.685–6.

16. J.B. Cohen, *Japan's Postwar Economy* (Bloomington, IN, 1958), pp.68–9; K. Kawahito, *The Japanese Steel Industry: With an Analysis of the US Import Problem* (New York, 1972), pp.22–3.

17. The authoritative work on the history of MITI is Johnson, *MITI*.

18. The other industries targeted in 1950 were coal, electric power, ship building and chemical fertilisers.

19. The fourth integrated steel company was the Nakayama Steel Works, which accounted for less than 1 per cent of Japan's steel output.

20. There is disagreement over whether, in the end, Kawasaki was reorganised under the SCAP Enterprise Reconstruction Law or voluntarily. See, for example, Institute for Iron and Steel Studies (IISS) and R.L. Deily (ed.), *Steel Industry in Brief: Japan 1977* (New Jersey, 1977), p.54; and S. Yonekura, 'Entrepreneurship and Innovative Behavior of Kawasaki Steel: The Post World War II Period' (Tokyo: Institute of Business Research, Hitosubashi University, Discussion Paper No.120, 1984), pp.5–15.

21. Japanese bureaucrats were primarily concerned with productive efficiency, not allocative efficiency. See E.M. Hadley, *Antitrust in Japan* (Princeton, NJ, 1970), pp.37–8 and 448.

22. R. Dore, *Flexible Rigidities: Industrial Policy and Structural Adjustment in the Japanese Economy 1970–1980* (Stanford, CA, 1986); Hadley, *Antitrust in Japan*, pp.390–407; C. Johnson, 'The Japanese Political Economy: A Crisis in Theory', *Ethics & International Affairs*, Vol.2 (1988), esp. pp.95–6; and 'Industrial Policy's Generation Gap', *Economic Eye*, Vol.7 No.1 (March 1986), p.22.

23. Official MITI documents frequently revealed this objective. For example, MITI wrote: 'When an excessive number of firms, for a given market size, is reduced by means of mergers and unification, it will lead to economies of scale and the ability to expand into a new technological frontier'. From 'A Proposal by MITI', quoted in K. Yamamura, 'Structure as Behavior', in I. Frank (ed.), *The Japanese Economy in International Perspective* (Baltimore, MD, 1975), p. 65. See also: 'The Positive Adjustment Policy for the Basic Materials Industries', MITI, (24 March, 1983), p.24; and *Economic Survey of Japan 1965–66* (Japan's Economic Stabilisation Board), pp.57 and 62.

24. The benefits of protectionism in infant industries under certain conditions is generally accepted in the development economics literature. For a discussion of the argument, see: H.G. Johnson, 'Optimal Trade Interventions in the Presence of Domestic Distortions', in R.E. Caves *et al.*, *Trade Growth and the Balance of Payments* (Amsterdam, 1965), pp.3–34.

25. The Japanese are prone to describe a variety of market conditions as 'excessive', 'needless' or 'desperate' competition. See, for example: *Economic Survey of Japan 1954–1955*, p.18; Hadley, *Antitrust in Japan*, pp.296–97 and 448; *Japan's Iron and Steel Industry 1953–1954*, p.91; Yamamura, *Economic Policy*, pp.49 and 72–3.

26. Johnson, *MITI*, p.79.

27. *Japan's Iron and Steel Industry 1953–54*, pp.69–72.

28. Ibid., pp.66–78; T. Kawasaki, *Japan's Steel Industry* (Tokyo, 1985), pp.59–80.

29. 'Greenfield' refers to an entirely new plant rather than a renovated or 'rounded out' plant.
30. For an account of this incident, see: *Japan's Iron and Steel Industry 1953–54*, pp.72–3; L.H. Lynn, *How Japan Innovates: A Comparison with the US in the Case of Oxygen Steelmaking* (Boulder, CO, 1982), pp.107–10; and Yonekura, 'Entrepreneurship and Innovative Behavior', pp.8–15.
31. *Japan's Iron and Steel Industry 1953–54*, p.72; and Yonekura, 'Entrepreneurship and Innovative Behavior', p.32.
32. *Japan's Iron and Steel Industry 1953–54*, p.73.
33. Ibid., pp.174 and 206. An additional 2 million tons of capacity were reported as out of operation, or under construction or repairs.
34. K. Yamamura, 'Success that Soured', in K. Yamamura (ed.), *Policy and Trade Issues of the Japanese Economy: American and Japanese Perspectives* (Seattle, WA, 1982), p.85; and M. Shinohara, *Industrial Growth, Trade and Dynamic Patterns in the Japanese Economy* (Tokyo, 1982). p.28.
35. *Economic Survey of Japan 1957–58*, p.105.
36. Speculation about Kawasaki in K. Imai, 'Iron and Steel Organization', p.218, in K. Sato, (ed.), *Industry and Business in Japan*, (New York, 1980); and *Japan's Iron and Steel Industry 1957*, p.179.
37. Industrial organisation economists have written extensively about the inclination of oligopolistic firms that recognise their interdependence to co-ordinate investment activities. See: R. Gilbert and M. Lieberman, 'Investment and Coordination in Oligopolistic Industries', *Rand Journal of Economics*, Vol.18 No.1 (Spring 1987), pp.17–33; and G.B. Richardson, *Information and Investment: A Study in the Working of the Competitive Economy* (New York, 1960).
38. K. Imai, 'Japan's Changing Industrial Structure and the United States-Japan Industrial Relations', pp.49–50; E.J. Kaplan, *Government Business Relationship* (Washington, 1972), p.146; and Yamamura, 'Success that Soured', in Yamamura, *Policy and Trade Issues*, p.85.
39. Interview with Mr Takashi Suzuki, Deputy General Manager, Business Research Department, Sumitomo Metal Industries Ltd., 15 Oct. 1984; and Sumitomo Metal Industries, *Annual Report* (1966), p.1.
40. *Japan's Iron and Steel Industry 1957*, p.98.
41. Lynn, *How Japan Innovates*.
42. T.K. McCraw, *Prophets of Regulation: Charles Francis Adams, Louis D. Brandeis, James M. Landis, Alfred E. Kahn* (Cambridge, MA, 1984), p.63.
43. From late 1950 until 1969, there was a nominal change in the industry's structure. In 1950, Japan's largest steelmaker, Japan Iron & Steel, was divided into two separate companies: Yawata and Fuji. In 1970, Yawata and Fuji merged – with MITI's endorsement – to form the Nippon Steel Co. which at the time of its formation, accounted for 38 per cent of Japan's steel production.
44. Mueller and Kawahito, *Steel Industry Economics*, p.7; and *Japan's Iron and Steel Industry 1976*, p.63.
45. Because 1960 was the last year in which the American Iron and Steel Institute made public capacity data, capacity utilisation statistics for the US steel industry after 1960 are estimates. It is generally held that US steel capacity was under-utilised. See Crandall, *Steel in Recurrent Crisis*, p.45.
46. Mueller and Kawahito, *Steel Industry Economics*, p.7.
47. For cost comparisons, see: D.F. Barnett, 'International Competitiveness in Steel and Dynamic Advantages', Working Paper, 15 Oct. 1977; C. Bradford, *The Japanese Steel Industry: A Comparison with its United States Counterpart* (1977); Council on Wage and Price Stability (COWPS), *Prices and Costs in the American Steel Industry* (Washington, 1977); Crandall, *Steel in Recurrent Crisis*; Federal Trade Commission, *Staff Report on the United States Steel Industry and Its International Rivals*; and Mueller and Kawahito, *Steel Industry Economics*.
48. T. Nakamura, *The Postwar Japanese Economy: Its Development and Structure*

(Tokyo, 1981), pp.25–6. The role of interfirm competition in Japan's contemporary market is a central theme in M.E. Porter, *The Competitive Advantage of Nations* (New York, 1990).

49. Office of Technology Assessment, Congress of the United States, *Technology and Steel Industry Competitiveness* (Washington, 1980), p.124.

50. An extensive literature is emerging on the subject of profitability and the cost of capital in Japan. See, for example: A. Ando and A. Auerbach, 'The Corporate Cost of Capital in Japan and the United States: A Comparison', in J.B. Shoven (ed.), *Government Policy Towards Industry in the United States and Japan* (Cambridge, MA, 1988), pp.21–49; C.Y. Baldwin, 'The Capital Factor: Competing for Capital in a Global Environment', in M.E. Porter (ed.), *Competition in Global Industries* (Boston, MA, 1986), pp.185–223; W.C. Kester and T. Leuhrman, 'Real Interest Rates and the Cost of Capital: A Comparision of the United States and Japan', *Japan and the World Economy* Vol.1 (1989), pp.279–301; and K. Kawahito, 'Relative Profitability of the US and Japanese Steel Industries', *Columbia Journal of World Business* (Fall 1984), pp.13–17.

51. R.H.K. Vietor, 'Energy Markets and Policy', in T.K. McCraw (ed.), *America versus Japan* (Boston, MA, 1986), esp. pp.226–8.

Serving America's Business? Graduate Business Schools and American Business, 1945-60

SUSAN ARIEL AARONSON
John Hopkins University and The American University

Since 1985, a diverse group of economists, engineers, business leaders, and policymakers have attempted to alert the American people that the nation's competitive edge was rapidly eroding.[1] Echoing Paul Revere, they warned that the US faced multiple dangers: a ballooning budget deficit; a stubborn trade deficit; and the potential loss of comparative advantage in key sectors such as aerospace and computers. These concerned citizens recognized that some decline in the US share of world trade was both positive and inevitable – a testament to the vitality of international competition. But the depth and scope of America's competitive crisis sparked a competitiveness movement, and triggered a search for its causes as well as solutions.[2]

This search focused not only on business and government actions, but also on the institutions and values underlying American economic practices. Some of the blame for America's declining competitiveness has been laid at academia's doorstep.[3] Although there is no direct relationship between business education and managerial success,[4] the role of America's graduate business schools in preparing American management and the relationship between academia and business deserve the careful scrutiny of historians.

America's graduate business schools grew in influence at the same time that American business experienced 25 years of enormous growth, followed by dramatic decline. MBA educated executives were a rarity in American business until the middle of the twentieth century. But during the 15 years following World War II, corporate recruiters increasingly turned to graduates of America's business schools to staff their flourishing operations.[5] These MBA educated managers changed the way Americans did business.[6] Their impressive credentials enabled them to get hired and promoted to management positions in growing numbers.

The post-war generation of MBA-educated executives assumed senior management responsibilities just as their companies began to encounter dramatic changes in markets and technology.[7] Yet many of these executives thought that the days of American economic dominance would never end. Because so many MBA-educated executives had difficulty managing their companies' response to such changes, I have tried to look carefully at how business education has influenced managerial attitudes and practices.

Like other forms of professional education, business education can be evaluated by how well it provided knowledge that is 'useful' to executives at all levels of management.[8] During this 15-year period, graduate business schools differed from other professional schools in *how* they conveyed such 'useful knowledge'. In other professional schools such as law, engineering, education, or medicine, in-class education was supplemented by outside practice in clerkships or internships. Moreover, in these professional schools, such real-world experience was reinforced in classes principally taught by practitioners. But graduate business schools adopted a different approach to educating business professionals.[9] MBA students were rarely instructed by executives and neither they nor their professors brought much business experience to their classroom discussion. Thus, at the same time that American business grew reliant on graduate business schools for their managerial pool, MBA students gained managerial training twice removed from real-world experience.

Professional business education can also be appraised by *how well* it prepared managers to make a wide range of decisions. In *Strategy and Structure*, Alfred D. Chandler noted that the role of managers is to plan and direct the use of corporate resources to meet short-term (operational decisions) and long-term (entrepreneurial decisions) developments in the market. When managers responsible for entrepreneurial decisions concentrate on short-term activities to the exclusion or detriment of long-range planning and co-ordination, they have failed to carry out effectively their role in their enterprise and in the economy. Those executives who fail to develop an entrepreneurial outlook hamper their companies' performance, and over the long-term, survival.[10] If their training was comprehensive, MBA-educated managers should have been able to respond flexibly to short-and long-term market fluctuations, and to make both operational and entrepreneurial decisions. My research indicates that America's graduate business schools generally did train students to make operational decisions. These schools were less successful in helping their graduates develop an entrepreneurial outlook. Hence, the reliance of American business upon graduate business schools may have had consequences for American business and the economy as a whole.

In this paper, two contrasting models of graduate business education are examined to ascertain how well professional business education served American business during the growth period and the more difficult years that followed.[11] The Graduate School of Business at Columbia University (CBS) and the Harvard Business School (HBS) had divergent approaches to business education and were two of the oldest, most prominent schools in the nation.[12] As large well-established business schools, they were major suppliers of MBAs and executive education programmes.[13] In 1956, of approximately 4,500 Masters degrees granted, these two schools produced 888 (almost one fifth of the total).[14] Because both schools were affiliated with prominent research universities, they were expected to produce scholarship and graduates that would add to their university's reputation. The two schools were located in major business cities and, therefore, had great potential to influence management practice at prominent companies headquartered nearby.

During the period of study, both schools established programmes and publications to train and involve business practitioners in their work. Their programmes were emulated by other business schools.[15] The two schools pioneered in developing training for business as a profession, and in balancing liberal and vocational studies within their respective university curricula.[16]

It is important to note that after the mid-1950s, new approaches to management education gained increasing influence on curricular and management practices. Graduate business schools such as Carnegie Mellon, the University of Chicago, and Wharton developed their own distinctive approaches to graduate management education. But because Harvard and Columbia had such a large share of the executive population; because their educational approaches were so influential; and because their publications were so widely read, the two case studies can serve to illuminate graduate business education in the postwar period.[17]

II

The Graduate School of Business at Columbia University

The Graduate School of Business at Columbia University (CBS) was uniquely positioned to serve business needs. Because CBS was located in New York, America's business capital, it had many opportunities to include business practitioners and business problems in its curriculum. Furthermore, the university fostered an environment conducive to research, including business research. However, during the 15 years following World War II, Columbia could not fully capitalise on these advantages.

All of Columbia University's departments and divisions were expected to emulate the university's proud tradition of providing 'liberal education'. Thus, in 1916, the founders of the Graduate School of Business concurred with the university's values: they hoped to use 'liberal educational' subjects and methods to mould competent, socially responsible business citizens. They believed that a liberal education was the best way to provide businessmen with the 'broad knowledge and special competence beyond that which experience alone can provide'. Businessmen must 'have knowledge of science, technology, . . . politics, sociology and related subjects'. Such a liberal educational approach would enable the school to 'improve human competence for the conduct of business and economic affairs'.[18]

'Liberal education' became the avowed strategy of the school. In 1949, undergraduate courses were abolished, and Columbia limited its programme to graduate professional education. In this way, the university reasserted the primacy of undergraduate liberal education. The business school recruited heavily at liberal arts colleges, in the belief that 'the highest standards of business training can hardly be attained unless the fruits of liberal education are preserved'. The school's catalogues advised potential applicants to obtain 'a suitable background in the liberal arts'. Although the majority of the school's students were white males (the traditional pool for corporate staff and line officers), the school also accepted a few women, minorities, and significant numbers of foreign students – all in line with its liberal orientation.[19] Moreover, the American Assembly (which CBS administered) provided a forum for the discussion of society's general problems, a liberal goal.[20]

Ironically, in spite of this 'liberal' emphasis, the school's programme was balanced heavily in favour of job-oriented coursework. Columbia's strategy was in fact job-specific/vocational. It prepared students for specific real world jobs such as personnel manager or accountant, rather than the generic profession of manager.[21] The triumph of vocationalism over liberal education stemmed primarily from the school's long-term devotion to faculty specialisation. Since its inception, CBS had fostered numerous areas of specialisation in business teaching and research. Specialisation enabled the business school faculty to emulate the *mores* of the university and perform in an academically respectable manner. Some of the faculty's specialised areas were attempts to make traditional liberal arts disciplines relevant to business, but most of these specialised areas arose out of the need to train students for real-world jobs. Consequently, many of these areas corresponded to actual jobs or careers, rather than functional business disciplines.[22] For example, courses in advertising included 'Problems in Advertising and Selling', 'Advertising Copy Research', and 'Media and Market Analysis', which prepared students for jobs as advertisers, copywriters, and marketing researchers, respectively.[23] Most CBS students concentrated their coursework in an area of specialisation corresponding to a desired first job.[24]

While there were 'liberal' courses sprinkled throughout the curriculum, the bulk of the school's offerings were in job-specific skills. For example, in 1946, the school offered: courses concerned with business techniques (accounting, statistics); courses dealing with business operations and management (finance, marketing); courses dealing with various specialised types of business (banking, transportation); and miscellaneous specialised courses or seminars on one topic (prices, group behaviour).[25] The curriculum had not changed much by 1957; although the school offered a greater variety of coursework, the bulk of the courses were still vocationally oriented. MBA candidates had to complete 60 points of coursework, by majoring in general administration or devoting their studies to one of the 14 areas of specialisation.[26]

The CBS curriculum had several noteworthy aspects. CBS had long focussed on the social responsibility of business. The school was also an early innovator in the study of international business, and it pioneered in emphasising the philosophical aspects of business.[27] In contrast with many other business schools of the period, Columbia maintained a constant focus on production management and manufacturing throughout this period.[28]

But on balance, CBS's focus was vocational, and during the 1950s the school's leadership became convinced this approach did not enable the school to achieve its goals. Too many students were concentrating their coursework in a single vocational area. There was no common curriculum. Because there was no shared curriculum, there was no common academic preparation for management.[29] Despite the school's adoption of liberal educational values and methods, CBS did not develop effective linkages to the general University community.[30] By the mid-1950s, the school appeared to be unravelling. Nationally-known faculty members departed; faculty morale declined; enrolment stagnated.[31] Clearly, Columbia needed a new approach to business education.

But many on the CBS faculty feared curricular change, and they used specialisation as a rationale for their opposition.[32] Ironically, they argued that any proposed changes to the areas of specialisation would conflict with the school's commitment to 'liberal education'.[33] They maintained that truly 'liberal education' could only be achieved through a 'normal' academic programme, which of course involved their specialties.[34]

As a result of faculty opposition, curricular reform was delayed until 1959. It took five years of prodding from the school's new dean, Courtney Brown.[35] After he inaugurated three faculty retreats to ease the way towards change, the faculty finally accepted an integrated core curriculum which limited the school's fields of specialisation.[36]

But even these curricular reforms did not end faculty specialisation, and as a result, the school was unable to balance its liberal and vocational goals effectively. Despite Dean Brown's leadership, CBS faculty members had enough power to maintain many of their areas of specialisation.[37] Because the faculty simply repackaged its courses as part of the new curriculum, vocationally-oriented education survived at Columbia.[38] After all, the faculty still set teaching standards and priorities. Since faculty appointment committees identified candidates, reviewed appointments, and recommended appointments and promotions, they could effectively sustain specialisation by controlling the faculty. As Dean Brown noted, 'The fourteen divisions were really fourteen little "czars" . . . Each academic division was more or less autonomous'.[39]

Faculty influence over the curriculum and personnel made it difficult for CBS to serve business. Professors determined courses based on their interests, not business needs. Business executives, including the trustees, had no direct input into these courses. Furthermore, many faculty members were unenthusiastic about teaching in the new core areas, such as quantitative methods (computer skills and statistics), which appeared unrelated to their specialities.[40] Although there was good reason to believe these core areas were necessary to keep American business 'on the cutting edge', many CBS faculty members were simply not interested in them.

Faculty control also effected the school's ability to produce research to meet the immediate and long-term needs of business. CBS did not produce either the quality or the diversity of research that its focus on 'liberal educational' values would lead one to expect.[41] CBS faculty members were well-trained and experienced in research, like their peers at Columbia's sister schools. In 1949, 28 of the 52 faculty members had doctorates (52 per cent); this increased to 57 per cent by 1959 (34 of the 60).[42] Yet only one of these doctoral degrees was in business! Thus it was no accident that the CBS faculty shared the academic values of the university's arts and sciences faculties. Like their peers in the university, the business school faculty was prolific: despite the stress of curricular reform, they produced over 100 articles and books during 1953–58.[43] But the business school faculty did not produce pathbreaking research. In the post-war era, many of the major contributions to 'leading-edge' business research were developed by interdisciplinary groups.[44] Despite ample opportunity, the business school faculty did not engage in such collaborative research with professors from the university's other highly regarded divisions and departments.[45] Columbia did not make major theoretical contributions to the study of business.[46] Although Columbia initiated studies on the internationalisation of American business and the role of multinationals in international trade, the school clearly fell short of its research potential.[47] The continued focus on vocational specialities led to research on esoteric issues, all too many of which were irrelevant to the actual problems confronted business executives. During this period, Columbia did not effectively meet the research needs of business.

In part, this reflects the fact that business practitioners had little influence on CBS' approach to education or research. Despite the school's 'unique access to America's greatest business center',[48] executives were seldom on campus. Columbia did not develop courses for business personnel until 1951.[49] The bulk of the university's programmes for executives were held off-campus.[50] Although students could meet business practitioners through the school's lecture programmes, most student contact with executives was at placement or alumni conferences.[51] The faculty had greater opportunities to interact with businessmen. They could open a business, consult, or serve on corporate boards, although none of this service counted towards promotion. There were no formalised incentives for faculty to research and apply the problems of business to the curriculum. This had important implications for what went on in the classroom. Columbia students were prepared for business with academically respectable theories and models; they rarely studied real business problems. In addition, these students learned about business from faculty members who generally had little practical business experience.[52] Their competence to train future business practitioners for the demands of market change appears questionable.

Business involvement in the affairs of the school remained minimal. Business leaders and alumni financed some of the school's research and established scholarships, fellowships and programmes for equipment donations.[53] But the School's Board of Visitors did not review the revised curriculum until 1960, after it had already been enacted.[54] And even this limited business interaction compromised the school's relationship with other divisions of the University. As Dean Brown noted, other departments looked upon the business school as merely a 'milk cow'.[55] This may help explain why the business school faculty bent over backwards to prove its academic legitimacy, in part by remaining committed to specialisation.

Despite these problems, during the 1945–60 period, Columbia Business School effectively met some of the needs of business. Columbia trained its students for many business professions, as well as to make operational decisions. With its skill-oriented coursework, the school served the immediate needs of corporate recruiters and helped students attain their first jobs.

Although the new curriculum helped make Columbia's programme more coherent, faculty power ensured that the school's vocational orientation was maintained. The faculty continued to focus their research on narrow areas of study, most of which were irrelevant to the real-world problems executives were confronting. The school's failure to prepare its students for the challenges presented by the globalisation of technology and industrial capacity in the postwar world may be explained by the faculty's reluctance to engage in path-breaking research. Because CBS maintained so many specialised areas of study, students still learned a skill-specific approach to management. The school did not effectively develop the broader perspective needed by entrepreneurial executives and organisations over a lifetime career.[56] This contrasted dramatically with Harvard's approach to business education during these years.

III

Harvard Business School

Harvard Business School (HBS) was affiliated with America's most prominent university. Yet its independence from Harvard University allowed the school to develop a unique tool for business teaching and research.[57] Like its sister school, the law school, HBS fashioned an integrated strategy for business education and research around the case method.[58] The use of cases for research enabled the faculty to develop relationships with many types of businesses. Furthermore, by using cases, both HBS faculty and students learned from actual business experience. The devotion to faculty-developed cases helped the school maintain a common sense of mission and develop a community among the faculty, students, business and alumni.

The Harvard Business School's approach to business education differed from that at Columbia in two major ways. HBS faculty were not concerned with providing a liberal education in business; they assumed that their students had already been liberally educated in college. Furthermore, HBS did not aim to teach the many professions which comprise business. Harvard trained its students for only one business profession – management. The curriculum emphasized integrated managerial concepts, rather than job or skill-specific concepts. Thus, Harvard trained what Alfred D. Chandler has termed 'good line men', executives who would make the major entrepreneurial decisions for corporate America.[59] Harvard's curriculum focussed on 'the administrator who is not and cannot be a specialist, but who must make use of specialists'.[60] Underlying this training was the notion that Harvard's graduates would become business leaders.[61]

HBS was the most influential graduate school of business in postwar America.[62] This influence stemmed from the quality and size of its classes, its share of MBA educated businessmen, and the breadth of its involvement with business.[63] Harvard dominated the hiring market for MBAs. It had the biggest alumni base in business to draw upon for contacts. By 1949, almost 50 per cent of all MBAs were Harvard graduates.[64] But sheer numbers are an inadequate measure of Harvard's influence. Harvard fostered its reputation by keeping business practitioners involved in the affairs of the school. HBS was able to draw upon the prestige of the Harvard name to develop and enlarge its business contacts. These factors were mutually reinforcing.

The Harvard Business School built its programme around the goal of moulding leaders in business, government, and education.[65] Harvard faculty and administration carefully selected students for their leadership skills and helped them succeed throughout their careers.[66] According to the Admission Statement in the 1954 catalogue, the school looked for men of 'character, intellectual capacity, seriousness of purpose, maturity, leadership potentialities and other favorable personal qualities'. In contrast with Columbia, which aimed to promote a more diversified pool of potential business leaders, Harvard sought students who already possessed the characteristics linked to success in leading American business.[67]

Every aspect of Harvard's approach to business education was designed to prepare its carefully selected group of students for leadership. They learned business from the vantage point of 'top management, where company-wide objectives are set'. Because of this perspective, the graduate, 'regardless of the management level in which he is located will . . . make the most effective contribution to the business as a whole'.[68] Harvard taught its students that they could learn to manage a diversity of skills, tasks, and people in a wide range of employment settings.[69] The underlying message to business was that Harvard's graduates were deemed fit for management and, ultimately, corporate leadership.

The Harvard Business School community worked as a team to help its graduates advance. Alumni throughout the country helped HBS place and track its graduates. The school nurtured an effective long-term relationship with these alumni.[70] Job placement services were always available to facilitate their movement up the career ladder, and HBS constantly surveyed its graduates to assess their success. HBS also utilised its focus on business-oriented cases to market its graduates to business and make business part of the HBS community.[71]

Harvard's curriculum was based on the idea that students could practice for management by learning from real world problems and solutions.[72] Thus, every course at Harvard was taught in the case method; texts and lectures were rarely utilised. The first-year coursework included courses cutting across functional areas ('Administrative Practices', 'Control') and process courses (finance, marketing). The second-year courses included one required course, 'Business Policy'. Students could take a wide variety of electives such as 'Business History', 'Factory Management', 'National Transportation Policy' and 'Problems in Collective Bargaining'.[73] In contrast with Columbia's experience in this period, the HBS curriculum remained relatively stable.

This curriculum had several innovative aspects. Since 1946, HBS had emphasised the role of management in society and business-government interaction.[74] Furthermore, the school was an early leader in stressing the importance of human relations and the different perspectives of individuals within business organisations.[75] Like Columbia, Harvard maintained a focus on manufacturing and production.[76] HBS also pioneered in offering corporate planning as part of the required course on 'Business Policy'.[77]

Despite these curricular innovations, however, the school's rigid adherence to the case method seems to have caused some problems. The faculty was ingrown; and while such insularity can lead to a greater degree of camaraderie, 'curriculum, teaching methods and attitudes towards research can become frozen if considerable new blood is not introduced from the outside'.[78] The devotion to cases necessitated a special type of teacher, one comfortable with the more democratic and applied nature of case discussion (rather than lecturing). As a result, HBS tended to hire Harvard MBA graduates, train them as case researchers, and nurture them through their doctoral studies. Harvard students learned about business from Harvard-educated scholars, rather than from business practitioners. In contrast with the Columbia faculty, the faculty members were scholars of business, rather than traditional academics.[79]

By the mid-1950s, however, this system had produced an inadequate supply of scholars, especially in such new areas of managerial studies as operations research and applied mathematics.[80] HBS had to hire outsiders.[81] These new faculty members had the potential to bring new perspectives to the program. But because they were directed to utilise the case method for their teaching and research, even these lecturers were moulded to fit the Harvard approach to business education.[82]

The reliance on cases limited the faculty's ability to teach business problems. In contrast with Columbia, Harvard faculty members believed that business theory and specific analytical models were subordinate to good managerial judgment.[83] As a result, Harvard's curriculum was more practical[84] and more 'business-oriented' than Columbia's. It effectively taught management and kept professors 'involved with the activities of real corporations'.[85] But, as previously noted, because the bulk of HBS faculty members were homegrown, few had any hands-on business experience. In addition, because cases were the only tool to teach business, the pool of ideas discussed in HBS classes was circumscribed by what had already happened to the corporations examined in Harvard cases. This, I believe, probably blinded many of the HBS faculty to the dramatic changes taking place in the world economy.[86]

The case orientation and HBS's system for evaluating and supporting research seems to have impeded the school's ability to sustain the record of innovative research it had gained after its famous Western Electric studies.[87] In contrast with Columbia, the school's approach to research forced the faculty to develop a unified conception of research on management. Research was centrally assessed and funded by a faculty peer group, which maintained a common conception of proper research. The dominance of Harvard trained faculty made HBS ingrown in its research orientation. The culture encouraged consensus, not intellectual controversy.[88] Furthermore, faculty were encouraged to use case research in order to keep in touch with immediate business problems. This made it harder for the faculty to focus on research projects with a long-term orientation. It also seems to have led faculty to select practical research topics capable of being assessed with case research.[89] As a result, Harvard was not in the vanguard of research-oriented business schools.[90]

The strength of the case method was the *entrée* it provided to the diversity of the business world. Groups of alumni and interested companies were solicited to enable HBS to examine a wide range of companies. Since 1944, the 'Associates' of the school had provided funding for project research and development. Additional funds for research came from companies interested in specific projects or from contributions to a general research fund.[91] HBS acknowledged these contributions in publications, conferences, invitations, and seminars, as well as in cases. These approaches enabled the school to excel in marketing the relevance of its research and in disseminating its research to business.

The case method also furnished businessmen with an effective mechanism for influencing the curriculum. When these businessmen/students participated in case discussions, faculty got immediate feedback from experienced executives. The advanced and middle management classes were held separately from those of the MBA students, but the teachers and coursework were often the same.[92] Faculty service on corporate boards, consulting, and lectures to business groups provided additional indirect mechanisms by which business could influence the affairs of the school.[93] In contrast with Columbia, this interaction between faculty and businessmen meant that in the classroom, students and faculty learned about business with the input, albeit indirect, of business practitioners.[94]

Harvard actively encouraged a dialogue between the school and the business community. Through the school's published cases as well as publications, business could respond to the faculty's research. These publications encouraged feedback from within the business community, by seminar discussions and letters to the editor. They attracted a diverse readership, including executives in small and foreign business, and stimulated discussion on economic, political, technological and social change as well as business problems.[95]

Harvard thus differed markedly from Columbia in its early development of an infrastructure to serve alumni and business. Alumni were kept involved with the affairs of the school through seminars as well as their service in the Associates; the HBS Association (which facilitated the school's relationships with students and alumni) and the school's Visiting Committee.[96] The administration of the school designated staff to maintain channels of communication with business and alumni.[97]

Harvard's reliance on the case method enabled the school to serve many immediate business needs. Students were given a broad conception of management and, as statistics show, went on to lead many of America's companies. Despite this success, it is questionable whether this perspective provided Harvard's graduates with a long-term vision of global economic change.

Although the case method facilitated Harvard's ability to involve business in its programmes, the case method also limited the school's ability to meet many of the long term needs of business. It was difficult for the faculty to use cases to anticipate problems that business had yet to encounter. Furthermore, since research was expected to culminate in cases or case books, the faculty did not focus research on long-term problems.

The business school's limited interaction with other departments at the university made it less up-to-date in those areas where science 'challenged genteel decision-making skill'.[98] Despite its excellent relationship with business, Harvard did not develop a curriculum or research which could prepare executives to anticipate major transitions in world markets or technologies. Consequently, the school provided its students with the confidence, but little of the information and experience, to make entrepreneurial decisions for their future companies.

IV

Graduate Business Education in Service to Business? Conclusion

In this paper, I have developed a two-part standard for appraising business education in the postwar period. Graduate business schools can be evaluated by the approaches they adopted to prepare America's future business leaders. Moreover, each approach to business education can be appraised by *how well* it provided managers with the skills, information and confidence to make both entrepreneurial and operational decisions.

With the Harvard and Columbia wrapping, young men (and at Columbia, women) were made acceptable to corporate recruiters. Companies saved money on their preselection and training costs by hiring students deemed fit for corporate management. But it appears that there were unforeseen costs to American business for its myopic attitudes regarding *how* these MBAs were trained.

Each business school had a special niche: Harvard produced graduates aiming for corporate leadership, while Columbia effectively met the needs of business recruiters for a wide range of specialists. Although the two schools chose different paths to educating executives, both schools effectively prepared their graduates for operational decisions.

These two approaches, however, did not successfully provide managers with the skills and information to make entrepreneurial decisions. Neither Columbia nor Harvard developed a curriculum and teaching methods that kept pace with global economic developments. Moreover, neither school focussed on developing leading-edge business research. The range of ideas discussed in the classrooms of both schools was limited by their respective approaches to education. Harvard students learned only from cases, while Columbia students learned from 'academically respectable' theories and models. These graduates learned an ivory tower, rather than practical conception of business. Without an understanding of the real world of business, they were less prepared to make the entrepreneurial decisions essential to long-term business success.

Columbia and Harvard taught their students how to make decisions in a multitude of environments. But their graduates were not trained to anticipate and flexibly respond to new technologies, production methods, competitors, or markets. Moreover, both schools imbued their graduates with the arrogant notion that if one knows how to manage, one can manage anything and anyone at any time.[99]

American business appeared remote from the schools that supplied them with their future employees. Executives rarely insisted that the MBAs they hired be prepared with actual business experience such as internships. Moreover, although these executives went to business schools as recruiters, guest lecturers and students, they rarely became full-time lecturers or professors. The bulk of faculty involvement with business at both schools was as consultants, not as hands-on managers. Faculty executive exchange programs, as well as student internships, could have helped make business education more relevant to actual business problems and needs.

As noted previously, there is no direct relationship between management education and corporate competitiveness. However, one wonders whether America might have been better off without such reliance upon business education for executive suite preparation. By delegating such training to an outside supplier, many American companies showed a lack of interest in the preparation of a key factor of production – people. In contrast, corporations in other nations such as Germany and Japan, took a more hands-on, in-house approach to training their future leaders.[100]

With greater involvement of business executives in business education, American managers might not have been better educated, since managers may not be effective teachers. With greater investment in the education of their future executives, America's companies may not have been more competitive than they are today. But America's 'whiz kids' may have been better prepared to confront the challenges of unavoidable market change. Meeting such challenges is the essence of entrepreneurial management.

NOTES

1. An earlier version of this article, 'Without Practice or Practitioners: Graduate Business Education, 1945–1960', appears in *Business and Economic History*, 2nd series, Vol.19 (1990), pp.262–70.
2. The competitiveness movement began with the formation of the Presidential Commission on Competitiveness (1985). It was followed by the Council on Competitiveness (1986); the Congressional Competitiveness Caucus (1986); and the Business Roundtable on International Competitiveness (1987). Moreover, numerous

competitiveness courses, a wide range of books on America's competitiveness problems, and legislation mandating a competitiveness impact statement, illustrate the emergence of competitiveness as a new issue for America's policymakers. Michael Porter provides a good sectoral overview of America's competitiveness in *The Competitive Advantage of Nations* (New York, 1990), pp.507–35.

3. Critics who have linked business education to competitiveness include P. Choate and J.K. Linger, *The High-Flex Society* (New York, 1986), and J.N. Behrman and R.I. Levin, 'Are Business Schools Doing Their Job?', *Harvard Business Review*, Vol.62 No.1 (1984). However, no form of education could have prepared students for the specific changes that have bedevilled the American economy since the 1970s.

4. This is discussed in J.S. Livingston, 'Myth of the Well-Educated Manager', *Harvard Business Review*, Vol.49 No.1 (1971).

5. The majority of graduates of graduate business schools receive Masters in Business Administration (MBA) degrees. On the increase in MBAs, see H.J. Muller, J.L. Porter and R.H. Rehder, 'Have the Business Schools Let Down U.S. Corporations?' *Management Review* (October 1988), p.24. From 1945–59 the number of graduate business schools increased dramatically, until by 1959 there were approximately 100 schools offering some form of graduate business instruction.

6. MBA training grew in influence as MBA-educated executives gained increased managerial responsibility for many prominent American companies and business magazines touted the MBA. See A.D. Chandler, 'Managerial Enterprise and Competitive Capabilities', pp.11–41 in this volume; idem, 'The Enduring Logic of Industrial Success', *Harvard Business Review*, Vol.68 No.2 (1990), pp.434–44. A 1959 study of 428 top executives in 1950 found that a majority had gone to college. Of the group with graduate degrees, 19 (approximately 4 per cent) had degrees in business administration. M. Newcomer, *The Big Business Executive* (New York, 1955), pp.68–9. The numbers of MBAs increased significantly by 1964. A study of 66 business leaders found 17 per cent had MBAs. F. Bond, D. Leabo and A. Swinyard, *Preparation for Business Leadership* (Ann Arbor, MI, 1965), p.65. A 1979 Harvard study, 'Success of a Strategy', p.3, found that by 1977, over 20 per cent of the top three officers of each of the Fortune 500 manufacturing companies was a graduate of the Harvard Business School. Ten years later, 225 of the chief executive officers at the top 1000 corporations had MBAs. 'A Portrait of the Boss', *Business Week*, Oct. 21 1988, p.28. The bulk of these executives attended business schools during the 1950s.

7. Because of the enormous market share, shrewd management, and technological edge of many American companies, many American managers (along with other executives, economists, and government officials) became arrogant about America's economic prowess. They assumed that the days of American economic dominance would never end. Choate and Linger, *The High-Flex Society*, pp.3,91; D. Halberstam, *The Reckoning* (New York, 1986), pp.726–8; and J. J. Servan-Schreiber, *The American Challenge* (New York, 1968), pp.3, 10, 11. A.D. Chandler notes the role of business schools and the press in contributing to this arrogance: 'Managerial Enterprise and Competitive Capability', p.38.

8. I have taken this definition from Robert Locke's new book. R.R. Locke, *Management and Higher Education Since 1940* (Cambridge, 1989), p.212.

9. Unlike engineering schools, graduate business schools found it difficult to integrate professional standards and practices into the business school curriculum. This is because business is not one profession, but many (such as investment banking, accounting, and personnel management). These professions do not share mutually developed professional standards. In further contrast with engineering schools, graduate business schools generally did not develop internship programmes to supplement classroom experience. As a result, academics, rather than executives, held the bulk of influence over business school curricula and research. See

D. F. Noble, *America by Design: Science, Technology and the Rise of Corporate Capitalism* (New York, 1977), pp.168–71, 185.

10. A.D. Chandler Jr., *Strategy and Structure* (Cambridge, MA, 1962), pp.11–16, 383, 396.

11. Although business historians have long looked at the role of managers in the modernisation of the American economy, few historians have examined the training of American managers or business school history. Exceptions include S. Sass, *The Pragmatic Imagination* (Philadelphia, 1982) and J. Cruikshank, *A Delicate Experiment: The Harvard Business School, 1908–1945* (Cambridge, MA, 1987). Robert Locke examined the rise of managerial education in several nations. R. R. Locke, *The End of the Practical Man* (Greenwich, CT, 1984). There are several influential studies of graduate business education during this period, such as R.A. Gordon and J.E. Howell, *Higher Education for Business* (New York, 1959) and F. Pierson, *The Education of American Businessmen* (New York, 1959). See also L. Silk, *The Education of Businessmen* (New York, 1960) and R.D. Calkins, 'Objectives of Business Education', *Harvard Business Review*, Vol.25, No.3 (1947).

12. Harvard Business School, founded in 1908, was the first graduate business school to require a bachelors degree for admittance. Columbia's Graduate School of Business was established in 1916. By 1955, the US had several well-established graduate schools of business (including Dartmouth, Carnegie Mellon, Chicago, Indiana, UCLA, Harvard, Northwestern, Stanford, New York University, Wharton, Michigan and Columbia), affiliated with major research universities.

13. The number of students receiving Masters degrees in business rose from 3,357 in 1948 to 5,204 in 1958. See Pierson, *The Education of American Businessmen*, pp.36–41. Business schools were increasingly viewed as vehicles of social mobility for those seeking to join the growing managerial class. R. Hofstadter and C.D. Hardy, *The Development and Scope of Higher Education in the United States* (New York, 1952), p.90.

14. See Pierson, *The Education of American Businessmen*, p.229 for total Masters degrees. These figures are inexact, because they include MSs as well as MBAs granted. For Harvard MBA enrolment figures see M. Copeland, *And Mark an Era* (Boston, MA, 1958), p.123. For Columbia MS and MBA figures, see Columbia Business School Records (hereafter CBSR), The Report of the Dean, Columbia Graduate School of Business, 1958, p.8.

15. Both institutions were singled out by the Ford Foundation as models for the rest of the nation. S. Schlossman, M. Sedlak and H. Wechsler, *The 'New Look': The Ford Foundation and the Revolution in Business Education* (Los Angeles, CA, 1987), pp.15, 83–94 and Pierson, *The Education of American Businessmen*, p.34. The Ford Foundation reports established criteria for business education. S. Schlossman and M. Sedlak, *The Age of Reform in American Management Education* (Los Angeles, CA, 1988), p.III.

16. America's approach to collegiate and university education was derived from the European tradition of 'liberal learning'. 'Liberal education' traditionally necessitated work in the three major divisions of higher learning (the natural sciences, the social sciences and the humanities) and aimed to teach analytical skills, logic and values. For the purposes of this study, 'liberal education' is defined as broad education based on the lessons of the humanities and social sciences. Vocational or professional training is defined as job or skill-specific training. Hofstadter and Hardy, *The Development and Scope*, pp.137–8 and 208–25. Despite their vocational orientation, graduate business schools were 'hampered by the need to be liberal'. See P. S. Hugstad, *The Business School in the 1980's* (New York, 1983), p.22.

17. The writer cannot generalise about all business schools as she examined only the major approaches to business education in this period. Schlossman, Sedlak and Wechsler; Hugsted; Pierson; and Gordon and Howell all note the influence of Columbia and Harvard on other graduate business school programmes.

18. Announcement of the Graduate School of Business, Columbia University,

1944–1945, pp.10–11, 1948–1949, pp.12–15 and 1949–1950, p.50. These documents were found in the CBSR, stored at the Dean's office. They were kindly made available to me by then-Acting Dean's Kirby Warren and Daiselle Crawford, Administrative Assistant and LEAP Co-ordinator at the Dean's office. In 1955, Columbia was singled out by the Brookings Institution to report on how business schools 'liberally educate' their students. Memo to the Committee on Instruction, Item No.199, April 18, 1955. See also Gordon and Howell, *Higher Education for Business*, pp.266 and 255n. On the American Assembly, see T. W. Van Metre, *A History of the Graduate School of Business, Columbia University* (New York, 1954), pp.11, 100, 102.

19. See *Yearbooks of the Columbia University Graduate School of Business*, 1947 and 1960, Unpaginated. Also see C. Brown, *The Dean Meant Business* (New York, 1983), p.155. This was also in line with the schools's 'liberal' orientation.

20. CBSR, Announcement of the Graduate School of Business, Columbia University, 1945–1946, 'Aims of the School', p.11 and Memo to the Committee on Instruction, No.90, 7 Sept. 1951.

21. Throughout much of this period, Columbia's students could prepare for jobs ranging from personnel specialist to traffic manager. See CBSR, Announcement of the Graduate School of Business, Columbia University, 1946–1947, 'Aims of the School', pp.12–13.

22. Some of the functional academic specialisations such as economic geography appeared unique to Columbia. However, the development of functional academic specialties also occurred in other business schools. S. Sass, 'The Managerial Ideology in Collegiate Business Education', in *Business and Economic History*, (Champaign-Urbana, 1985), p.20. In 1945, areas of specilisation included traffic management, retail merchandising or consular service. In 1949–50, areas of specialisation included bank management, insurance and urban land use. CBSR, Announcement of the Graduate School of Business, 1945–1946, p.18; 1949–1950, pp.31–7.

23. CBSR, Announcement of the Graduate School of Business, 1952–1953, p.37. In 1949, there were 24 areas of specialisation and by 1956 there were 26 areas. According to Assistant Dean Robert Senkeier, the faculty's research interests led to additional specialised courses. See R. Senkier, *Revising a Business Curriculum: The Columbia Experience* (New York, 1962), p.10.

24. Students tended to use all of their electives to take courses in their field of specialisation. CBSR, Announcement of the Graduate School of Business, 1950–1951, p.25.

25. The curriculum included a few 'liberal' courses such as business cycles and economic geography. CBSR, Announcement of the Graduate School of Business, 1945–1946, p.12.

26. CBSR, Announcement of the Graduate School of Business, Columbia University, 1957–1958, p.15.

27. Brown, *The Dean Meant Business*, pp.157–64; Gordon and Howell, *Higher Education for Business*, p.267; and Schlossman, Sedlak and Wechsler, *The 'New Look'*, p.242.

28. Many other business schools abandoned courses in manufacturing to focus on marketing and finance. At Columbia however, manufacturing was a required course for the MBA until 1949. CBSR, Announcement of the Graduate School of Business, 1944–1945, p.18 and 1947–1948, p.33. Production management courses were available throughout this period. Ibid., 1952–1953, p.25; 1957–1958, p.15. It remained an area of specialisation in the new curriculum. Ibid., 1960–1961, p.23.

29. CBSR, The Report of the Dean, 1958, p.15.

30. Many university faculty members thought Columbia had already moved too far from the 'scientific' and 'theoretical' to the 'professional' and 'technical'. They resented the business school. See Van Metre, *A History*, p.20. For information about the disputes over the school's curriculum and mission, see Brown, *The Dean Meant Business*.

Even Dean Brown admitted he had difficulty reconciling 'liberal education' with business education, p.142.
31. Brown, *The Dean Meant Business*, pp.139-40.
32. See for example, CBSR, Minutes of the Committee on Instruction 7 Nov. 1951, Memo No.190, pp.1-2; and Memo to the Committee on Instruction, Minutes of the Committee on Instruction, 16 March 1956, No.205.2. File No.205.2. File No.205.2 contains several other memos on this issue. One professor justified specialisation by saying 'I have known several students who selected Columbia over Harvard because of this opportunity'. Memo to Dr Fisher from Dr Hance, p.2. The political tenor of the times may provide a further reason for faculty reluctance to abandon specialisation. The drive to reform Columbia's curriculum occurred during the McCarthy era, a time of great stress for many universities. Like many of their academic brethren, business school faculty members may have believed they were preserving academic freedom by ensuring their academic control.
33. For example, in 1951, the school's Dean Young complained that 'traditional departmental compartmentalism fails to give the students an integrated approach to the problem of business management'. In 1953, the Beckhart Committee noted, 'Although there are only 15 recognized divisions in the School, there are 26 possible fields of specialisation. This . . . is . . . not consistent with the general policy of the School'. (Here again we have the conflict between the espoused strategy and its real world results.) Senkier, *Revising a Business Curriculum*, pp.11, 13-15. Although four committees were organised in the 1950's to introduce curricular changes, Columbia's faculty thwarted reform until 1959.
34. They stated, 'our faculty must of necessity be an aggregation of specialists'. These reasons were cited in the Report of the Beckhart Committee, 1955, as quoted in Senkier, *Revising a Business Curriculum*, p.13.
35. Columbia's curriculum revision was initiated by a memo from Dean Brown in March, 1955 and consummated in September, 1960. The Dean seemed to be the perfect leader for reform at Columbia. He had received a doctorate from the school and had years of high-level business and government experience. He was not well-liked, however. According to former Assistant Dean Senkier, some faculty expressed reservations because he was not an 'academic man'. 'If the new Dean makes an attempt to apply business methods in the operation of this institution', they said, 'it will be resented'. See Ibid., p.17.
36. Senkier, *Revising a Business School Curriculum*, pp.18, 23, 70, 88. The new curriculum emphasised breadth of education rather than technical preparation for business. It represented a concensus on the functional areas of business in which all students should be literate. This included balancing core areas of study of management with the areas of specialisation. The core curriculum included eight required courses: 'World Resources'; 'Conceptual Foundations of Business'; 'Business Decision-Making'; 'Human Behavior in Organisations'; 'Quantitative Methods'; and 'Policy Determination and Operations'. Core courses totalled 29 of 60 required credits. CBSR, Announcement of the Graduate School of Business, 1960-1961, p.15. Students could take 15 points of electives and 15 points in an area of specialisation. Available electives included economics; maths; political science; philosophy; and history. Areas of specialisation included banking; business economics; finance; industrial relations; international business; marketing; production; and management. See CBSR, Report of the Dean, 1960, p.11.
37. Senkier, *Revising a Business Curriculum*, p.17.
38. Brown, *The Dean Meant Business*, p.160-3. See also CBSR, Committee on Instruction, Memorandum, 4 Nov. 1955, Item No.213, 'Proposed Curriculum Changes in the Field of International Business'.
39. CBSR, Report of the Dean, 1958, p.17 and Minutes of the Committee on Instruction, 11 May 1959, Item No.280, pp.1-4. Promotion criteria may have changed slightly during this period. See Brown, *The Dean Meant Business*, p.192.

40. CBSR, Minutes of the Committee on Instruction, Item No.298, Memo from Dr William Newman, p.1.

41. The ostensible purpose of academic research in all disciplines is to 'add to knowledge'. Gordon and Howell, *Higher Education for Business*, p.380 and Hofstadter and Hardy, *The Development and Scope*, p.57. For this study, I have divided business research into three areas: pure research creates new, more efficient modes of management or new understanding (e.g. data processing, human relations); adaptive research facilitates business adaption to changing technologies and markets (e.g. studies of ways to increase steel industry productivity); and finally, predictive research develops models used to anticipate economic or technological changes (e.g. research on the ageing of America and how this will increase demand for preventative medicine). Adaptive research is often done by consultants. All three types of research serve business.

42. In 1949, the faculty included 3 BAs; 3 BSs; 3 MAs; 3 MSs; 2 MBAs; 4 CPAs; 1 LLD; 4 LLBs and 28 Ph.D.s. In 1959, the faculty included 1 BA; 6 MSs; 1 MA; 3 MBAs; 4 CPAs; 5 LLBs; 1 LLD; 5 Ph.D./LLDs; 1 DCS (a doctorate in Commercial Science from Harvard); and 33 Ph.Ds. See CBSR, The Announcement of the Graduate School of Business, 1949–50, pp.8–10 and 1959–60, pp.5–8.

43. CBSR, Report of the Dean, Appendix, Faculty Publications, 1953–1958.

44. During this period, Carnegie Mellon and the University of Chicago had the most notable research records. Carnegie Mellon's reputation was derived from its work in organisational behaviour and from strong interdisciplinary research. The University of Chicago was noted for its work in bridging business and the social sciences, as well as its orientation toward scientific work in the study of business. See Schlossman, Sedlak and Wechsler, *The 'New Look'*, pp.18–19, 27, and 36–7; Pierson, *The Education of American Business*, p.313; Gordon and Howell, *Higher Education for Business*, p.391; and telephone interview with Professor William Newman, Columbia University Graduate School of Business, 29 Dec. 1988.

45. During the post-war decades, Columbia University had an outstanding reputation as a research university. Its leading departments included physics and sociology, as well as the faculties of law, engineering and medicine. The business school frequently used professors from other departments to teach at CBS, including sociology, engineering, mathematics and economics. Such fields were important and frequent contributors to research in business. Gordon and Howell, *Higher Education for Business*, p.381. However, interdisciplinary research was rare at CBS in this period. See CBSR, Report of the Dean, Appendix, Faculty Publications, 1953–1959, and telephone interview with Professor William Newman, Columbia University Graduate School of Business, 29 Dec. 1988. Collaborative work would later bloom at Columbia's business school, especially in sociology.

46. Schlossman, Sedlak and Wechsler, *The 'New Look'*, and Brown, pp.149, 152. In my opinion, the work of Eli Ginzberg on labour economics, William Newman and Leonard Sayles in management and Otto Serbein on health care were notable exceptions during this period. The faculty of the international business division also stands out in their early recognition of the need for coursework in how different cultures affected business. CBSR, Minutes of the Committee on Instruction, No.213, Memo from Dr Roy Blough to the Chairman of the Curriculum Committee, 4 Nov. 1955.

47. Schlossman, Sedlak and Wechsler, *The 'New Look'*, p.27. Also telephone interview with Professor William Newman, 29 Dec. 1988.

48. CBSR, Announcement of the Graduate School of Business, 1952–1953, 'Special Advantages', p.10.

49. Some low-level executives were allowed to matriculate part-time at the school, allowing some full-time students to interact with business practitioners. Van Metre, *A History*, pp.99–100.

50. Ibid., pp.100–101; CBSR, Report of the Dean, 1958, pp.24–5. The programme was held at Arden House, off the business school campus.

51. Van Metre, *A History*, pp.81 and 102.
52. There was one important exception where CBS students did solve real business problems. Columbia had a course where an executive would present a problem, which the students would assess, and then make recommendations. See Pierson, *The Education of American Businessmen*, p.290. Some businessmen served as guest or adjunct faculty. Two of the most famous were Harlow S. Person, an expert on management and Benjamin Graham, an expert on securities analysis. Van Metre, *A History*, pp.74–75.
53. Brown, *The Dean Meant Business*, pp.149–50 and Van Metre, *A History*, p.112.
54. Senkier, *Revising a Business School Curriculum*, p.90. On the recommendation of the University Trustees, the Visiting Committee was established to advise the School on its programme. Ironically, even 'the Council members expressed the hope that the School's new program will prove liberal'.
55. Its main function 'was to be a financial contributor . . . to the more important facilities of the University'. Brown, *The Dean Meant Business*, p.144.
56. Even the school admitted that the curriculum trained students for the first job through an emphasis on facts and skills. See Senkier, *Revising a Business School Curriculum*, p.92 and Gordon and Howell, *Higher Education for Business*, p.299 and 299n. Until 1959, Columbia's students were directed towards one 'best' functional approach to managing business (accountants got a bottom-line focus; personnel a labour-relations focus; and so on), rather than a unified managerial perspective.
57. The business school (HBS) sits apart from the university on the Boston side of the Charles River, closer to Boston's business district. Its physical distance from the university is symbolic of its financial and administrative independence.
58. The case method is a tool for studying business practice through the history of a particular incident or problem confronted by one or several firms. For example, a steel industry case can be written from the perspective of a steel worker or steel company president. Students analyse these situations, make recommendations for business policy and actions, and weigh the implications of their recommendations in class. In class discussions, students gain an understanding that there is no one correct managerial answer. It is probably as close to practical experience as one can get in a classroom.
59. Interview with Professor Alfred D. Chandler, Jr., Harvard Business School, 10 Jan. 1989. Other business schools would produce the corporate staff: accountants, financial managers, or public relations executives. Harvard graduates would be trained to manage many different types of employees, products and services. For a definition of line and staff, see A. D. Chandler, Jr., *The Visible Hand* (Cambridge, MA 1977), pp.106–107.
60. This means good 'line men'. See Cruikshank, *A Delicate Experiment*, pp.159, 198.
61. Because of this focus, HBS graduates would not reap the full benefits of their training until some 15 years after their graduation. Schlossman, Sedlak and Wechsler, *The 'New Look'*, pp.22–23 and Copeland, *And Mark an Era*, pp.148–9.
62. L. Shames, *The Big Time* (New York, 1986), p.18; Silk, *The Education of Businessmen*, p.17; and Schlossman, Sedlak, and Wechsler, *The 'New Look'*, p.21. The Ford Foundation noted that Harvard's standing in the business community was unequalled.
63. Pierson, *The Education of American Businessmen*, pp.287, 429, 725–726; Shames, *The Big Time*, pp.17–18, 27; Copeland, *And Mark an Era*, pp.122–3.
64. Shames, *The Big Time*, p.18.
65. Harvard Business School Catalogue (hereafter HBS Catalogue), 1959–1960, pp.21–22 and 'Success of a Strategy,' (1979) p.1. Of these three functions, Harvard clearly stressed the first two. See HBS Catalogues, 'Objectives of the School', for the years 1945, 1960. All of the HBS catalogues and course outlines are available in hard copy or on microfiche at Baker Library (hereafter BL). I am grateful to Florence Lathrop, Curator, and Elise Thall, Assistant Curator, for their assistance.

66. Interview with Professors Kenneth Andrews and Harry Hansen, Harvard Business School, 9 Jan. 1989. My study of the school's yearbooks indicates that women were not perceived as potential leaders during this period.

67. BL, HBS Catalogue, 1953–1954, p.65; 1957–1958, p.48; 1959–1960, p.51. HBS attempted to study the personal characteristics linked to the business success of its earlier graduates and replicate these qualities in new candidates for admission. Gordon and Howell, *Higher Education for Business*, p.337n.

68. Description of the required second-year course, 'Administrative Policy' in BL, HBS Catalogue, 1948–1949, p.32.

69. Interview with Professor Alfred D. Chandler, Jr., 10 Jan. 1989. A brochure to potential recruiters, 'Selecting Tommorow's Management Leaders from Today's Graduates' (1960), pp.3, 5 in BL noted that all of the business school's students had been 'carefully prescreened . . . Their two years of graduate study of close to 100 cases . . . will have developed their analytical abilities . . . and understanding of management problems'.

70. BL, HBS Catalogue, 1949–1950, 'Placement Section', p.93.

71. With these mechanisms, HBS was able to perpetuate the success of its graduates. BL, 'Selecting Tommorow's Management Leaders from Today's Graduates', pp.3, 5.

72. 'In the business world . . . it is the ability . . . to weigh diverse influences that leads to sound judgement; and that ability can be developed only through practice'. BL, HBS Catalogue, 1959–1960, p.23.

73. BL, *Planning for Change, Report of the MBA Study Committee*, (Graduate School of Business, Harvard University Sept. 1961), pp.14–15, 27–28; Copeland, *And Mark An Era*, pp.176–8.

74. BL, HBS Catalogue, 1949–1950, p.34; 1959–60, pp.29, 36–37, 48. These courses included 'Government and Business', 'Economic Aspects of Public Policy', and, after 1959, 'Business Responsibility in American Society', 'Business Policy' and 'Business, Society and the Individual'.

75. BL, HBS Catalogue 1949–1950, p.23; 1958–1959, pp.45–46, 124–126, 138.

76. Production was a required part of the first-year coursework. BL, HBS Catalogue, 1954–1955, p.33; 1959–1960, p.31. In 1947, it was part of the 'Elements of Administration'. BL, 'Elements of Administration, Production, Volume I, 1946–1957.

77. BL, 'Success of a Strategy', p.19. This course was offered throughout the 1950s. HBS relied solely on cases to explore the planning process. But because cases can only deal with problems business has already experienced, such cases cannot adequately deal with future changes.

78. Gordon and Howell, *Higher Education for Business*, p.346.

79. M. McNair, *The Case Method at the Harvard Business School* (New York, 1954), pp.99, 178–87, 285–90. Also interviews with Professors Kenneth Andrews and George Lombard, 9 Jan. 1989. Most of these home-grown faculty members had never worked in business.

80. Gordon and Howell, *Higher Education for Business*, pp.349–53 and Cruikshank, *A Delicate Experiment*, p.194.

81. BL, HBS Catalogue, 1949–1950, pp.10–11; 1959–1960, pp.14–16. Of a sample of 40 professors in 1949–1950: there were 2 BAs; 6 MAs; 8 MBAs; 1 had a Doctor of Philosophy; 9 Ph.Ds (for some reason this was listed differently than Doctor of Philosophy); and 12 had a DCS. (Doctorate of Commercial Science from HBS). Of a sample of 51 faculty members in 1959–1960: there were 9 BAs; 3 MAs; 11 MBAs; 1 M. Phil.; 9 Ph.D.s; 2 LLBs; 2 MDs; 6 DCSs; and 7 DBAs (doctorates in Business Administration). As this reveals, Harvard's faculty had become more diverse.

82. HBS professors were expected to teach large classes and develop research in the case method. Gordon and Howell, *Higher Education for Business*, p.404; BL, 'Success of a Strategy,' pp.26–7. They were also expected to be interchangeable, especially at the junior levels. Thus, a Harvard professor might teach 'Business Policy' one year, do case research the next, and teach Marketing the subsequent semester. HBS

faculty members were expected to be research and teaching generalists. After several years of experience, they were also expected to do specialised or project research. Many on the faculty, whether junior or senior, were given the title Professor of Business Administration, rather than a specialist's title. Cruikshank, *A Delicate Experiment*, pp.139–40, 175, 270. Also interviews with Professors Harry Hansen, Kenneth Andrews and George Lombard on 9–10 Jan. 1989.

83. Even in teaching theoretical disciplines such as economics, faculty members relied principally upon cases. Collateral readings were rarely assigned. The school utilised the findings of related disciplines, but kept its instruction free from their intellectual control. Copeland, *And Mark an Era*, pp.176–7.

84. BL, 'Success of a Strategy', pp.1, 26–29.

85. Ibid., p.27.

86. A HBS faculty committee admitted that dependence solely upon cases made it difficult to teach problems of increasing scope (such as technological obsolescence) and newly emerging techniques (such as linear programming and sampling). BL, 'Planning for Change, The Report of the M.B.A. Study Committee', p.20.

87. Cruikshank, *A Delicate Experiment*, pp.165–7 and 170–5, describes the Western Electric Studies. These studies influenced business practice in the area of Human Relations.

88. Interview with Professor Keith Butters, 24 Jan. 1989. See also Copeland, *And Mark an Era*, pp.187–8 and pp.238–53; Gordon and Howell, *Higher Education for Business*, pp.32 and 386.

89. Interviews with Professors Alfred D. Chandler, George Lombard, Harry Hansen and Kenneth Andrews, 9–10 Jan. 1989. See also Copeland, *And Mark An Era*, pp.183–6 and 227–36; BL, 'Success of a Strategy', p.27; and Schlossman, Sedlak, and Wechsler, *The 'New Look'*, p.68.

90. The faculty generally produced adaptive, not highly innovative research. The school led, however, in researching government regulation of business and the social responsibilities of business. In addition, HBS innovated in human relations and business history.

91. BL, HBS 'Annual Report' of 1954, p.17.

92. As at Columbia, students and executives did not mingle in class, although these classes were held on campus during the school year. Copeland, *And Mark an Era*, p.127–8.

93. Interviews with Professors Alfred D. Chandler, George Lombard and Kenneth Andrews, 9–10 Jan. 1989. See also BL, 'Success of a Strategy', p.4; Copeland, *And Mark An Era*, pp.125–31. The Advanced Management Program for Businessmen began in 1945, the Middle Management Program began in 1954.

94. Harvard did not include many practising executives on its faculty during this period. Like Columbia, Harvard did have some notable exceptions, such as George Doriot. Most faculty business experience was as consultants, however, not as hands-on managers.

95. Alumni and research publications were widely disseminated. In 1944–48, over 85,000 copies of Harvard research materials were distributed. See BL, 'Success of a Strategy', p.29; Pierson, *The Education of American Businessmen*, pp.577–608; Gordon and Howell, *Higher Education for Business*, pp.368, 370–1. But the *Harvard Business Review* was HBS' most prominent publication, growing in circulation from 15,000 to 60,000 by 1960. Ninety per cent of its readers were businessmen, but only ten per cent were HBS graduates. BL, *HBS Alumni Bulletin*, March/April 1966, pp.7–10.

96. BL, *HBS Alumni Bulletin*, Sept./Oct. 1963, p.27.

97. For example, HBS had a full-time Director of Alumni Relations, an Associate Dean for External Affairs, and a Director of Placement. BL, *HBS Alumni Bulletin*, Sept./Oct. 1963, pp.28–9; Copeland, *And Mark an Era*, pp.326–38.

98. Harvard played catch-up in the new management sciences. Sass, 'The Managerial Ideology', p.205.

99. Although Harvard and Columbia had radically different ideas of proper management, training at both schools may have led to management arrogance. Harvard students may have been deluded into thinking their work would lead them to senior management. Columbia's functional orientation may have led to a functional management bias. See Pierson, *The Education of American Businessmen*, p.242–5. Such management arrogance may have been reinforced by the market for MBAs and the ease with which such executives moved up the corporate ladder. This gave MBA training a seal of approval and market advantage that may not have been fully deserved. In 'The Enduring Logic of Industrial Success', p–442, Alfred D. Chandler, Jr. notes that managers were 'told by academics that management was a general skill'. In 'Managerial Enterprise and Competitive Capabilities', earlier in this volume, he identifies business schools in the 1960s as encouraging management arrogance, leading to the conglomerisation trend. Conglomerates are large corporations composed of many different divisions, which are not necessarily related by product line, technology, production method or markets. Also see interview with Alfred D. Chandler, 10 Jan. 1989.

100. Robert Locke has provided a good overview of how other nations educated their future business leaders in *Management and Higher Education Since 1940*. Clearly, many non-US companies have flourished without business schools training their management. However, it is very difficult to speculate if those nations would have been better off with or without business schools. For example, my research is not on the British case. But there is reason to believe that prior to 1960, the UK might well have benefited, not so much from graduate business schools, but from having recognized the need for a higher degree of professionalisation of management based on ability, not pedigree.

Regulatory Responses to the Rise of the Market for Corporate Control in Britain in the 1950s

RICHARD ROBERTS

University of Sussex

On both sides of the Atlantic the post-war years have seen 'the coming of an institutionalised market for corporate control'.[1] For the first time it became possible for the ownership of public companies to be determined simply by stock market transactions and for control to pass thereby to parties previously unconnected with a firm. Chandler identifies this development, the buying and selling of companies, as one of the factors undermining 'the dynamics of managerial enterprise' in post-war America. In Britain the market in corporate control began in the 1950s, rather earlier than in the United States. It is the responses of the 'authorities' – the commonly used shorthand for the Bank of England and the government departments concerned with economic affairs – and the City to this development which is the subject of this article.

I

Mergers between firms are as old as the joint stock company and a natural feature of a market economy. Besides regular annual occurrences, there have been surges in merger activity in the 1880s, at the turn of the century, immediately after the First World War, in the late 1920s, in the mid-1930s, following the Second World War, in 1953–54, 1959–61, 1968, 1972, 1978–79 and 1984–87.[2] Merger activity between 1949 and 1962 is depicted in Figure 1. Prior to the 1950s mergers were effected by private negotiations between boards of directors and no need was perceived for a set of rules for their conduct beyond the minimal framework provided by the Stock Exchange rule book, the Companies Acts, and the law of the land on fraud. Though the inter-war amalgamation waves aroused expressions of concern about competition, no significant anti-trust measures were introduced.[3] The post-war Labour government was more concerned about the abuse of market power by companies than previous administrations and in 1948 it enacted the Monopolies and Restrictive Practices (Inquiry and

Control) Act which established the Monopolies and Restrictive Practices Commission.[4] This body was charged with investigation of cases referred to it by the Board of Trade to establish whether restrictive agreements between firms or dominant market positions operated against the public interest. However, it was not until 1965 that the impact of amalgamations became a subject of special scrutiny, which was signalled by the change of name to the Monopolies and Mergers Commission. The Companies Act of 1948 was a milestone in many aspects of company regulation, but its provisions regarding the conduct of amalgamations were scant.[5] One other statutory constraint warrants mention, the Prevention of Fraud (Investments) Act, 1939, which specified channels of communication with shareholders, but it was not intended and did not act as a brake on amalgamations. In summary, effectively there were no statutory regulatory obstacles to the conduct of mergers during the 1950s and companies could in theory be bought through the stock market virtually without hindrance.

The early 1950s saw the emergence of a new phenomenon – the 'take-over'. A take-over, a term which became current in 1953, was the acquisition of a publicly quoted company by the purchase of a majority of its shares by another firm without the agreement of the directors of the acquired company. 'Offers made over the heads of the Boards concerned', was a working definition adopted at the time.[6] It was with the advent of the take-over that the market in corporate control came into being. Chandler has identified a link between the emergence of institutional shareholders as the principal owners of American firms and the development of the market for corporate control. Britain experienced a similar transformation of the pattern of ownership of public companies but the take-over anticipated these changes and is explained by other factors.

Hannah has drawn attention to the more stringent financial disclosures required of company accounts by the 1948 Companies Act, which for the first time provided the basis upon which corporate predators could make reasonably accurate estimates of asset values and earnings and thus launch bids without the co-operation of the prey.[7] Contemporary explanations of the advent of the take-over bid stressed the 'abnormal circumstances' of the post-war years.[8] 'Why was there a spate of startling take-over bids in the years after the World War II?', asked Bull and Vice, a pair of financial journalists, in 1958.[9] 'The brief answer is that various factors combined, after the war, to produce exceptionally favourable opportunities for the bidder'. They identified four such factors.[10] First, and 'most important and all-embracing', were the structural changes to the British economy during and since the war – changes which

FIGURE 1

EXPENDITURES ON ACQUISITIONS ON SUBSIDIARIES AND EQUITY PRICE INDEX,
1949–1962

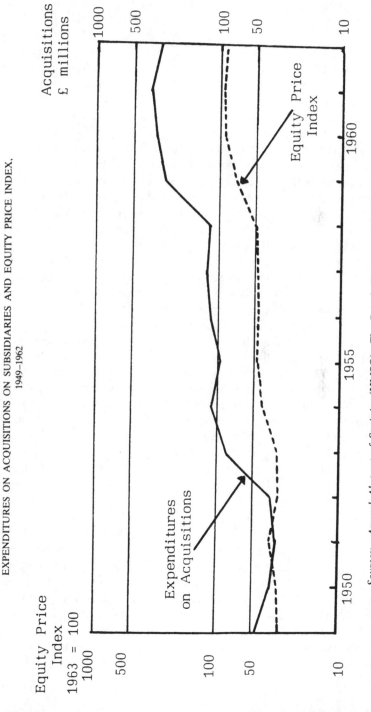

Sources: Annual Abstract of Statistics (HMSO); *The British Economy: Key Statistics
1900 – 1970* (London and Cambridge Economic Service, 1972), Table M.

had created a gulf between the most and least efficient firms which 'was where the bidder saw, and seized, his opportunities'. Second, the increase in company taxation from 37 per cent of gross trading profits in 1938 to 56 per cent in 1952, which led to a reduction in the proportion of profits distributed in dividends to shareholders from 52 per cent in 1938 to 20 per cent in 1952 in order to retain adequate funds for the business. Share prices reflected the reduced pay-outs rather than the increases in asset values and earnings which made it cheap to buy assets and earnings, by buying companies. Third, the large cash reserves prudently held by many companies because of inflation and uncertainty were tempting treasures for raiders. Fourth, the eagerness of shareholders to realise tax-free capital gains rather than highly-taxed dividend income. A list of factors compiled by the Oxford economist J.F. Wright a couple of years later made the same points plus a few more, in particular the role of dividend restraint in depressing share values and the attraction to bidders of cash and liquid assets in an era of restrictions on bank borrowing and access to the capital market because of the Capital Issues Committee.[11] Of course, most contemporary comment paid no heed to such matters and ascribed the phenomenon to the dynamism and ruthlessness of a new breed of financiers. In the popular press, where take-overs received plentiful attention in the 1950s, they were portrayed as swashbuckling duels whose 'distinctive flavour' was the regular trouncing of the Establishment by buccaneer outsiders.[12]

The first of the sensational take-overs was Charles Clore's bid for J. Sears & Co., the parent company of the shoe shop chain-store Freeman, Hardy & Willis, in the spring of 1953. Clore, the son of a Jewish immigrant East End tailor who was already a self-made millionaire from business and property ventures, launched his attack on being informed by a partner in the estate agents Healey & Baker that Sears' balance sheet underestimated the real estate value of the firm's 900 high street stores by £10 million.[13] He immediately began to establish a shareholding by buying in the market and set his own staff to work on the bid, which was conducted without the services of a merchant bank, as were all his take-over operations in the 1950s. The bid was conducted over the heads of the Sears board by mailing offer documents direct to shareholders, a tactic hitherto impossible because of paper rationing. The Sears directors, who were taken entirely unawares, retaliated by announcing the tripling of the dividend. Shareholders were astonished by this sudden largesse which was perceived as a desperate and irresponsible act on the part of the management. Faith in the incumbent board being thoroughly undermined, there was a rush to sell to Clore, who quickly acquired control of the company. 'We never thought anything like this would happen to us', were the Parthian words of the outgoing Sears chairman.[14]

The struggle for Sears prompted the Bank of England to consider its attitude towards take-overs, and an internal document was prepared which examined their causes and consequences.[15] It was acknowledged that a case could be constructed, as had been done by some financial journalists, that take-overs promoted the efficient use of corporate assets, but the author was sceptical about the ability of 'syndicates of financiers' to judge what was in the best interest of firms and deplored the pressure upon management to abandon prudent conservative accounting practices. 'This kind of manoeuvre', he warned, 'may mean the break-up of businesses which are making an important contribution to the country's needs'. Moreover, take-overs constituted a threat to macro-economic management since they undermined adherence to the government's policy of dividend restraint and were inflationary. As for motives, bidders were simply out to realise non-taxable capital gains through the manipulation of share prices and property assets, a sort of peacetime profiteering. In the spring of 1953 the Bank's sympathies plainly lay with the 'victim companies' and take-overs were regarded as against the national interest.

Take-overs were back in the headlines that autumn when it became known that someone was building up a shareholding through nominees in the Savoy Hotel Co., the owner of the famous Savoy, Claridge's and Berkeley hotels and Simpson's Restaurant in the Strand.[16] Clore was the prime suspect, though not the only one, and during October the Savoy directors endeavoured to establish his intentions and to identify the purchaser of the company's shares. Early in November the Prime Minister, Winston Churchill, received a request from the chairman of the Savoy, Hugh Wontner, for a meeting to discuss the company's situation.[17] Churchill was a long-standing *habitué* of the Savoy – the venue for the fortnightly gatherings of The Other Club, his favourite dining club which he and F.E. Smith had founded in 1911 – and a friend of Wontner, who had let him know early on that the firm was 'in trouble'.[18] The meeting took place on 10 November and immediately afterwards Churchill asked the Chancellor for a briefing note about take-over bids, expressing particular concern about the Savoy.[19] Reginald Maudling, the Economic Secretary to the Treasury and charged with the preparation of the note took up the question with the Governor of the Bank of England, Cameron Cobbold, who in turn consulted Sir John Braithwaite, Chairman of the Stock Exchange, Lord Aldenhan, Chairman of the Westminster Bank, and Sir Alan Rae Smith, a chartered accountant who was financial adviser to the government and a director of the Savoy Hotel. Maudling's note, delivered on 13 November 1953, read:

> It creates a bad public impression when large capital profits are seen to be earned by mere financial manipulations. It is also a danger to the Chancellor's policy of voluntary restraint, both of wages and dividends. The Boards of companies whose shareholders are likely to be approached in this manner are tempted to increase their dividend distributions substantially in the hope of increasing the Stock Exchange valuation of their shares, so making the take-over bid less attractive, though in some cases this can be bad from the long-term interests of their companies.
>
> But, while the process is distasteful, and may be politically embarrassing, it is difficult to see anything that the Government can do about it. It is impossible by legislation to prevent individuals offering to buy the property of other individuals. Yet, short of such legislation, there is really nothing that would hamper the process, nor is it possible to do anything to dry up the source of finance for the speculators concerned.
>
> I have consulted the Governor of the Bank of England, who shares our dislike for many of these operations, but tells me that so far he himself, despite much thought on the subject, has reached the same conclusion, that there is no action that either the Government or the Bank can properly take in the matter.[20]

On the same day Churchill also received a memorandum from Peter Thorneycroft, the President of the Board of Trade, on the Savoy Hotel Co. share purchases. Referring to that situation in relation to the department's responsibility for the enforcement of the Companies Acts, Thorneycroft told Churchill that 'there is nothing that the government can do under existing legislation to check operations of this kind, in the absence of fraud'.[21] He informed the Prime Minister that following consultations with the Chairman of the Stock Exchange Council and the government Law Officers he had explained to Wontner the form in which an application could be made under Section 172 of the 1948 Companies Act for the appointment of an inspector to establish the true identities of the Savoy's nominee shareholders. Wontner had immediately made such an application. 'This is the first time that this section of the Act has been invoked for the purpose of an enquiry into this kind of situation', reported Thornycroft. He also registered that the Board of Trade had 'solid objections' to legislation to restrict take-overs.

In summary, by mid-November 1953, galvanised by Churchill's concern about the Savoy Hotel, the authorities were agreed that take-overs were politically undesirable and economically harmful. The obvious remedy was legislation to ban or curb hostile bids, but this was ruled out for practical and ideological reasons. However, officials were not content to let the matter rest and explored informal ways of curtailing take-overs. At the Bank of England attention focused upon restrictions on the use of nominee names on share registers, but the scheme foundered because of doubts about its effectiveness and because it required an amendment to the 1948 Companies Act which, as a Bank official put it, 'would not be especially welcome to HMG'.[22]

Meanwhile, the Treasury was pursuing a different and ultimately fruitful line of thought. 'We must have an answer to the question "why cannot you control the raising of money by Clore & Co?"', wrote the Treasury official Edmund Compton to Sir Kenneth Peppiatt, executive director at the Bank of England.[23] 'First', continued Compton, 'have you any positive information as to who the lenders may be? Secondly, have you any comment to make on the suggestion that influence might be brought to bear on those lenders to withdraw support from the less reputable take-over operators?' Peppiatt's reply identified three possible sources of bidders' finance besides their own funds: British banks, foreign banks and the insurance companies.[24] But British banks were bound by the Chancellor's 'request' of December 1951 not to lend for the purpose of speculation, which was deemed to include the finance of take-over bids, and he informed Compton that he was aware of several occasions on which bridging finance for bids had been denied. On the other hand, he had also heard that American, French and Belgian banks had provided funds for take-overs. Even more important were the insurance companies which advanced funds to bidders and then purchased from them prime commercial properties acquired through the take-over, which provided the bidders with the means of repaying their borrowings. The authorities determined to plug these sources of funds, and, on 3 December 1953, after consultations in the City, the Governor sent a letter to the banking and insurance industry associations reminding them of the Chancellor's request regarding the finance of speculation of two years earlier. Privately it was made clear to the chairmen for relay amongst their members that the authorities regarded the finance of take-overs as speculation and wished it to stop, a classic example of the Bank of England exercising informal regulatory control over the City of London.

On 7 December 1953, the *Daily Telegraph* ran an article headlined 'Insurance Companies Warned by the Bank' which revealed the dispatch of the Governor's letter and reported that its purpose was to curb the support for take-overs provided by American banks and British insurance companies. The source of the *Telegraph* story was a loose-tongued assistant general manager of one of the insurance companies, but an officially contrived leak could not have been more effective in achieving the Bank's objectives.[25] Spokesmen for the American banks protested to the Bank that the report was 'totally unfair and misleading', but in an audience with the Deputy Governor the manager of the Bank of America, which was known to have participated in financing both the Sears and Savoy bids, sheepishly admitted involvement in 'two or three takeover bids', appearing 'uncomfortable and clearly worried'.[26] A few days later the Governor received a letter which amounted to a remarkable collective supplication by the American banks in London, assuring him that they were 'glad to co-operate and to be guided by the wishes which had been expressed'.[27] The episode demonstrates that in the 1950s foreign banks operating in the City were as susceptible to a nod from the Governor of the Bank of England as their British counterparts, suggesting that it was not the influx of foreign firms but the intensification of competition which led to the demise of the informal 'gentlemanly' form of regulatory control over the City by the Bank of England from the 1960s.

The insurance industry was also deeply disconcerted by the public revelation of the Governor's displeasure. The chairman of the British Insurance Association arrived in the office of the Deputy Governor in a state of great agitation complaining that his members were being unfairly pilloried. Only with difficulty was he persuaded from 'stoking the fire', as the Governor put it, by issuing a vindication of the insurance industry to the press.[28] Cobbold was aware that the Labour Party was beginning to perceive political advantage in the issue of take-overs and there was concern at the Bank about the Parliamentary Question tabled by the Labour shadow Chancellor, Hugh Gaitskell, for 15 December 1953. Cobbold hoped that his actions would satisfy the opposition and put paid to 'these transactions (which) are disruptive to the community and bad for the City's prestige'.[29]

Meanwhile, the struggle for the Savoy Hotel had been resolved. The report of the Board of Trade inspector, published on 1 December, revealed that it was the Land Securities Investment Trust, chaired by Harold Samuel, which was stalking the Savoy and controlled almost 40 per cent of the equity, about as much as the Savoy directors. A day later the Savoy board announced that the company's principal assets were to be transferred to the Worcester Buildings Co., a private company whose equity was owned by the Savoy staff pension fund whose trustees were on the side of the Savoy board. This was a tactic to ensure that even if Samuel secured a majority of the equity he would be unable to control the assets. City reaction was 'sharply hostile', reported the *Financial Times*, because of the scheme's 'inequitable nature and the dangerous precedent it sets in separating ownership of assets from their control'.[30] Although the scheme was subsequently approved by the Board of Trade it was never implemented since on 10 December 1953, to the astonishment of observers, it was announced that the Savoy board was purchasing Samuel's shareholding. This solution satisfied both the Savoy directors, who retained their company, and Samuel, who made a handsome profit. The Bank of England was happy at the prospect of the end of such episodes and a few days later the Governor concluded some words on take-overs to a Stock Exchange audience with the remark that 'I hope that this little storm may be dying down and that what I have said may be in the nature of a postscript'.[31]

Cut off from credit, bidders had to rely on their own resources to mount cash bids and were constrained from offering payment in shares by capital issue consent requirements and the bearish stock market. Bids did not cease, but most likely they were fewer in number and smaller in scale than would otherwise have been the case. The effect of the authorities' action in December 1953 was to ensure that take-overs did not become 'normal commercial exercises' in the mid-1950s but remained 'financial curiosities'.[32]

II

The merger wave of 1959–61 was a product of the bull market of these years (Figure 1). The relationship between rising stock markets and upsurges in merger activity has been noted on both sides of the Atlantic and stems from the disparity in valuations between highly-rated companies and poor performers, enabling the former to use their shares to acquire the latter.[33] A feature of the merger wave of 1959–61 was the spate of take-over bids unprecedented in number and size. Behind the bid boom lay two new factors. The first was the availability of external finance, which came about because of the relaxation of controls on bank lending in July 1958 and the abolition of the necessity for Capital Issues Committee consent for securities issues in February 1959. The second was a change in the attitude of the 'financial Establishment', which hitherto 'had tended to regard the bidder as an outsider'.[34] The origins of this shift were discerned by Bull and Vice in the scramble by the clearing banks to control the City's major hire purchase houses following the abolition of lending limits in February 1958, setting an example which suggested 'that take-over bids were more respectable than many had supposed'.[35] Remaining reservations in the City were rudely swept away by the outcome of the great bid battle for the British Aluminium Co. which filled the headlines at the end of 1958 and the beginning of 1959.

The struggle for control of Britain's major aluminium company began in September 1958 with an approach to the British Aluminium board by Reynolds Metals of Virginia, an American aluminium manufacturer, and Tube Investments (TI), a British engineering and metallurgical firm, which made an offer to purchase the company through a joint subsidiary owned 49 per cent by Reynolds and 51 per cent by TI. The British Aluminium board, led by the pre-eminently Establishment figures Lord Portal, former Chief of Staff of the Royal Air Force, and Geoffrey Cunliffe, son of a former Governor of the Bank of England, rejected the bid and instead arranged for the Aluminium Company of America (Alcoa) to take a controlling interest. However, Reynolds/TI, advised by the merchant banks Warburgs, Helbert, Wagg, and Schroders, were not prepared to accept the board's decision and soon acquired a substantial shareholding through purchases in the market. British Aluminum's advisers, Lazards and Hambros, were outraged and appalled that leading City firms should endorse and orchestrate a bid against the recommendations of an incumbent board of directors, a feeling which was widespread in the City. On New Year's Eve it was revealed that a 'City Consortium', comprising 14 of the most respected names in the Square Mile including the merchant banks Morgan Grenfell, Samuel Montagu, M. Samuel, Brown Shipley and Guiness Mahon and the leading brokers Cazenove and Rowe & Pitman, had been assembled to contest the issue.[36] The British Aluminium bid had become a civil war in the City.

The government became involved in the struggle because both bids required capital issue and foreign exchange consents which were within its power to withold. In December 1958 and early January 1959 the matter was discussed several times in Cabinet and it took up a considerable amount of the time of the Prime Minister, Harold Macmillan, who dealt with it personally because the Chancellor, Heathcote Amory, was a Tube Investments shareholder.[37] Ministers came under pressure to announce decisions on the consents favourable to the Alcoa bid to support the stand of the City Consortium. However, the issue which concerned the Cabinet was not the conduct of take-over bids but the future of the British aluminium industry. By this criterion the Reynolds/TI bid was preferred 'on grounds of national interest . . . mainly because legal control would remain in British hands'.[38] So the Cabinet decided 'to do nothing' knowing 'that Reynolds would continue to buy shares in the market . . . and therefore ensure their success'.[39] On the morning of the announcement of the Reynolds/TI victory, Lord Portal called on Macmillan and expressed 'a very bitter feeling'. 'I did not think it was worth arguing with him about what we had done', noted the Prime Minister.[40]

The Cabinet's decision to favour the Reynolds/TI bid had consequences for the regulation of take-overs which were much more far-reaching than Macmillan probably realised. The humiliation of the City Consortium changed City attitudes to take-overs overnight and henceforth financial advisers added hostile bids to their repertoire of merger and acquisition techniques. Had the authorities still regarded take-overs with the misgivings expressed in the Bank of England's internal memorandum of the spring of 1953 this would have presented a problem, but their attitude had undergone a profound change. Their revised thinking was expressed by Leslie O'Brien, Chief Cashier at the Bank, in a memorandum to the Governor summarising the position in July 1959. 'Developments since 1953', wrote O'Brien, 'have tended to support the view that take-over bidders generally perform a useful function. Mr Clore, for example, appears to have improved the retail shoe trade of the country, Mr Fraser the Barkers Group of shops. Neither they, nor Mr Wolfson nor Mr Samuel, have operated for short-term capital gain, as their critics alleged they would, and all have built up prosperous businesses and helped to develop assets more efficiently . . . In present circumstances Directors generally have only themselves to blame if they are dispossessed by more enterprising rivals'.[41]

O'Brien's memorandum was occasioned by Clore's bid in May 1959 for the 'sleeping giant' of the brewing industry, Watney Mann.[42] The bid was controversial at several levels. The authorities were aroused because it was the first use of outside funds since 1953.[43] In the City it shocked even those who were prepared to defend bids between firms in the same industry on the grounds of rationalisation, since Clore had no brewing interests.[44] For the man in the street it was beer and pubs, matters close to his heart, which were at issue and the episode received enormous press coverage, the public being treated to the spectacle of the senior figures of the brewing industry heaping abuse upon the 'financial raiding party' for its 'preposterous and deplorable' bid.[45] Clore was no stranger to vilification, but this time he decided that discretion was preferable to valour and on 19 June 1959 he withdrew the bid, his first take-over defeat. The reason given by Clore's deputy was the 'preposterous' price of Watneys' shares in the market; but the decision was consistent with the 'considerable feeling of public concern' identified by a *Financial*

Times leading article and the episode marked a turning point of general significance in the development of the take-over.[46]

By the spring of 1959 a general election was in prospect and the controversy over the Watneys bid turned take-overs into a party political issue. The City had long been a *bête noire* of some Labour politicians, and take-overs provided a 'live issue on which to arraign the Government'.[47] As soon as the House resumed after the Whitsun recess a 'barrage of criticism' erupted from the Labour benches.[48] Take-overs were 'economic gang warfare' declared Sydney Irving, the member for Deptford, one of the leaders of the assault which culminated in a Commons debate on the issue on an Opposition motion on 29 June 1959 in which the Chancellor, Heathcote Amory, and Harold Wilson, his Labour 'shadow' led their respective sides. Wilson got the better of the argument and Harold Wincott, the redoubtable *Financial Times* columnist, reported the view that on a free vote the Labour motion would have been carried by a majority of two to one. 'The average person . . . is so offended by the trappings of some bids and mergers that he tends to be sickened by the whole process', wrote Wincott. 'Get hold of a copy of *Hansard* for June 29 and read Harold Wilson's speech. It contains just about the only issues on which the Socialists could win an election these days'.[49]

In the summer of 1959 take-overs became part of the political agenda. During the election campaign Labour politicians called for the establishment of a statutory body along the lines of the US Securities and Exchange Commission (SEC) to police the City and by polling day both Labour and the Conservatives were committed to the conduct of inquiries, which led to the Jenkins Report on Company Law. Furthermore, the Institute of Directors, the Association of British Chambers of Commerce and the Leeds Chamber of Commerce announced the establishment of inquiries into take-over bids. Most importantly of all, the Governor of the Bank of England was spurred to convene a conference out of which emerged an initiative to instigate self-regulation of the market in corporate control amongst City take-over practitioners.

III

The Governor's conference was held at the Bank in secret on 10 July 1959. It was attended by Cobbold and his deputy and the chairmen or deputy-chairmen of the Stock Exchange, the Committee of London Clearing Bankers, the British Insurance Association, the Association of Investment Trusts, the Accepting Houses Committee and the Issuing

Houses Association.[50] Cobbold opened the proceedings by stating the Bank's view of the situation, that take-overs 'had on balance proved beneficial to the economy', but there were some 'troublesome features' of bids and 'the public relations aspect was deplorable'. He then asked the others present at the meeting for their views and suggestions. The City luminaries expressed 'full agreement' with the Bank's assessment of the generally wholesome effects of take-overs, a measure of the transformation of City attitudes in the first six months of 1959 since many of them must have been former supporters of the City Consortium. From Sir Edwin Herbert, chairman of the Association of Investment Trusts, came the observation that 'there was in many quarters a genuine desire for guidance', and by the end of the meeting agreement had been reached to produce 'some code of conduct . . . [for] . . . dissemination in the City'. A body, which became known as the City Working Party, comprising representatives of each of the practitioner organisations present, but *not* the Bank of England, was established to supervise the production of the code of conduct.

The lead was seized by the Executive Committee of the Issuing Houses Association (IHA) which on 17 July 1959, a week after the conference at the Bank, established its own working party to draw up a draft document.[51] At the top of its priorities was 'to find an alternative name for "take-over" as this has been brought into disrepute', which was the origin of the use of the term 'amalgamations'. A first draft was prepared by the chairman of the IHA, J.S. French, a director of the London and Yorkshire Trust who was a former City editor of the *Sunday Times*. After discussion and amendment the document was eventually approved at a meeting at the Bank on 15 October 1959.[52] Evidently it contained nothing unexpected, for O'Brien reported to the Governor that it scarcely required comment. 'Not a very bold document', was his verdict.[53]

While the experts were at work on the code of conduct, a general election was announced on 8 September. Labour politicians made much of City abuses during the campaign and their denunciations of the 'spiv's paradise' appeared to be vindicated by the major City scandal which erupted in the middle of the campaign, the Jasper Affair, involving take-over malpractice and the misuse of building society funds, which, in Cobbold's words, led to a 'song and dance about take-over bids'.[54] Lord Hailsham resourcefully counter-attacked with the accusation that Labour's policy amounted to a take-over bid for Britain.[55] Despite the controversy raging amongst the politicians, no hint whatsoever was given that the City was itself considering the question of take-overs, perhaps because it might have been construed as substantiating the charges of its detractors. It was not until mid-October that the first reports of the preparation of the guidelines appeared in the press; by which time the election was long over.[56]

The 'Notes on Amalgamations of British Businesses' was published on 31 October 1959. It was an an anonymous pamphlet available from the Secretary of the Issuing Houses Association, price 6d. (2¹/2p.) Its eight pages comprised a brief history of 'amalgamations' amongst British companies followed by a statement of four principles governing the conduct of take-overs and a dozen recommendations regarding practice. The principles began with the statement that 'there should be no interference with the free market in shares and securities', which might have been taken as a disavowal of the whole exercise. The others were laudable but vague assertions of shareholder rights. The most venturesome of the suggestions as to practice were those which expressed disapproval of partial bids and the finance of take-overs by the issue of non-voting shares. The frequent use of such phrases as 'it is generally desirable' or 'as a general rule' provided plenty of opportunity to argue exemption.

The press gave a warm welcome to the 'Notes on Amalgamations': 'sensible, concise and well-written', commented the *Economist*; 'strikes a fair balance between the bidder and the bid-for', observed *The Times*; 'encouraging and valuable', was the verdict of the *Financial Times*.[57] The problem of the enforcement of codes of conduct was discussed in a leading article in the *Financial Times* which raised and rejected the idea of a Securities and Exchange Commission for Britain as 'cumbrous and unwieldy' but foresaw the need for a small expert body to review the situation, the first suggestion of the Take-over Panel. The Issuing Houses Association was greatly gratified by the 'wide publicity and favourable comment' and in the month following publication 11,100 copies of the pamphlet were distributed.[58]

With the benefit of hindsight it is plain that the 'Notes on Amalgamations' made almost no difference to the conduct of take-overs in Britain. 'Given little publicity and heeded even less', was the verdict of one authority.[59] In 1963 following a 'minor sensation' over the favour shown to institutional shareholders in the take-over of Whitehead Iron the City Working Party was reconvened.[60] A new document was produced entitled 'Revised Notes on Company Amalgamations and Mergers' – once again the word 'take-over' was eschewed – which took account of developments and adopted a more forthright stance on the equal treatment of all shareholders during bids. The City Working Party was convened, once again, in the summer of 1967 following yet another upsurge of controversy over take-overs. This time it produced a rule book, entitled *The City Code on Take-overs and Mergers*, which defined proper practice for bids. To enforce compliance, the Panel on Take-overs and Mergers, a body with a full-time director-general and staff, was established in 1968.[61] 'This is our last chance before legislation', remarked one of the practitioners responsible for the new arrangements.[62]

IV

The regulatory framework adopted in 1959 for the conduct of mergers and take-overs conformed to the 'self-regulatory' form traditional to the City and to many other aspects of British life. The alternative was the US model of statutory regulation enforced by an independent agency.[63] Labour Party politicians were not the only ones to advocate a British SEC in the summer of 1959 and even the British Chamber of Commerce espoused this course of action, leading the Bank of England to suggest that its enthusiasm should be 'toned down'.[64] The 'Notes on Amalgamations' established self-regulation as the regulatory form for mergers and take-overs, an important extension of the practice. The publication was the first step in the process which led to the establishment of the Panel on Take-overs and Mergers, a body which 'perhaps more than any other, typifies the role and nature of self-regulation in Britain'.[65]

The reaction of the authorities, the City and industry to the first stirrings of the market in corporate control in Britain in the 1950s was suspicion and hostility. The measures taken in 1951 and 1953 to curb 'speculation' restricted the growth of the market in corporate control for most of the decade. The actions of the authorities in 1958 and 1959 had the opposite effect and created the conditions for the take-over booms of the 1960s. First, the government engineered defeat of the City Consortium led the merchant and investment banks to adopt the hostile bid as a quotidian technique for securing control of firms, institutionalising the market in corporate control. Second, by handing over regulation to City practitioners the authorities ensured the least restrictive form of regulatory regime. It is implausible that the experienced officials of the Bank of England believed that a vague voluntary code of conduct would prove a constraint upon the conduct of take-overs – nor did it. But that was the point, because by then the authorities had come to regard take-overs as a means of promoting industrial rationalisation and instilling discipline in management. Chandler, on the other hand, suggests that a market in corporate control may contribute to the neglect of long-term considerations by firms, which can undermine the industrial base of a nation by 'the weakening of the organisational capabilities of managerial enterprises'.[66] Chandler's essay is consistent with a growing body of criticism of 'short-termism', which is alleged to have characterised corporate governance in Britain and the US since the war. In this perspective it is possible that any enhancements of the efficiency of British firms which arose from the advent of the take-over were outweighed by long-term handicaps, in which case the actions of the authorities in the late 1950s which contributed to the rise of the market in corporate control in Britain may come to be regarded as a *faux pas*.

NOTES

I am grateful to Dr David Kynaston for his helpful comments on a draft of this article.

1. A.D. Chandler, 'Managerial Enterprise and Competitive Capabilities', pp.11–41 in this volume.
2. See L. Hannah, *The Rise of the Corporate Economy* (2nd ed. 1983); J. Scouller, 'The United Kingdom Merger Boom in Perspective', *National Westminster Bank Quarterly Review* (May 1987), pp.14–30.
3. P. Craig, 'The Monopolies and Mergers Commission: Competition and Administrative Rationality', in R. Baldwin and C. McCrudden (eds.), *Regulation and Public Law* (1987), pp.202–5.
4. Craig, 'Monopolies and Mergers', p.205; J. Fairburn, 'The Evolution of Merger Policy', in J. Fairburn and J. Kay, *Mergers and Merger Policy* (Oxford, 1989), pp.193–4.
5. D.G. Rice, 'Take-over Bids and the Law', *Banker*, Vol.109 (1959) pp.606–7; J. Charlesworth, *The Principles of Company Law* (6th ed., 1954), pp.290–8.
6. Bank of England, C40/971, f.11, Take-over Bids, Note of Meeting at Bank of England on Friday 10 July 1959.
7. L. Hannah, 'Takeover Bids in Britain Before 1950; An Exercise in Business "Pre-History"', *Business History*, Vol.16 No.1 (1974) p.75.
8. (Issuing Houses Association), *Notes on Amalgamations of British Businesses* (1959) p.3.
9. G. Bull and A. Vice, *Bid For Power* (1958), p.14.
10. Ibid., pp.14–18
11. J.F. Wright, 'The Capital Market and the Finance of Industry', in G.D.N. Worswick and P.H. Ady (eds.), *The British Economy in the Nineteen-Fifties* (Oxford, 1962), pp.465–6.
12. Ibid., p.464.
13. C. Gordon, *The Two Tycoons: A Personal Memoir of Jack Cotton and Charles Clore* (1984), p.51.
14. D. Clutterbuck and M. Devine, *Clore: The Man and His Millions* (1987), p.69.
15. Bank of England, C 40/970, f.2, 'Memorandum on Real and Fictitious Share Bids', 18 March 1953.
16. See Bull and Vice, *Bid For Power*, pp.29–46.
17. PRO, PREM/656, Note from J.C. Colville, Prime Minister's Office, to the Prime Minister, 5 Nov. 1953.
18. M. Gilbert, *Winston S. Churchill: Never Despair, 1945–1965*, Vol.VIII (1988), p.318.
19. Bank of England, C 40/970, f.4, Governor's note on meeting with Reginald Maudling, Economic Secretary to the Treasury, 13 Nov. 1953.
20. PRO, PREM/656, Letter from the Economic Secretary to the Treasury, Reginald Maudling, to the Prime Minister, 13 Nov. 1953.
21. Ibid., Memorandum from the President of the Board of Trade, Peter Thorneycroft, to the Prime Minister, 13 Nov. 1953.

22. Bank of England, C 40/970, f.7, Memorandum to the Governor, 19 Nov. 1953.
23. Ibid., f.7, Letter from E.G. Compton, Treasury, to Sir Kenneth Peppiatt, 19 Nov. 1953.
24. Ibid., f.11, Memorandum from Sir Kenneth Peppiatt, Bank of England, to E.G. Compton, Treasury, 23 Nov. 1953.
25. Ibid., f.60, Deputy Governor's Note, 7 Dec. 1953.
26. Ibid., f.61, Deputy Governor's Note, 8 Dec. 1953; f.64, Memorandum of Chief Cashier to Governor, 9 Dec. 1953.
27. Ibid., f.65, Letter from John M. Wallace, Chase National Bank, to Governor, 10 Dec. 1953.
28. Ibid., f.75, Governor's Note, 11 Dec. 1953.
29. Ibid., f.84, Extract from Governor's Speech at Stock Exchange Lunch, 15 Dec. 1953.
30. *Financial Times*, 8 Dec. 1953.
31. Bank of England, C 40/970, f.84, Extract from Governor's Speech at Stock Exchange Lunch, 15 Dec. 1953.
32. Bull and Vice, *Bid For Power*, p.240.
33. See, for instance, Scouller, 'Merger Boom in Perspective', p.24.
34. Bull and Vice, *Bid For Power*, p.237.
35. Ibid.
36. D. Kynaston, 'A City at War with Itself', *Financial Times*, 7/8 Jan. 1989.
37. PRO, PREM 11/2020, Letter from the Chancellor of the Exchequer, Heathcote Amory, to the Prime Minister, Harold Macmillan, 2 Dec. 1958.
38. Ibid., Memorandum from the Economic Secretary to the Treasury to the Prime Minister, Harold Macmillan, 3 Jan. 1959.
39. Ibid.
40. PRO, PREM 11/2020, 'Note For The Record' of conversation between Harold Macmillan, Prime Minister, and Lord Portal, Chairman of the British Aluminium Company, 9 Jan. 1959.
41. Bank of England, C 40/971, f.10, Memorandum from Leslie O'Brien, Chief Cashier, to the Governor, 8 July 1959.
42. Clutterbuck & Devine, *Clore*, p.81.
43. Bank of England, C 40/970, Memorandum Leslie O'Brien to Governor, 1 June 1959.
44. *Financial Times*, 3 June 1959.
45. Clutterbuck and Devine, *Clore*, p.82; Gordon, *Two Tycoons*, p.53.
46. *Financial Times*, 23 June 1959.
47. 'The City and the Election', *Banker*, Vol.109 (1959) p.579.
48. *Financial Times*, 3 June 1959.
49. *Financial Times*, 7 July 1959.
50. Bank of England, C40/971, f.11, Note of Meeting at the Bank on Friday 10 July 1959.
51. British Merchant Bankers' Association, Issuing Houses Association Executive Committee Minutes, 17 July 1959.
52. Bank of England, C40/971, f.79, Minutes of Meeting, 15 Oct. 1959.
53. Ibid., f.71, Memorandum Leslie O'Brien to Governor, 14 Oct. 1959.
54. Ibid., f.62, Governor's Note, 28 Sept. 1959.
55. D.E. Butler and R. Rose, *The British General Election of 1959* (1960), p.57.
56. Bank of England, C40/971, f.79, Minutes of Working Party, 15 Oct. 1959; *Economist*, 17 Oct. 1959.
57. *Economist*, 31 Oct. 1959; *The Times*, 31 Oct. 1959; *Financial Times*, 31 Oct. 1959.
58. British Merchant Bankers' Association, Issuing Houses Association Executive Committee Minutes, 20 Nov. 1959; 11 Dec. 1959.
59. D. Gooch, *Certified Accountant*, Vol.66 (1974), p.92.
60. Stamp and Marley, *Accounting Principles*, p.9.

61. For accounts of the origins of the Take-over Panel see M. Clarke, *Regulating The City: Competition, Scandal and Reform* (Milton Keynes, 1986), pp.105–7; Sir Alexander Johnston, *The City Take-over Code* (Oxford, 1980), pp.8–18; E. Stamp and C. Morley, *Accounting Principles and the City Code* (1970), pp.3–10.

62. Johnston, *City Take-over Code*, p.41.

63. See, M. Moran, 'Regulating Britain, Regulating America: Corporatism and the Securities Industry', in C. Crouch and R. Dore (eds.), *Corporatism and Accountability: Organised Interests in British Public Life* (Oxford, 1990), pp.103–124.

64. Bank of England, C40/971 f.88, Note For Record re British Chamber of Commerce, 20 Oct. 1959.

65. B.A.K. Rider, 'Self-regulation: The British Approach to Policing Conduct in the Securities Business, with Particular Reference to the Role of the City Panel on Take-overs and Mergers in the Regulation of Insider Trading', *Journal of Comparative Corporate Law and Securities Regulation*, Vol.1 (1978), p.319.

66. A.D. Chandler, 'Managerial Enterprise and Competitive Capabilities', op.cit.

INDEX